The Informal Regulation of Criminal Markets in Latin America

This book explains how states informally regulate drug markets in Latin America. It shows how and why state actors, specifically police and politicians, confront, negotiate with or protect drug dealers to extract illicit rents or prevent criminal violence. The book highlights how, in countries with weak institutions, police act as interlocutors between criminals and politicians. It shows that whether and how politicians control their police forces explains the prevalence of different informal regulatory arrangements to control drug markets. Using detailed case studies built on 180 interviews in four cities in Argentina and Brazil, the book reconstructs how these informal regulatory arrangements emerged and changed over time.

Hernán Flom is Visiting Assistant Professor at Trinity College.

T0370697

The Informal Regulation of Criminal Markets in Latin America

HERNÁN FLOM

Trinity College, Hartford, Connecticut

CAMBRIDGE
UNIVERSITY PRESS

CAMBRIDGE
UNIVERSITY PRESS

Shaftesbury Road, Cambridge CB2 8EA, United Kingdom

One Liberty Plaza, 20th Floor, New York, NY 10006, USA

477 Williamstown Road, Port Melbourne, VIC 3207, Australia

314–321, 3rd Floor, Plot 3, Splendor Forum, Jasola District Centre, New Delhi – 110025, India

103 Penang Road, #05–06/07, Visioncrest Commercial, Singapore 238467

Cambridge University Press is part of Cambridge University Press & Assessment, a department of the University of Cambridge.

We share the University's mission to contribute to society through the pursuit of education, learning and research at the highest international levels of excellence.

www.cambridge.org
Information on this title: www.cambridge.org/9781009170703

DOI: 10.1017/9781009170710

© Hernán Flom 2022

First published 2022
First paperback edition 2024

A catalogue record for this publication is available from the British Library

ISBN 978-1-009-17072-7 Hardback
ISBN 978-1-009-17070-3 Paperback

Additional resources for this publication at www.cambridge.org/9781108488822

Contents

Figures

Tables

Acknowledgments

The road to publishing this book was anything but straightforward. It had multiple stops, detours and restarts along a six-year trip back and forth between the United States and Argentina. A journey that long guarantees that there are many people to thank along the way, but I think it makes sense to start with the person whose contribution was the longest and greatest. Belén Fernández Milmanda (Bel Mil), the most amazing partner I could ask for, provided the essential support that made this book happen. She read through every chapter, proposal and key emails; was both a sharp critic and staunch supporter; and gave me the resources, time and encouragement I needed to finish this book. For everything, thank you for being (in) my life.

This book began as my doctoral dissertation at Berkeley.[1] For their unwavering support and sharp insights throughout, I thank Alison Post, Leonardo Arriola, Ruth Berins Collier and David Collier, as well as my doctoral colleagues, with a special shout out to the Argentine Mafia, Tomás Bril, Eugenia Giraudy, Andrés Schipani and Rodrigo Zarazaga. Between 2013 and 2015, I carried out fieldwork in Argentina and Brazil. My special thanks to all those who generously gave up their time for the

[1] Later, portions of this book were originally published as "State Regulation of Organized Crime: Politicians, Police, and Drug Trafficking in Argentina," *Latin American Politics and Society* 61 (3), Fall 2019: 104–28; and as "Controlling Bureaucracies in Weak Institutional Contexts: The Politics of Police Autonomy," *Governance* 33 (3), Jul 2020: 639–56. Parts of the chapters on Rio de Janeiro and São Paulo are derived from an article, "The Politics of Police Violence: Political Competition and Police Killings in Brazil," published in *Journal of Urban Affairs*, Feb 15, 2022, copyright The Urban Affairs Association, available online: www.tandfonline.com/10.1080/07352166.2021.2018935.

interviews that constitute the primary evidence material for this book. I acknowledge the funding by the Institute on Global Conflict and Cooperation (IGCC) and the Institute for International Studies at Berkeley, which made such fieldwork possible.

Large portions of the dissertation which made up the basis for this book were written in the computer labs at the Harvard Department of Government and benefited from the brilliant insights of all members of the Harvard and MIT Latin American Working Groups.

The book began to take autonomous form during my stay at the Kellogg Institute at the University of Notre Dame between August 2016 and May 2017. I thank all Kellogg professors and staff for setting up a wonderful community to live and work as well as my cohort fellows for their sharp and enthusiastic comments in the early stages of this process. It was undoubtedly enriched by a fantastic seminar I organized with Guillermo Trejo, one of the most astute minds and kindest people in this field. For their companionship, suggestions and support throughout, I specially thank the members of that seminar: Juan Albarracín, Stefanie da Souza, Leslie MacColman, Camilo Nieto-Matiz and Lucía Tiscornia.

After Kellogg, I returned to Argentina to work in the National Ministry of Security. While being in a policymaking role forced me to shelve the manuscript for most of this time, the experience I gained working directly with police officers was invaluable. It allowed me to put many of my hypotheses to the test, and to see the personal stories of many people with whom I had brief but deep interactions while writing the book. For this opportunity, I thank Alberto Föhrig, Patricia Bullrich and the late Juan Carlos Pugliese. For being an exceptional team to work with, thanks to Flavia Carbonari, Pia Ferreyra, Gonzalo García, Evelyn Garrote, Ale Gricman, Juan Jalif, Federico Manolio, Marcelo Reidman, Santiago Rodriguez Melgarejo and Federico Tassara.

After my government tenure ended, I joined my wife in Hartford, Connecticut, in early 2020, where this book's revision began in earnest, just as the world was turning upside down due to the COVID-19 pandemic. The possibility of secure employment at Trinity College undoubtedly allowed this book to materialize, and for that I especially thank Stefanie Chambers, Sonia Cardenas and the wonderful staff. For their advice, companionship and support, thanks to all members of the Political Science Department. I also appreciate the assistance provided by the College's Research Completion Grant. As I neared the final drafts, I was lucky enough to find kind souls who not only were willing to revise the manuscript but also offered brilliant suggestions to improve it. Many thanks to Desmond Arias, Marcelo Bergman, Eduardo Moncada, Brian Palmer-Rubin and Lucía Tiscornia.

As the 2020 winter neared, I finally sent out the manuscript. I sincerely thank Sara Doskow for her championing of this project as well as for sending it to two amazing reviewers, whose suggestions I hope to have done justice to in this final version. Thanks to Jadyn Fauconier-Herry for shouldering on the project and everyone at Cambridge University Press for their assistance and guidance throughout the production of this book. Thanks to Rudy Leon for her masterful work at indexing this volume.

None of this would be possible without the support, encouragement and love of my family. Whether in Argentina or the United States, I am grateful for every moment we spend together and for having you in my life. Thanks to the Fernández Milmandas (César, Mariela, Pablo, Sebastián and Guady) for the family we've built. To my parents, Marta and Jorge, thank you for always having my back and helping me find the path forward as well. I'm blessed to have had you as parents and mentors.

As if her academic and personal support was not enough, Belén also gave me the most wonderful gift a person could get. Our daughter, Elena, was born in November 2020, just as I sent out the manuscript for review. While her direct contribution is perhaps harder to pinpoint, since she has yet to read a single chapter (or read at all), seeing her smile each morning is the best reward possible for the work this project involved. I love you both more than words can say. This book is for you.

Abbreviations

Brazil

ADA	Amigos dos Amigos (Friends of Friends, Rio de Janeiro)
BOPE	Batalhão de Operações Especiais (Special Operations Battalion, Rio de Janeiro)
BPM	Batalhão da Polícia Militar (Military Police Battalion)
CIED	Centro Integrado de Educação (Integrated Education Center, Rio de Janeiro)
CPI	Comissão Parlamentar de Inquérito (Parliamentary Inquiry Commission)
CV	Comando Vermelho (Red Command, Rio de Janeiro)
DEIC	Departamento Estadual de Investigações Criminais (State Department of Criminal Investigations)
DENARC	Departamento Estadual de Prevenção e Repressão ao Narcotráfico (State Department of Prevention and Repression of Narcotics, São Paulo)
DHPP	Delegacia Estadual de Homicídios e de Proteção à Pessoas (State Division of Homicides and Personal Protection, São Paulo)
GPAE	Grupos de Policiamento de Áreas Especiais (Police Groups for Special Areas, Rio de Janeiro)
ISP	Instituto de Segurança Pública (Institute of Public Security)
PCC	Primeiro Comando da Capital (First Command of the Capital, São Paulo)
PCERJ	Polícia Civil do Estado do Rio de Janeiro (Civil Police of the State of Rio de Janeiro)
PDS	Partido Democrático Social (Social Democratic Party)

PDT	Partido Democrático Trabalhista (Democratic Workers' Party)
PMDB	Partido do Movimento Democrático do Brasil (Brazilian Democratic Movement Party)
PMERJ	Polícia Militar do Estado do Rio de Janeiro (Military Police of the State of Rio de Janeiro)
PSB	Partido Socialista Brasileiro (Brazilian Socialist Party)
PSDB	Partido da Social Democracia Brasileira (Brazilian Social Democratic Party)
PT	Partido Trabalhista (Workers' Party)
ROTA	Rondas Ostensivas Tobias de Aguiar (Tobias de Aguiar Ostensive Rounds, São Paulo)
SESEG	Secretaria de Segurança (Security Secretary, State of Rio de Janeiro)
SSP-SP	Secretaria de Segurança Pública (Secretary of Public Security, São Paulo)
TC	Terceiro Comando (Third Command, Rio de Janeiro)
UPP	Unidade de Polícia Pacificadora (Police Pacification Unit, Rio de Janeiro)

Argentina

ALIANZA	Alianza para el Trabajo, la Justicia y la Educación (Alliance for Work, Justice and Education)
AMIA	Asociación Mutual Israelita Argentina (Argentine–Jewish Mutual Aid Society, Buenos Aires)
CEVARESO	Centro Varelense de Rehabilitación Social (Varela Center for Social Rehabilitation, Florencio Varela, Buenos Aires)
DSV	Double Simultaneous Vote (also Ley de Lemas, Santa Fe)
FPCS	Frente Progresista Cívico y Social (Progressive Civic and Social Front, Santa Fe)
FPV	Frente para la Victoria (Front for Victory), also PJ (Partido Justicialista)
FR	Frente Renovador (Renovation Front, Buenos Aires)
FREPASO	Frente País Solidario (Front for a Country in Solidarity)
GBA	Greater Buenos Aires
PJ	Partido Justicialista (Justicialist Party), also Peronist Party, Peronism
PS	Partido Socialista (Socialist Party, Santa Fe)
UCR	Unión Cívica Radical (Radical Civic Union)

Informal Regulation of Criminal Markets in Latin America

POLICE, POLITICIANS AND DRUG MARKETS

"We simply entered favelas at night, killed two or three traffickers, seized a couple of weapons, and that was our measure of success."[1] Former Rio de Janeiro Military Police Captain Rodrigo Pimentel said this quite matter-of-factly, as we sat in his office at O Globo headquarters in Leblon, an upscale neighborhood of the City of Rio. He was referring to the years when he worked in the notorious BOPE, the elite squad of Rio de Janeiro's Military Police. He did not boast or bemoan this reality. It was just the way things were – and continued to be.[2]

This phrase could mostly sum up Rio de Janeiro's response toward drug trafficking since redemocratization in the 1980s. Each year, violent, anarchic confrontations between military police and heavily armed criminal gangs rampage city life and cost thousands of lives. Police in Rio are not only overtly violent but also heavily corrupt. Extortion of drug dealers is commonplace. Police often intimidate, kidnap or torture traffickers to obtain bribes for a supposed "protection" they mostly do not deliver. For most of the democratic period, Rio de Janeiro has represented the crudest epitome of the drug war fought in Latin American cities outside of Colombia and Mexico (Lessing 2017).

However, a quick comparison with the neighboring state of São Paulo depicts a different scenario. In Brazil's most populous state, the police

---

[1] Interview by author with former Police Captain Rodrigo Pimente l, Rio de Janeiro, September 8, 2014. Pimentel was the inspiration for Colonel Nascimento, the protagonist of the hit movie *Elite Squad*, played by Brazilian actor Wagner Moura.
[2] All translations in this book are the author's own unless otherwise indicated.

have reached an informal agreement, an *acordo*, with the main drug gang, the Primeiro Comando da Capital (PCC, First Command of the Capital), to maintain relative peace in the urban area. As a Military Police (PM) lieutenant told me, "[After 2006, when the agreement began] the PM never again raided a prison, or entered a cell to look for weapons, drugs, or cell phones. [PCC] prisoners have more freedom to have these things, to talk on their cell or to use the Internet in the prison. It's part of the agreement (*acordo*) with the government."[3] Unlike in typical narratives of monetary exchanges between Mexican and Colombian drug lords and their state protectors, this agreement is not primarily based on corruption but on toleration. Police and criminals restrain their mutual aggression, enabling drug transactions on the one hand, and maintaining order on the other. São Paulo, once extremely violent, has been one of the most peaceful Brazilian states for decades.

Informal agreements with criminals are not exclusive to monopolistic drug markets like São Paulo. The state police in Greater Buenos Aires, the largest metropolitan area of Argentina, collected illicit protection rents with the complaisance or even complicity of governing politicians,[4] and thus offered credible protection to certain drug dealers. As a former vice-minister of security told me, "Where there are better business opportunities, they [i.e., the provincial government] send better business managers [i.e., police commanders]. The police are a source of financing."[5] At the same time, the police managed to maintain relative order despite an extremely fragmented drug market.

However, such informal pacts are not always sustainable. The neighboring Argentine province of Santa Fe exhibited a similar pattern to Buenos Aires until it collapsed in the 2000s to make way for particularistic covenants between police and drug dealers, especially in Rosario, its largest metropolitan area. As a federal judge described, "Drug trafficking in Rosario became scandalous because police protection, which always existed but was contained, became decentralized, so every police precinct ran three or four bunkers."[6] Violence in Rosario – and the province – reached unprecedented levels.

---

[3] Interview by author with Military Police lieutenant, São Paulo, October 30, 2014.
[4] I use "rents" in this book to refer to the share of the revenues accrued from drug trafficking and other illicit activities collected by police officers (or other state actors) from criminals.
[5] Interview by author with Marcelo Sain, Buenos Aires, July 25, 2013.
[6] Interview by author with federal judge Vera Barros, Rosario, June 24, 2014.

As these examples show, police in Latin America do not just fight drug trafficking; they deal with it in multiple ways. None of these approaches are codified in written laws or procedural manuals. Rather, they illustrate the various *informal regulatory arrangements* that state officials in Latin America and other regions with weakly institutionalized polities systematically apply to administer illicit markets.

This book addresses the puzzle of how weakly institutionalized democracies can control drug markets and produce order in Latin American metropolitan areas. If the idea of ordered illicit markets sounds contradictory in and of itself, it seems particularly bizarre in Latin America, the most violent region in the world, which hosts 10 percent of the world's population but 33 percent of global homicides (Muggah and Tobón 2018). Furthermore, police in Latin America are widely regarded as abusive of citizens and complicit with criminals, an obstacle rather than a solution to security (Bergman 2018; Yashar 2018). Argentina and Brazil are no exception in this regard.

However, illicit markets in Argentina and Brazil exhibit great variation in violence not only between but also within these areas over time. While some initially turbulent districts managed to quell violence, in other more tranquil settings it spiraled out of control. Rio de Janeiro's predatory police provoked retaliation by traffickers, competitive violence between drug gangs and overall insecurity in marginalized neighborhoods. In the early 1990s, homicide rates in the city were above 60 per 100,000. Decentralized protection deals in Santa Fe also doubled homicide rates between 2008 and 2013, reaching an unprecedented 21 homicides per 100,000 people. By contrast, police in Buenos Aires and São Paulo were able to reduce criminal violence through collusion or nonaggression agreements with criminal gangs, respectively: in Buenos Aires, homicide rates were one-third the level of Santa Fe while in São Paulo they decreased from 50 to below 10 per 100,000 individuals and have remained low for more than a decade. I will show that such fluctuations in criminal violence can be understood as the embodiment of different state strategies to informally regulate illicit markets. While multiple scholars have explained variation in criminal violence in Latin America, very few have defined or explained informal regulatory regimes that govern illicit markets. Such is this book's premise.

Informal regulation involves the intentional exercise of authority by a public agency to monitor market participants and enforce nonwritten, shared standards. In this case, the public agency is the police, who are at least formally subordinate to elected politicians. However, whether and how politicians control their police is another central question, whose answer depends on politics. This book unpacks the relationship between elected politicians and police to explain the politics behind the different drug market regulation regimes in Latin American metropolitan areas.

I argue that political competition influences whether and how politicians manage to control their police, that is, the autonomy of police departments, which then affects how police officers employ toleration, protection and predation in relation to drug dealers. These systematic police responses produce different *informal regulatory arrangements*, with differing levels of violence by both criminals and police. This book presents a subnational comparative analysis of the four main metropolitan areas in Argentina and Brazil to show how these regulatory regimes emerge, persist or collapse. In doing so, I show how state regulation became more or less coordinated over time, and how this affected drug market stability and levels of violence. I also show how even corrupt police and politicians can produce order and shape illicit markets.

Drug trafficking is by far the most lucrative illicit market in Latin America (Reuter 2014). All countries in the region are involved in the drug trade, whether as producers of marihuana, cocaine or heroin;[7] transshipment routes; exit ports or money laundering sites (UNODC 2012). Drug consumption in the region has also increased dramatically during the last two decades, according to a report by the Inter-American Observatory on Drugs (CICAD 2015). This illicit economy is also a major albeit contingent source of the violence in the region. Political scientists have explained variation in drug-related violence through the cohesion of the state's security apparatus (Snyder and Durán-Martínez 2009; Durán-Martínez 2015), drug geography (Yashar 2018), the state's conditional repression of trafficking (Lessing 2017) and the political alignment between different levels of government (Dell 2015; Osorio 2015; Trejo and Ley 2020).

This book proposes an alternative narrative of how state actors produce order in weakly institutionalized contexts with deeply embedded and potentially violent illicit markets. It makes two central contributions. First, I present a broader set of state responses to illicit markets. I specify four types of informal regulatory arrangements that encapsulate the different combinations of toleration, protection and predation that police can apply with respect to criminal markets: *coordinated coexistence,*

---

[7] For example, all of the world's cocaine is grown in three countries: Bolivia, Colombia and Peru (Bagley 2012).

protection rackets, particularistic negotiations and *particularistic confrontations.* By the end of each case analysis in Chapters 3–6, the reader will appreciate how these arrangements emerged and shifted over time in each subnational district due to changes in political competition and police autonomy. I show that systematic patterns of state regulation of illicit markets prevail in each metropolitan area during a substantial period. In contrast with other works, which focus on criminal or rebel governance (Arjona 2016; Arias 2017), this book brings the state's governance of illicit markets and criminal violence back to the forefront.

The second key contribution of this book is a theoretical framework that connects political competition, police autonomy and drug trafficking regulation. These three components have rarely been analyzed in conjunction. On the one hand, there are innumerable studies on security forces in Latin America; although many of them refer to political competition, they mostly neglect the linkage between police politics and criminal violence. Meanwhile, most studies on the impact of political competition on criminal violence overlook tensions between police and elected politicians, hardly irrelevant in a region where police forces exhibit systematic corruption, inefficiency and abuse of human rights that jeopardize democratic legitimacy and politicians' electoral prospects. I posit that, to understand how states shape illicit markets in developing democracies, we first need to analyze the relationship between politicians and their security apparatus. In short, police responsiveness to incumbents in developing democracies should be explored rather than assumed (Post 2018).

I argue that increases in political competition over time (turnover) and between political actors (fragmentation) decrease incumbents' capacity to control the police and thus expand police autonomy. Autonomous police are more likely to regulate drug markets through *particularistic negotiations* or *confrontations,* which consist primarily of predatory techniques that (re)produce violence. By contrast, entrenched governments are more capable of controlling the police, whether to further their own interests (politicization) or to subject police to the rule of law (professionalization). Entrenched governments with concentrated power (less fragmentation) are more likely to politicize the police, while governments with dispersed power (more fragmentation) are more inclined to professionalize the force. Politicized police, on the one hand, regulate drug trafficking through *protection rackets* based on coordinated corruption. Professionalized police, on the other, employ coordinated toleration to stabilize drug markets through *coordinated coexistence* regimes. Both arrangements feature low violence by criminals and police. This book thus offers a novel theoretical framework to explore the relationship between democracy, policing and illicit markets. The remainder of this chapter situates this study within literatures on the state, police politics and criminal violence; describes the four types of regulatory regimes; presents the research design; and provides a roadmap for the rest of the book.

INFORMAL STATES, POLICE POLITICS AND CRIMINAL VIOLENCE

This book contributes to three interrelated yet often estranged literatures in political science and social sciences more broadly. First, the informal side of states in developing democracies; second, the relationship between elected politicians and police – and bureaucratic agencies, more generally; and, finally, the causes and consequences of criminal violence, especially in relation to drug markets. While most of these studies center on Latin America, some of their findings might also apply to other developing regions.

Regulation and the Gray Zones of Criminality

Many scholars from various disciplines have uncovered the hidden layer of states in the developing world. Whether due to resource scarcity or political calculation, many developing democracies have failed to build strong formal institutions and egalitarian enforcement of the rule of law. The dramatic increase in crime – often fueled by the state – in Latin America since the 1990s fits into this narrative. Guillermo O'Donnell famously referred to spaces within the national territory where the state did not enforce the rule of law and fostered low-intensity citizenship as "brown areas" (O'Donnell 1993). Since then, several scholars have ushered innovative concepts to describe the informal (or illicit) traits of Latin American states, such as "parallel polities," "grey zones," "violent democracies," "clandestine orders," "forbearance," "criminal governance," "ambivalent states" or "the gray zone of criminality" (Leeds 1996; Auyero 2007; Arias and Goldstein 2010; Dewey 2015; Holland 2016; Arias 2017; Auyero and Sobering 2019; Trejo and Ley 2020).

This book aligns with these authors' premise that state illegalities are more than simply a matter of capacity. Informal regulation does not equate to state absence or weakness. On the contrary, regulation implies that state actors can credibly enforce the law against the criminals they monitor. Although police in most developing countries certainly lack fundamental resources to perform their duties, such as proper wages, equipment and working conditions, the relative territorial fixedness of retail drug dealing in metropolitan areas affords police ample opportunities to detect and repress this criminal activity. In other words, the politics of regulation implies that state actors can choose when and how to enforce the law.

However, this book departs from these works by distinguishing and accounting for the systematic patterns by which states govern illicit markets, or different informal regulatory regimes. Where other authors see undifferentiated patterns or micro-level regimes, I show that there are relatively stable and internally coherent regulatory arrangements that account for the state's varied responses to drug markets. I also propose a theory of the influence of political competition and police autonomy in the emergence and collapse of these regimes, showing how they can vary over time, even in the same metropolitan area.

Police: From Destabilizers to Regulators

Police perform the quintessential task of the modern Weberian state: preserving the monopoly of legitimate violence within a given territory. Nonetheless, political scientists, even in the criminal violence literature, have often undertheorized how the relationship between elected politicians and their police forces affects the evolution of state responses to illicit activities. In this book, I apply the concept of police autonomy, understood as police's ability to control their internal governance and external operations without political interference, to analyze police–government relations in developing democracies. In these contexts, police autonomy does not depend solely on legal statutes but on the distribution of political power. With varying levels of autonomy, police regulate drug trafficking in diverse ways, applying different dosages of violence and corruption and provoking distinct levels of violence by criminals.

The main research on police in political science has come from the literature focused on the police reforms undertaken in Latin America and other third-wave democracies (Hinton and Newburn 2009). Police reforms refer to legal changes in the structure, organization and functions of the police to make it more accountable to the law, respectful of human rights and responsive to citizens (Bayley 2006, 23). Encompassing police reform has been the exception rather than the rule in Latin America. Reforms have typically floundered due to police resistance, partisan turnover (Davis 2006), corrupt linkages between police and politicians from different levels of government (Hinton 2006; Eaton 2008), societal clamors for punitive policies following violent crimes (Ungar 2009; Holland 2013) or politicians and bureaucrats' attempts to avoid blame for such crimes (Flom and Post 2016). Meanwhile, successful reforms rely on multiple idiosyncratic factors such as social activism (Fuentes 2005; Moncada 2009), mobilized scandals following police malfeasance (González 2020) or political and police commitment to reform (Arias and Ungar 2009). While extremely insightful, this literature explains the onset rather than the persistence of reform and has mostly overlooked the multiple patterns of accommodation between police and their political superiors (see as exceptions Beare and Murray 2007; Prado et al. 2012). Additionally, it has rarely addressed the impact of reform on drug markets and criminal violence (Sabet 2012 as exception). Through the examination of police autonomy, this book addresses these gaps, providing theoretical and practical recommendations to rethink policing in Latin America and beyond.

Within this literature, Yanilda González's book, *Authoritarian Police in Democracy*, stands out not just for its ground-breaking theoretical framework of institutional change but also for recasting the importance of policing as a basic state function. My study, however, focuses on how political competition impacts aspects purposefully omitted by her framework, such as the implementation, effectiveness, durability and outputs of different efforts by politicians to control the police (González 2020, 36). Moreover, I cover not only formal policies but also informal mechanisms, such as sharing rents from corruption, by which politicians achieve this objective.

Criminal Violence

Finally, this book builds on insights from a vast literature on criminal violence, in turn inspired by civil war and ethnic conflict studies. Most scholars in this burgeoning field have focused on the Mexican case, highlighting the destabilizing effect of increased political competition on criminal violence. They have shown that the decentralization of the national government and the state security apparatus (Ríos 2015; Durán-Martínez 2017), unconditioned repression by the state (Lessing 2017), lack of partisan coordination between national and local states (Dell 2015; Trejo and Ley 2020) and increased electoral competition due to democratization (Osorio 2013) are associated with greater conflict between state and criminals and higher overall criminal violence.[8] However, these studies rarely refer to the actual implementation of security policies by the state's security apparatus – especially the state and local police.

Ben Lessing's ground-breaking book, *Making Peace in Drug Wars*, is an exception in this regard. I share his premise that "few things shape cartels' incentives as thoroughly as state policy" (Lessing 2017, 3). However, I would add that, in addition to formal laws and policies, the state's *informal* regulation also shapes criminal actors' incentives as well as the overall dynamics of illicit markets.

This book also finds common ground with Angélica Durán-Martínez's *The Politics of Drug Violence*, since it focuses on the interactions between the same actors (politicians, police and criminals). Nonetheless, not only do I analyze different countries (in her case, Colombia and Mexico; in my case, Argentina and Brazil), but I also place greater emphasis on tensions between politicians and police rather than on other sources of state incoherence.

Furthermore, I focus on a different outcome than most of this literature since I do not concentrate primarily on criminal violence but rather on the different arrangements through which states regulate drug markets. I argue that political competition affects criminal violence indirectly, through police autonomy and drug trafficking regulatory regimes, which are built on different combinations of police violence and corruption. The following section will clarify this concept and introduce the argument.

INFORMAL REGULATION OF ILLICIT MARKETS

We are accustomed to hearing about regulation with regard to various activities. In the public policy, political science and economics domains, regulation refers to a government agency's[9] monitoring, direction or supervision of certain economic activities[10] like finance, telecommunications, energy and cybersecurity. Regulation can also entail protection of workers and consumers against exploitative labor practices, business cartelization or shoddy product quality. Overall, we tend to equate regulation with formal rules and instruments: laws, codes, procedures, checklists, manuals and so on. By contrast, it is rarer to think about informal

---

[8] See Kalyvas (2015) for an illustrative summary of this literature.

[9] Non-state actors, both economic and otherwise (NGOs, social movements, citizen organizations, etc.), might also perform regulatory activities internally (self-regulation) or with respect to a specific segment of society.

[10] Government regulation can also apply to noneconomic spheres, such as the family, education, health and reproduction.

regulation in the context of illicit markets, except to show how criminals evade the state's oversight (see as exceptions Beckert and Dewey 2017; Sain 2019). However, the core definition of regulation as "the intentional use of authority to affect behavior of a different party according to set standards" (Black 2001) can also apply to the state's *informal* response to drug trafficking and illicit markets more generally.

What Does It Mean That States Regulate Drug Trafficking?

While most countries' national legislation prohibits drug trafficking, states enforce these rules differently across their territory and over time. Drug trafficking is primarily an illicit market, which means that state actors, as business regulators, can seek to restrict its supply or demand and reduce its potential negative externalities. Police, as the main regulatory agency of the state security apparatus, can employ formal and informal enforcement mechanisms to affect criminals' behavior and the market in general.[11] Much of Latin American states' formal responses to drug trafficking have centered on militarized struggles to reduce supply (crop eradication, interdictions, arrests, etc.) while devoting scant resources to demand reduction strategies (prevention, treatment, rehabilitation and harm reduction).[12] Governments have sought to reduce the drug trade's main negative externality – criminal violence – through different crime control strategies, from "zero tolerance" to community policing or hot-spot policing. Some governments have adopted more draconian measures, such as the "kingpin strategy" in Mexico – arresting or killing the heads of different drug cartels to dismantle their organizations (Calderón et al. 2015).

This book focuses on the *informal* responses applied by the state to control drug trafficking. Legality is often a blurry line when fighting organized crime. Some of the formal responses mentioned earlier can also deviate from the law or break it entirely. For instance, police might kill a drug trafficker as part of a sanctioned operation or via unauthorized summary executions. However, the main premise of informality is that states do not simply repress but *regulate* drug trafficking. This involves different degrees of toleration, protection and predation of drug dealers to

---

[11] Other state agencies beyond the security sector also implement drug policies but have much fewer direct interactions with drug dealers.

[12] Rarer still is the implementation of formal decriminalization or legalization of various aspects of the drug trade. The Uruguayan model, in this sense, is still an exception in Latin America.

change their behavior, whether to contain their violence, absorb part of their revenues or eliminate them from the market.

Informal regulation, which police carry out through unwritten yet entrenched practices of violence and corruption, enables the state to partially affect drug supply and demand. State enforcement agents may dictate when and where drug dealers may or may not sell their product and make it harder or easier for dealers to expand their operations outside of their original territory. While state enforcement might not modify the retail price or "quality" of drugs being sold (Caulkins et al. 2006; Keefer et al. 2010), it can affect the extent to which drug dealers resort to violence to settle market disputes and the number of licensed distributors (Gambetta 1996). Like Marcelo Bergman proposes in his book, *More Money, More Crime: Prosperity and Rising Crime in Latin America,* I also argue that the regulatory capacity of law enforcement agencies to keep crime under control can explain variation in violent crime (Bergman 2018, 21). Again, our stories differ in that I focus on the *informal* regulatory capacity of the state, which relates to the degree of coordination its police have in tolerating, protecting, or preying upon drug dealers. These differences in coordination yield distinct regulatory regimes.

How States Regulate Drug Trafficking: Informal Regulatory Regimes

Drug trafficking regulatory regimes are the set of actions by which state officials enforce formal and informal norms to constrain drug traffickers' behavior and structure drug trafficking markets. These regimes differ in their respective levels and coordination of police violence and corruption and have different implications for criminal violence.

A few minimal conceptual clarifications are in order. Throughout this book, I refer to police violence as events involving lethal interventions by police officers.[13] While this is clearly a subset of the total acts of police violence, it is the most extreme and most easily measurable by governments or non-governmental organizations. Police corruption refers to different instances by which police use their authority for means other than their legally specified mission.[14] In Chapter 2, I elaborate the four main ways in which police deviate from their legal role: toleration,

---

[13] For my theory, it makes no difference a priori whether the act of police lethality was justified or not, accidental or intentional, or carried out while the police officer was on duty or off duty.

[14] Instances of corruption thus might not necessarily entail economic profit and serve a purported "greater good" (e.g., reducing violence).

protection, predation and criminal entrepreneurship. Finally, criminal violence is the act of inflicting deadly bodily harm on a person.[15] I measure criminal violence through homicide rates, which represent the most reliable indicator of this phenomenon.

I distinguish between four regimes: two coordinated types – *coordinated coexistence* and *protection rackets* – and two uncoordinated variants – *particularistic negotiation* and *particularistic confrontation*.

Coordinated coexistence occurs when politicians and police forces jointly broker explicit or implicit agreements with criminal actors to restrain their mutual conflict. Following Staniland's definition, in coordinated coexistence "neither side makes a total attempt to destroy the other" and "violence ... follows the implicit rules of engagement about what is and is not acceptable to each side" (Staniland 2012, 251) to avoid the escalation of violent conflict. In this scenario, police repression of drug traffickers is coordinated, selective and targeted – as opposed to uncoordinated, indiscriminate and arbitrary (Kalyvas 2006). Police might confront traffickers when they violate the rules of engagement by killing fellow officers, women, children or other persons not involved in the drug trade. Criminals might also strike at police who torture or summarily execute members of their organization or who threaten their families or communities. Nonetheless, violent actions should target specific offenders and end rapidly rather than lead to prolonged spirals. Consequently, when coordinated coexistence prevails, criminal and state violence should decrease or remain low. Meanwhile, state corruption, although present, is restricted to low-level police officers or individual politicians, including those outside the administration, acting separately from each other – hence its uncoordinated nature. Material payoffs for state actors are not a fundamental aspect of this regime, which is based on the toleration of drug markets.

While admittedly rare, there are several examples of coordinated coexistence in Latin America and other regions. During the late 1980s, the Cali cartel set up a modus vivendi with the Colombian state that distinguished it from its more brutal Medellín counterpart (Arias 2017, 23; Durán-Martínez 2017). Nonetheless, in Medellin – once the most dangerous city in the world[16] – homicides decreased in part because of a pact between the state and the head of the local drug cartel, Don Berna, who ordered his clique to restrain its violent acts to avoid extradition to the

---

[15] These incidents do not involve police officers or other state security forces, except when explicitly noted.

[16] During the peak of the war against Pablo Escobar's Medellín cartel, Medellín had 6,500 homicides in 1991, with a homicide rate of 381 per 100,000.

United States. This regime was termed "donbernabilidad," a sardonic twist on the notion that the criminal boss guaranteed governance.[17] In El Salvador, the government temporarily stemmed violence by brokering a truce between the main gangs in 2012, in which imprisoned gang leaders received improved living conditions in return for instructing their subordinates to cease their confrontation with their rivals (*The Economist* 2013). While these coexistence arrangements were brief, others have lasted for generations. Aside from a brief battle in the early 1990s, the Sicilian mafia has thrived mostly without fighting the Italian state (Gambetta 1996; Lessing 2017, 51), while the relationship with the Neapolitan Camorra has been more conflictive (Saviano 2010). In Japan, the national government has coexisted with the central criminal organization, the Yakuza, for the better part of a century, implicitly tolerating its activities in exchange for its regulation of violence (Hill 2006).

In a second type of coordinated regulatory regime, politicians and police jointly run *protection rackets*, in which they charge criminal groups for protection not just from rivals but from the state itself (Tilly 1985, 170–71). In protection rackets, state corruption is extensive but coordinated between street-level officers, high-ranking commanders and political authorities. Police enable dealers to operate relatively undisturbed by rival criminal groups or other enforcement agencies, although they also seize drugs and shut down some drug trafficking operations to signal their credibility as enforcers. In this regime, state and criminal violence should remain low.

The epitome of this regime was during the PRI hegemony, when Mexican politicians and law enforcement officials – from the attorney general and security ministers to the heads of the federal and state police – protected traffickers in exchange for succulent payoffs and the promise to keep criminal violence down (Snyder and Duran-Martinez 2009; Rios 2012). Some authors portray similar dynamics in post-Communist Russia, where there are multiple collaborative ties between criminal syndicates and state law enforcement or intelligence officials (Volkov 2002; Taylor 2013).

While coordinated coexistence and protection rackets involve coordination by state actors, in the two remaining regulatory regimes, the police fail to organize their corruption or violence toward dealers. In *particularistic negotiations*, various police units and officers collect bribes from

---

[17] Source: Insight Crime, www.insightcrime.org/colombia-organized-crime-news/don-berna. See also the 2011 Washington Office on Latin America report on Police reform (WOLA 2011, 7–8).

drug dealers without internal coordination or centralized protection from political incumbents. The police's high and disorganized corruption destabilizes the drug market as organized criminal groups (OCGs) seek to expand their operations into different territories, retaliate violently against aggression by rival groups and are unable to secure order in their turf, which generates spirals of violence. Criminal violence therefore increases in this regime, as occurred in Mexico after the end of the PRI hegemony, when centralized protection deals with drug cartels became harder to sustain (Snyder and Duran-Martinez 2009, 263–65).

Finally, the most violent regulatory regime, *particularistic confrontation*, consists of systematic yet uncoordinated attacks by state security forces against drug trafficking organizations. Indiscriminate police violence is accompanied, and often preceded, by similarly anarchic police corruption. State violence fuels criminal violence, as criminal groups confront the police, invade each other's territory and victimize the local population to deter (or punish) cooperation with the police. The conflict in Colombia between the state and Pablo Escobar's Medellín Cartel (1984–1993) often exhibited this dynamic. During this confrontation, the Colombian state sanctioned extrajudicial killings of Escobar's associates, carried out by a special police unit and a paramilitary death squad composed of Escobar's enemies. In retaliation, the Medellín Cartel and other unaffiliated groups killed thousands of people, including hundreds of police officers (Bowden 2002). The current drug war undertaken by President Rodrigo Duterte in the Philippines, which has killed over 5,500 people between 2017 and June 2019 (Johnson and Giles 2019), is another example of this bloody and corrupt arrangement. Table 1.1 summarizes the key features of these regulatory regimes.

TABLE 1.1. *Central features of drug trafficking regulatory regimes*

	Coordinated coexistence	Protection rackets	Particularistic negotiation	Particularistic confrontation
Police corruption	Low and Uncoordinated	High and Coordinated	High and Uncoordinated	High and Uncoordinated
Police violence	Low and Coordinated	Low and Coordinated	Low and Uncoordinated	High and Uncoordinated
Criminal violence	Low	Low	High	High

Source: Author's elaboration

RESEARCH DESIGN

This book carries out a subnational analysis in two countries since the return of state-level democratic elections in the 1980s: the Argentine provinces of Buenos Aires and Santa Fe; and the Brazilian states of Rio de Janeiro and São Paulo.[18] Over nearly forty years, these subnational governments have gone through several administrations, shifted their public security approaches and experienced multiple drug trafficking regulatory arrangements. In other words, there is a substantial variation not only *across* these cases but also *within* each case over time. I use process tracing to show how my independent and intervening variables (political competition and police autonomy) affect the regulation of drug trafficking, as well as the mechanisms that connect them. I marshal qualitative and quantitative evidence to explain variation within each case while addressing alternative explanations (Bennett and Checkel 2015).

The combination of a subnational comparative research design with within-case analysis lends greater analytical leverage to my findings for two reasons. First, within each subnational unit, I can obtain multiple causal process observations, in other words, "insights or piece(s) of data that provide information about context or mechanism" (Brady and Collier 2010, 184). This expands the number of cases beyond just the four subnational districts, as each gubernatorial term could be thought of as a distinct data-set observation: At least every four years there is the possibility of a change in the person or party in the governor's seat that may produce turnover,[19] and a reshuffling of cabinets and legislatures that can alter the level of fragmentation.[20] The persistence of different arrangements over time in each case yields at least two different scores of the dependent variable (*informal regulatory arrangements*) in the more than three decades analyzed (see Table 1.2).

Second, conducting this procedure in each of the four subnational units included in this study allows me to compare trajectories across cases, an analysis that I develop more fully in Chapter 7. The fact that different

---

[18] In Argentina, national and state democratic elections resumed simultaneously in 1983. In Brazil, by contrast, direct state elections occurred in 1982 but national *indirect* elections took place only three years later; hence, this book takes 1982 as the starting point for analyzing the Brazilian cases.

[19] Turnover may also occur before the four-year term ends if the governor were to resign for different reasons and her successor comes from a different party or faction.

[20] Fragmentation can also change every two years if there are midterm elections instead of concurrent elections every four years or more rapidly if there are substantial changes in the governor's cabinet.

TABLE 1.2. *Scores of different case-periods*

Case-period	Turnover	Fragmentation	Police autonomy	Informal regulatory arrangement
Rio de Janeiro, 1983–2007	*High*	*High*	*High*	*Particularistic confrontation*
Rio de Janeiro, 2008–2014	*Low*	*High*	*Low (professionalization)*	*Coordinated coexistence*
Santa Fe, 1983–1997	*Low*	*Low*	*Low (politicization)*	*Protection rackets*
Santa Fe, 1997–2015	*High*	*High*	*High*	*Particularistic negotiation*
Buenos Aires, 1983–1996	*Low*	*Low*	*Low (politicization)*	*Protection rackets*
Buenos Aires, 1997–2003	*High*	*High*	*High*	*Particularistic negotiation*
Buenos Aires, 2004–2015	*Low*	*Low*	*Low (politicization)*	*Protection rackets*
São Paulo, 1982–1994	*High*	*High*	*High*	*Particularistic confrontation*
São Paulo, 1995–2014	*Low*	*High*	*Low (professionalization)*	*Coordinated coexistence*

Source: Author's elaboration.

subnational districts similarly exhibit the hypothesized patterns strengthens the analytical thrust of this framework.

Additionally, this subnational comparative research enables controlling for national level factors which might condition state responses, such as the federal constitutional structure, national penal codes and the configuration of the state's security apparatus (Snyder 2001). It also enables a finer-grained focus than a cross-national comparison, especially when retail illicit markets and criminal violence are concentrated in each country's main metropolitan areas (Moncada 2013; Giraudy et al. 2019).

Case Selection

Studying drug trafficking in Argentina and Brazil might initially seem surprising. These countries are not drug producers, like Colombia, Bolivia and Peru, or the primary routes to the main consumption market – the United States – as Mexico or countries in the Central American Triangle. Furthermore, a comparison between Argentina and Brazil might seem odd given their respective levels of violence. The national homicide rate in Argentina in 2019 was around five homicides per 100,000 individuals, much lower than Brazil's 26 per 100,000. However, this disparity becomes less relevant when comparing the chosen *subnational* units.

First, in the 2010s, homicide rates in the province of Santa Fe were in the low 20s per 100,000 people, higher than in the state of São Paulo for most of the 2000s and in Rio during Pacification. Second, homicide rates can spike very rapidly in one state while hardly moving in its neighbor. Changes in regulatory regimes might not explain overall levels of violence but they do help us understand temporal shifts in patterns of violence, by both state and criminal actors. While homicide rates doubled in Santa Fe in the mid-2000s, they remained constant in Buenos Aires. Whereas criminal violence decreased dramatically and remained stable in São Paulo in the 2000s, it fluctuated radically in Rio. National-level differences in violence between Brazil and Argentina are less relevant for this discussion than the common shifts their subnational states exhibit from uncoordinated to coordinated regulatory regimes (or vice versa) over time.

Furthermore, when considering retail drug markets, Argentina and Brazil are two of the main drug transshipment and consumption hubs of Latin America, illustrating the growing consumption trend in the region (CICAD 2015). Brazil is the largest consumer of cocaine behind the United States, while Argentina has experienced a significant growth in marihuana and cocaine consumption in the last two decades (UNODC 2012).[21] While they do not have drug cartels, both countries feature state and local-level criminal groups involved in the wholesale and retail distribution of narcotics. Criminal factions or drug gangs in Brazil are clearly more organized and powerful than in Argentina, although in both cases gangs' territorial control is limited to informal neighborhoods in urban peripheries. Currently only the PCC in São Paulo resembles a drug trafficking organization in that they control the wholesale import and export of illicit drugs in Brazil.[22] However, retail distribution in São Paulo is outsourced by the PCC to multiple, small, unconnected groups who pay dues to the central command inside São Paulo's prisons (Lessing and Willis 2019). In this sense, despite its greater power, the PCC's retail distribution pattern looks like that of criminal groups in the other cases analyzed in this book.

Argentina and Brazil also share multiple political similarities. Both experienced limited democracies and brutal dictatorships until the 1980s, and regained democracy in the early years of the Third Wave. These newly democratized regimes increased popular participation,

---

[21] In both countries, the poor are the greatest consumers of cocaine base residue, locally called *paco* (Argentina) or *crack* (Brazil). I should note that UNODC statistics suffer from multiple deficits in data collection, so it is necessary to take them cautiously.

[22] The CV in Rio de Janeiro used to have this capacity but, as Chapter 3 will illustrate, such hegemonic control faded as a result of their confrontation with the state government.

amplified constitutional rights and promised greater equality, fairness and abidance with the rule of law. Unfortunately, both countries have under-performed in these regards. Brazil is one of the most unequal countries of Latin America while Argentina is continuously mired by economic instability. Political polarization has ballooned in recent decades. In both countries, several presidents have exited office before the end of their term, whether due to resignations following social protests or impeachments based on alleged corruption. This formal institutional weakness encompasses their police forces, which are often marred by arbitrary use of force, rampant corruption and weak external accountability (Méndez et al. 1999; González 2020, 15). As the case chapters will discuss, neither country substantially democratized its police during the early transition period.

Furthermore, Argentina and Brazil are among the wealthiest countries in the region and possess relatively high state capacity. Unlike their Andean or Central American counterparts, these states control their territories, especially urban areas. Although their formal institutions are weak and state corruption is pervasive, they are not failed or "narco states" captured by drug traffickers nor is criminal governance pervasive beyond the neighborhood-level. Even in the marginalized neighborhoods where drug dealing proliferates, the state – and particularly the police – is not absent but present in "convoluted," "selective, contradictory and intermittent" or "ambivalent" ways (Arias 2013; Auyero and Berti 2015; Auyero and Sobering 2019). Both countries have the capacity to regulate illicit markets, especially in the selected subnational districts, which makes the question of how they do so more relevant.[23]

Additionally, Argentina and Brazil are federal countries in which subnational governors are the political authorities primarily responsible for providing public security. Unlike other federal countries, such as Mexico or the United States, they do not have autonomous local police departments.[24] Brazilian states, unlike Argentine provinces, have two separate police forces, a Military Police, in charge of preventing and repressing crimes, and a Civil Police, tasked with investigating crimes. In both countries, the state police far outnumber their federal counterparts, who investigate specific, major crimes. Despite drug trafficking being a federal crime, subnational police often carry out the lion's share of drug

---

[23] Foreign influence is also negligible. For instance, the United States' role in shaping drug policy in Argentina and Brazil is much smaller than in Colombia or Mexico.

[24] In fact, in Latin America, Mexico is the only country in which local police enforce security, which highlights the importance of exploring interaction between national and subnational actors.

enforcement due to their daily interactions with street-level dealers. This subnational comparison underscores how the design and implementation of informal strategies varies within the same national context.

These cases are also illustrative of the security problems that urban areas in the region face. Argentina and Brazil have thirty-three of the fifty most populated metropolitan areas in South America. The subnational cases selected include the main metropolitan provinces in each country – Buenos Aires[25] and Santa Fe in Argentina, Rio de Janeiro and São Paulo in Brazil.[26] Because of their demographic size, they provide a greater domestic consumer base for drug retail distribution and feature several marginalized neighborhoods in which drug gangs store and distribute their product. These neighborhoods are also, for several reasons, typically the sites of greatest violence in each metropolitan area, which makes them the primary focus point of police interventions.

Within each subnational district, I conducted fieldwork in specific municipalities to understand the state's drug trafficking regulation on the ground. In Brazil, I focused on the metropolitan areas of Rio de Janeiro and São Paulo, which contain most of the state's population,[27] and are also the seat of the state-level government, which afforded me direct access to subnational political authorities and top security officials. In Buenos Aires, I carried out multiple interviews in the capital city of La Plata, where government offices are located, but since the population is widely dispersed through the metropolitan area, I selected two additional municipalities – San Martín and Florencio Varela – to examine responses to drug trafficking at the local level.[28] Finally, in Santa Fe, I focused on the city

[25] I do not include the Autonomous City of Buenos Aires in this study. Even though it technically constitutes part of Greater Buenos Aires (GBA), it has different political authorities and has been under the purview first of the Federal Police and then had its own security force. In this book, when speaking of the GBA, I only refer to the twenty-four municipalities surrounding the city.

[26] São Paulo, Rio de Janeiro and Buenos Aires are the three most populated areas in South America, in that order.

[27] According to the 2010 census, 78 percent of Rio's population live in the metropolitan area and 45 percent in the case of São Paulo. I use the terms "Rio de Janeiro" and "São Paulo" to refer to the state rather than the metropolitan area or the capital cities, unless explicitly noted.

[28] These municipalities are in different zones of Greater Buenos Aires (San Martín in the Northwest and Florencio Varela in the South) and, at the time, exhibited different political alignments with the provincial government: San Martín was governed by a major who had joined the opposing Peronist faction and had greater alternation in power throughout this period. Florencio Varela's mayor, by contrast, was aligned with the provincial government and had been in power for more than twenty consecutive years.

of Rosario – the province's largest metropolitan area,[29] and recent epicenter of drug-related violence – and also conducted interviews with public officials in the capital city of Santa Fe,[30] where the state government is located.

Interviews and Other Sources

The central claim of this book is that informality permeates linkages between police and politicians as well as how police regulate drug markets. Official documents and statistics are therefore insufficient to analyze these interactions and processes. This book thus relies primarily on the insights of key informants who participated in or observed police politics or drug market regulation from various perspectives since the 1980s. During various field trips to Argentina and Brazil, between September 2013 and July 2015, I conducted 178 interviews. In total, I spoke with 86 politicians, 44 police officers of various ranks – excluding five individuals who held both roles in succession, typically police officers then serving in elected or appointed political positions – as well as multiple judges, prosecutors, representatives from civil society, journalists and academic experts (see Table 1.3).

With respect to politicians, my priority was to interview security department officials from different administrations. To balance incumbents' viewpoints, I interviewed politicians from different opposition parties, contacting the members of parliamentary public security commissions through institutional channels. Interviews with acting police officers were harder to attain as they formally cannot give interviews without their superior's authorization. Sending a researcher through this bureaucratic route is a pretext to make sure the interview never takes place. Commanders are especially hard to reach since they are rarely in their offices. Therefore, I contacted police officers through three main channels: previously interviewed political authorities; police union websites in Argentina; and city council meetings in different neighborhoods in Brazil, especially in São Paulo. From there, I proceeded using a snowball method, alternating between politicians and police with differing partisan inclinations and limiting the number of interviewees contacted through a single source.

When conducting the interviews, I could not directly ask, "What is the nature of the police's involvement with drug trafficking?"

---

[29] With over 1.3 million people, the metropolitan area of Rosario concentrates 42 percent of the province's population (2010 census).

[30] Through the book, I use Santa Fe to refer to the province rather than the Capital City, unless explicitly noted.

TABLE 1.3. *Summary of interviews*

Category	Buenos Aires	Santa Fe	Rio de Janeiro	São Paulo	Total
Police	8	5	12	19	44
Politicians	36	27	10	13	86
Mixed[a]	1	0	1	3	5
Others[b]	11	8	20	4	43
Total	56	40	43	39	178

[a] "Mixed" refers to former police officers currently serving as elected or appointed government officials.
[b] Includes NGO representatives, journalists and academic experts.
Source: Author's elaboration

Rather, I included indirect prompts such that the subject would be brought up by the interviewee himself.[31] All interviews were semi-structured (Leech 2002), guided by specific preformulated themes such as how interviewees perceived the evolution of drug trafficking and criminal violence in their district, what policy initiatives were taken to tackle these problems and what kind of interaction the police have with drug dealers. I conducted interviews in government offices, cafés and people's homes, often having up to four interviews a day. Interviews lasted between fifteen minutes to more than three hours in length. In most cases, I was able to record the interviews, after asking for the respondent's permission.[32]

I triangulated these interviews with additional quantitative and qualitative evidence. I collected statistics on homicides and deaths from police interventions from annual reports by government security offices and human rights organizations since they became available, sometimes as far back as forty years.[33] I also searched national and local newspaper articles since the late 1980s, as well as secondary literature, to have additional data on the types and modalities of police corruption. This data helped illuminate certain mechanics of police corruption, such as how many officers took part in specific compacts with dealers, what district or divisions they belonged to and what was the nature of their relationship with dealers.

[31] Most interviewees were male, reflective of the limited role afforded to women in both police departments and political security offices in Latin America; therefore, I refer to interviewees in general through male pronouns (he/him/his).
[32] When speaking with low-ranking police officers or civil society representatives, I did not record or even ask to, so as to not condition their answers. I took handwritten notes and transcribed them once I returned to my room or in a café.
[33] This analysis has the advantage of capturing long-term trends, beyond specific years that might have been exceptional.

ROADMAP

This chapter has introduced the concept of informal regulation and the four predominant regulatory arrangements of retail drug markets in Latin America. I have also unveiled my argument that these regimes vary according to political competition and police autonomy. In Chapter 2, I develop this theoretical framework more extensively. I first outline the motivations and incentives of politicians, police officers and criminals and then define the three main conceptual building blocks of this research: political competition, police autonomy and drug market regulation. I then deploy my two-step argument: First, I discuss how political turnover and fragmentation affect police autonomy; second, how different variants of police autonomy shape different drug trafficking regulatory regimes.

The subsequent four chapters analyze the different patterns of political competition, police autonomy and drug trafficking regulation in each subnational district since democratization in the 1980s. Each chapter highlights the variation in regulatory regimes over time as well as the processes and mechanisms at play. The reader will not only be able to follow the argument in each case but also compare parallel sequences and divergent pathways across cases. Chapters 3 and 4 illustrate the two uncoordinated regimes – particularistic confrontations and negotiations – through the cases of Rio de Janeiro and Rosario, respectively. The following two chapters (5 and 6), by contrast, focus on coordinated regimes: protection rackets (Buenos Aires) and coexistence (São Paulo). Although a specific regime predominates in each case, there has also been substantial within-case variation during these more than three decades of democratic rule.

Chapter 3 shows how politicians repeatedly failed to reduce police autonomy in Rio de Janeiro due to high turnover and fragmentation since democratization. This failure resulted in *particularistic confrontations* featuring rampant police violence and corruption, as well as unbridled criminal violence in the Rio metropolitan area. This arrangement shifted temporarily due to the continuous tenure of the Party of the Brazilian Democratic Movement (*Partido do Movimento Democrático Brasileiro*, PMDB) in the late 2000s, which professionalized the police, regulated drug markets with greater tolerance and decreased criminal violence through the Pacification program.

Chapter 4 illustrates how Rosario, the main metropolitan area in the Argentine province of Santa Fe, drifted toward *particularistic negotiation*. Following democratization, the dominant Peronist party (*Partido*

Justicialista, PJ) politicized the police and centralized its rent extraction. However, this regime crumbled with the growing conflict between Peronist factions in the late 1990s and toppled with the arrival in power of the Socialist party in 2007. Police thereafter regulated the expanding drug market via dispersed agreements with dealers. This lack of credible protection fragmented and destabilized the drug market and led to unprecedented criminal violence in Rosario, the province's main metropolitan area.

Chapters 5 and 6 focus on coordinated regulatory arrangements, centered on the protection and toleration of illicit activities, respectively. In Chapter 5, I show how entrenched governments with low fragmentation can politicize the police and employ it to run *protection rackets*, as illustrated by most administrations of the Peronist party in Buenos Aires, Argentina, between 1987 and 2015. This regime featured high yet centralized corruption and low violence by police and criminals. While this arrangement prevailed for most of this period, temporary factional splits in the PJ in the late 1990s and early 2000s generated, as in Santa Fe (Chapter 4), uncoordinated corruption and greater criminal violence. As the PJ reunited in the mid-2000s, its administrations regained control over the police and reinstated protection rackets.

Chapter 6, meanwhile, shows how governments can professionalize the police and regulate drug markets through *coordinated coexistence*. The Brazilian Social Democratic Party (*Partido da Social Democracia Brasileira*, PSDB) governed São Paulo uninterruptedly between 1994 and 2018, yet always faced high legislative fragmentation, which inhibited the government from centralizing illicit protection rents. The increasing professionalization of the SP police facilitated its coordinated coexistence with criminal actors, which culminated in a truce with the main drug gang, the PCC, that decreased violent confrontations between police and criminals as well as overall violence in the state.

Finally, Chapter 7 summarizes the variation *across* as well as within the cases explored in the preceding chapters. I then extend the argument to other developing democracies in Latin America and other regions. I also outline the main theoretical and policy implications of these findings and lay out a future research agenda on the state and illicit markets in weak institutional contexts.

2

A Theory of Drug Market Regulation

Economic regulation is the exercise of public authority to align market actors' behavior with set standards. In the cases examined in this book, market actors (the regulated) are individuals involved in drug dealing in metropolitan areas, the public authorities (the regulators) are the police and the politicians to whom they are formally subordinated, and the set standards are implicit norms to conduct drug dealing in relatively peaceful terms. Informal regulation refers to the use by police of unwritten instruments such as violence and corruption to control drug dealers. To understand why and how regulation occurs, it is necessary to explain what these actors' incentives are; how these incentives and the constraints they face shape their respective interactions; and how these interactions produce different regulatory arrangements. In this chapter, I present my theoretical framework, which integrates these elements.

I argue that political competition, namely turnover and fragmentation, condition whether and how politicians can reduce police autonomy and shape different drug regulation regimes. Turnover refers to whether the same party or faction remains in power from one election the next. Fragmentation describes the extent to which power is concentrated by the governor during their term, in other words, whether they have a cohesive cabinet and a legislative majority that enables them to make decisions without substantial obstacles.

Under high turnover, efforts to curb police autonomy are thwarted and police regulate drug dealing through particularistic confrontations or negotiations, characterized by uncoordinated violence and corruption. In this case, political fragmentation is not decisive. While high fragmentation can increase policy incoherence or veto points and obstruct

24

reforms, low fragmentation is not sufficient to subdue the police when politicians are rotating in and out of office.

By contrast, low turnover ensures policy continuity, reduces transition costs and makes police commanders perceive incumbents as "the only game in town," subordinating the police to the administration. Fragmentation affects *how* that subordination takes place. Higher fragmentation can imply greater accountability checks and/or competition for illicit rents, motivating politicians to professionalize the police and regulate drug distribution through coordinated coexistence arrangements. Meanwhile, low fragmentation can motivate incumbents to politicize the police and use it to extract rents from criminal activities, regulating illicit markets through coordinated protection rackets (see Table 2.1).

TABLE 2.1. *Political competition, police autonomy and regulation of illicit markets*

Political turnover	Political fragmentation	Police autonomy	Police regulation of illicit markets
High Policy instability, transition costs	High fragmentation increases incoherence and veto points, but low fragmentation is insufficient to consolidate policy	*High* No reform (no increase in capacity, accountability)	*Particularistic confrontation and negotiation* Uncoordinated violence and/or corruption
Low Policy continuity, "only game in town"	High – greater accountability and competition for rents	*Professionalization* Increase in capacity and accountability to objective criteria	*Coordinated coexistence* Tolerance, controlled violence and corruption
	Low – lack of accountability and competition for rents	*Politicization* No increase in capacity, increasing accountability to political rulers	*Coordinated protection rackets* Controlled violence and centralized corruption

Source: Author's elaboration

The informal regulation of drug trafficking involves three groups of actors engaged in two main sets of interactions. On the one hand, there are the subnational politicians and police officers who design and apply formal and informal regulatory instruments, whose own relationship is often fraught by subtle tensions or overt conflicts. On the other hand, police target criminal actors involved in drug retail distribution and exercise informal regulation through different combinations of corruption and violence. In this chapter, I introduce these actors and outline their main incentives, preferences and motivations, as well as the content of their respective interactions. I then define the central concepts of my framework: political competition, police autonomy and regulatory regimes. Finally, I illustrate the dynamics and mechanisms of my argument in two steps: First, I explain how political competition affects police autonomy, and second, how police autonomy shapes informal regulatory arrangements.

ACTORS: POLITICIANS, POLICE AND CRIMINALS

Politicians

This category includes elected politicians and appointed officials who aspire to obtain votes to attain or remain in office. Crime has consistently ranked as one of the two main societal concerns in Latin America since the mid-1990s, along with unemployment (Lagos and Dammert 2012). Therefore, most elected executives, regardless of their party or ideology, aspire to claim credit for greater security in their districts or, at least, prevent salient crimes that may damage their political prospects. Politicians, at least partially, rely on their police to achieve this purpose.

In addition to reducing or containing crime, police can also contribute to incumbents' electoral ambitions in another way. Police can also supply incumbents with rents from various illicit markets, from illegal gambling or prostitution to drug trafficking, that can help finance politicians' increasingly expensive electoral campaigns, engross their personal fortunes, or cover other off-the-books expenses.[1] Police might also mediate

---

[1] This practice is common not only in Latin America but also in other developing regions (Raghavan 2002; Gerber and Mendelson 2008; Altbeker 2009; Hinton and Newburn 2009; Hope 2016) where political parties rely heavily on informal and illicit sources of finance (Freidenberg and Levitsky 2006; Kitschelt and Wilkinson 2007). Police rent extraction from crime was also extensive in US cities prior to the Progressive reforms at the end of the nineteenth century as "whoever dominated the police ... shared in the

between politicians and the underworld actors who participate in cliente-listic networks and party machines (Auyero and Sobering 2019).

Of course, politicians can deal directly with high-level traffickers. However, I focus on police as middlemen or brokers rather than on the direct relationship between politicians and criminals. Politicians would typically avoid these interactions because they risk being exposed for associating with criminal elements and because street dealers are usually not so important to merit such exposure. Meanwhile, it is more normal for police to interact with dealers as a normal part of their job.[2] In other words, politicians can usually count on the police to do their dirty work for them, since the benefit of plausible deniability is usually greater than the agency cost this implies.

That said, police may also become a liability for politicians. Scandals involving police violence or corruption may harm politicians' electoral aspirations. Although politicians might strategically use police repression to their electoral advantage (Wilkinson 2006), they are likely to face massive protests when police strike the "wrong" victims, usually middle-class or wealthy individuals.[3] Furthermore, police lethality might not only fail to reduce criminal violence but may actually spark or reinforce it, undermining politicians' claim of bringing order to their districts.

Police corruption also poses a dilemma for governing politicians (Geddes 1994). Some incumbents may seek to curb police corruption, in the hopes of strengthening institutions, reducing crime and improving citizen confidence in the force. However, while this initiative entails uncertain, long-term benefits, it carries certain, short-term costs. Police can resist these changes by dragging their feet, threatening reformist politicians, or exploiting their underworld connections to increase crime and spur a public outcry for tougher security policies. Given the historical entrenchment of police corruption and citizen distrust toward police in Latin America, meaningful changes will take long to materialize (Tulchin and Ruthenburg 2006). Hence, even if they do not necessarily profit from police corruption, politicians might decide to tolerate it because the cost of controlling it seems too great.

---

underworld's payoffs and earned its political support" (Fogelson 1977, 21; see also Varese 2013, 9, 106–11).

[2] I thank Eduardo Moncada for bringing this to my attention.

[3] Police violence might also put governments under the scrutiny of international human rights organizations, which may tarnish the incumbent's reputation and career prospects.

Alternatively, incumbents might eschew police reform and opt to politicize their security apparatus, which enables them to appropriate the rents police capture from criminal activities. This choice poses a different principal – agent quandary. On the one hand, these rents might bolster politicians' electoral machines or personal pocketbooks. On the other hand, police may shirk their obligation to control crime or be exposed in corruption scandals, which can provoke social protests, impeachment, or criminal investigations against the incumbent (González 2020). Incumbents might consequently opt to restrict police autonomy to reduce agency losses and preserve their electoral chances.

Politicians, therefore, have incentives to control the police, whether through professionalization or politicization. These incentives are particularly strong in weak institutional contexts, where police have historically exhibited vast inefficiency, corruption and human rights abuses (Hinton and Newburn 2009). In this book, I focus on how politicians attempt to reduce police autonomy in relation to two outputs: the use of lethal force (police violence) and the extraction of rents from criminal activities (police corruption), which are the main instruments police use to informally regulate crime. Police, however, will usually not allow these encroachments on their autonomy without resistance.

Police

Police are complex organizations. Not only do most countries, especially those with different tiers of government, have several police forces,[4] but each police force is also internally divided according to territorial and functional criteria (Reiss 1992). Territorially, police are divided into departments or regions, municipalities and precincts, while functionally they are organized according to major crime categories, such as homicides, property crime, organized crime and so on, along with administrative and support functions, such as training, human resources and planning departments (Bayley 1985, 109–13). This book focuses on state-level police forces, specifically, officers at the precinct-level who prevent and repress drug dealing and its associated violence. I also look

---

[4] For example: Argentina has four federal police forces and twenty-four state-level police forces; Brazil has one federal police force and twenty-seven state forces; Mexico has one federal police force for all thirty-two states and thousands of local-level police departments; the United States has more than 19,000 law enforcement bodies.

at specialized divisions in charge of investigating drug trafficking and organized crime.

Despite these nuances, there are strong commonalities across different police internal sectors and subcultures. Police officers' basic motivations are personal safety, tenure security and career advancement.[5] Often, as Peter Moskos recounts in his ethnography of policing in Baltimore, the most pressing goal of rank-and-file officers is to survive their shifts (Moskos 2009). This motivation should be stronger in Latin America, where police face greater risks than in the United States.

Furthermore, in weak institutional contexts, these basic motivations make rent extraction from illicit activities appealing for most police, for three main reasons. First, informal rents compensate for scant paychecks. In many developing countries, rank-and-file police have poor salaries and abject working conditions. Police in Latin America, for instance, earn on average 16 percent less than the rest of the public sector (Ortega 2018). They often work 24-hour shifts plus overtime, and even then, require side jobs – usually in the private security sector – to make ends meet. Police stations are derelict and patrol vehicles lack maintenance or fuel. Notice the exposed wiring, cramped space and battered walls in the police stations portrayed in Figure 2.1, from a Military Police precinct in the Eastern Zone in São Paulo. Keep in mind this is one of the wealthiest cities in Latin America. Most police stations in the region are in worse shape.

Many officers thus feel justified in collecting side payments from crime given the disparity between the risks they face and their formal compensation (Azaola 2009). Watching other state actors (e.g., politicians or the judiciary) profit from corruption surely does not promote police integrity.

Second, rents can influence police career advancement. In developing democracies, indicators such as clearance rates or citizen confidence rarely determine police officers' career prospects (Skolnick 2011, 149–50). Contrarily, funds from police protection of criminal activities can grease the wheels of internal bureaucratic processes: they allow police officers to obtain paid leave, bullets for their service weapon, promotions, or transfers to desired locations (Goldstein 1975, 21; Sherman 1978).

Finally, rent extraction might also reduce the risk of armed confrontation between police and criminals. Police may prefer to gather funds

---

[5] As criminologist Jerome Skolnick put it, "The police officer ... may well enjoy the possibility of danger, especially its associated excitement, while fearing it at the same time" (Skolnick 2011, 44).

FIGURE 2.1. (a) and (b) Military Police Station in the Eastern Zone (*Zona Leste*) of the City of São Paulo
Source: Photographed by the author.

from individuals involved in drug dealing and other "victimless crimes," especially when dealers are more heavily armed than the police itself. Such discretionary enforcement also relieves police from constantly arresting individuals and filling out paperwork for petty crimes only to see detainees released shortly afterward (Moore and Kleiman 1989; Reiner 2010). Police may also tolerate petty crimes to recruit confidential informants, who can provide information on more important criminal activities in their turf (Reuter 1982).

Police officers' illicit rent extraction may spike different tensions with political incumbents. On the one hand, reformist politicians may shut down officers' rackets. On the other hand, rent-seeking politicians may pressure police commanders to kick up a share of their illicit revenues in exchange for career advancement or protection from prosecution. Consequently, police have reason to suspect politicians' attempts to encroach on their autonomy. These tensions affect how police interact with the third actor in this plot: criminals themselves.

In Latin America, police violence is also recurrent, for multiple interrelated reasons. First, police carry out their duties in contexts of high preexisting conflict and violence. The region's dramatic social inequality, its exposure to illicit economies, including the drug trade, as well as other structural and cultural factors, generates a high violence benchmark.[6] Social and racial inequality also leads state officials, including police, to identify specific communities as havens for criminals, which justifies violence against them (Caldeira 2000; Brinks 2003). Most Latin American countries are scarred by legacies of political violence, whether in the form of civil wars or military dictatorships, which decreased confidence in and generated animosity toward police and security forces (Cruz 2011). Second, police officers are often unprepared and poorly trained. Officers are typically individuals from poor backgrounds with low education and few labor prospects (Casas et al. 2018). They are often put in the streets with little to no preparation and forced to interact with populations that distrust, fear or hate them: On average, only 30 percent of Latin Americans express trust in their police (Muggah and Tobón 2018, 17).[7] In such contexts, excessive use of force can occur due to officers' anxieties and their need to reaffirm their authority. Finally, police officers are often the targets of violence by individual or collective criminal actors, especially when they are off duty, such as when they return home to marginalized neighborhoods similar to the ones they patrol. These attacks often heighten their sense of corporate solidarity, triggering violent responses against the alleged perpetrators (Denyer Willis 2015).

Politicians' need to establish order in their districts can put them at odds with police officers accustomed to use force to discipline and punish specific communities or to extort protection rents from criminal actors. Reformist politicians may want to curtail police violence so that police respect the human rights of citizens of all social classes. Therefore, they typically promote alternative policing strategies, such as community policing (Malone and Dammert 2021) and endorse training in conflict de-escalation techniques. Alternatively, conservative politicians might initially view police repression as the most effective tool to reduce crime and give police greater leeway but change their tune when police violence targets the "wrong" victims, attracts the attention of the media, social movements or international organizations, or fuels rather than contains crime. In short, entrenched corruption and violence in Latin American police is bound to generate tensions between police and vote-seeking politicians.

---

[6] For a comprehensive review of factors that explain criminal violence in Latin America see Bergman (2018).

[7] Furthermore, police training actually seeks to make police feel different (and apart) from "average" citizens (Sirimarco 2009).

Criminal Actors

State actors' regulation of drug trafficking affects the behavior of criminal actors. I focus on those individuals whose main illicit economic activity is the retail distribution of drugs.[8] This illicit market includes a range of organized criminal groups, from drug trafficking organizations that dominate entire regions to drug gangs that control specific neighborhoods. Despite their differences in size and power, these groups share four defining characteristics. First, their primary activity is the sale of illegal drugs, even if they may have other occasional or permanent sources of income, such as car theft, extortion, kidnapping, trafficking of other goods (or even persons) and so on. Second, these groups control a defined territorial area, or at least aspire to do so. Territorial control enables criminals to store, refine and distribute illicit drugs. Because it is such a coveted resource, it is also, accordingly, one of the main sources of violence between criminal groups (Papachristos et al. 2013). Third, these criminal actors are willing and able to use violence to resolve market conflicts, discipline their troops or citizens in their turf and, if necessary, confront the state. Fourth, and perhaps most importantly, these actors require state toleration or protection to survive and maximize their profits, since the state can credibly shut down their operations or, at least, inflict serious damage to their organizations via arrests and seizures (Trejo and Ley 2020, 38). This feature distinguishes them from other armed non-state actors whose primary purpose is to confront the state, such as guerrilla movements or rebel groups. While law enforcement agencies may fail to shut down drug trafficking *markets*, they can take down most drug trafficking *organizations*.

Most criminal groups seek to avoid conflicts with the state. Confrontation is costly. Preparing for armed struggle requires significant investments (e.g., purchasing weapons, surveillance equipment and technology, hiring enforcers) under shrinking profit margins as buyers are scared away and supply chains are disrupted. Furthermore, proceeds from drug sales also allow dealers to distribute private or club goods to their communities, which enhances their prestige, legitimacy and power,

---

[8] The academic and policy literature on transnational organized crime has focused alternatively on criminal *organizations* or *activities/markets*. Examples of the most renowned organized criminal groups are the Sicilian Mafia, the Calabrian N'drangheta, the Russian vory v zakone, the Colombian Medellín and Cali cartels, the Japanese Yakuza and Chinese Triads. Organized criminal activities include drug, human, organ and arms trafficking, goods counterfeiting, extortion, piracy and gambling. See Paoli (2014) for an extensive review.

whereas continuous clashes with the police jeopardize such initiatives. Finally, most traffickers and dealers want to stay in business for the maximum available time. That requires, first, staying alive and, second, (usually) staying out of jail.[9] Both outcomes are more likely when dealers have the toleration or protection of state authorities. Criminal actors, therefore, have strong incentives to avoid confrontation with state actors.

Criminals who can count on state cooperation have a comparative advantage over their rivals, as they can anticipate raids, or have the police arrest or kill their competitors. Consequently, criminals have incentives to maintain that collaboration by paying rents for police toleration or protection and controlling violence in their turf. Depending on whether police protection is credible or not, criminals might decide whether to pay taxes that reduce their short-term profit but enable them to persist longer in business or that can be traded for information on – or action against – their rivals.[10] Additionally, criminal groups have inducements to contain violence on their turf as it attracts police attention, which means drug seizures, arrests or armed confrontations, all of which inhibit economic profits and jeopardize criminals' territorial governance. Thus, criminals have incentives to comply with the government's informal regulation of their activities.

To sum up, politicians and police are likely to clash regarding how much (and what type of) autonomy the former is willing to give the latter. How this tension is resolved will influence how police regulate drug trafficking, and subsequently, the degree to which criminals will resort to violence to settle market disputes and other problems. The next sections define the central concepts of this theoretical framework (political competition, police autonomy and regulatory regimes) and specify its dynamics and mechanisms.

CONCEPTS: POLITICAL COMPETITION, POLICE AUTONOMY AND REGULATORY REGIMES

Political Competition

Political competition is intrinsic to democracy. In democratic regimes, politicians subject themselves to the rules of the electoral process to access

---

[9] Many gangs in Latin America continue to control their operations from inside the penitentiary system. See Denyer Willis and Lessing (2019) as well as this book's chapter on São Paulo.

[10] This logic borrows from Olson's (1993) explanation of why people pay taxes to stationary bandits.

and exercise power. Politicians know that they will have to give up their office eventually upon defeat and that they might have to share power with other parties or factions to govern. In this book, I focus on two main components of competition: One refers to how different individual or collective actors hold power over time (turnover) and the other to how power is distributed among different political players in a given term (fragmentation). I argue that these factors condition the decisions politicians can make with respect to the police.

Political Turnover

Political turnover occurs when a different party or faction gains access to executive power at the end of a given term. Although this event technically occurs once every four years, it has implications for the entire mandate. On the one hand, politicians' decisions during the first weeks or months in office can set the pace for their entire term. Upon taking office, politicians have had more time to prepare the policies they want to implement than they ever will. Other politicians and citizens might also be more accepting of their decisions during this "honeymoon" period. On the other hand, gaining office carries multiple unforeseen administrative, political and financial obstacles, which can hinder policy formulation during this period. Politicians might spend months to figure out their budget allocations and to fill all the required positions.

Turnover is particularly relevant in weakly institutionalized contexts. Whereas in some advanced democracies, institutions and even some public officials are unlikely to change when a new party comes into office,[11] in most developing democracies that usually does not happen. Furthermore, the exiting administration does not always leave the office in the best shape. Incoming occupants might find troves of information to review, insufficient financial or human resources, and arcane bureaucratic structures. Thus, most incumbents have incentives to reshape the administration in their own image.

A couple of caveats are in order. First, while turnover usually refers to rotation between different parties, it can also include alternation between factions from the same party. In dominant or hegemonic party systems, the incumbent's main source of opposition could be a rival faction within her own party (Greene 2009). Second, and relatedly, instances of turnover might not necessarily occur every four years:

---

[11] In part, this might occur because of greater institutional veto points that inhibit policy replacement.

A governor might resign due to health reasons, political scandals or to run for higher office before her term concludes. In such instances, if her vice-governor belongs to a different party or faction, she could easily implement policies that clash with the preferences of her predecessor. The cases of Rio de Janeiro (Chapter 3) and Buenos Aires (Chapter 5) include examples of such transitions.

Political Fragmentation

The possibility of turnover implies a potential expiration date for democratic politicians' mandates. Political fragmentation relates to the fact that, in democracies, incumbents usually have to share power with other parties or factions. When this does not occur, either because electoral competition is biased in favor of the incumbent or because the incumbent cracks down on the opposition, the democratic nature of the regime is imperiled. Political fragmentation, thus, refers to the distribution of power among different parties or factions within a single term.

There are two different arenas in which the allocation of power affects the incumbent's capacity to govern. First, within the executive there might be a diverse coalition, represented by a multi-party cabinet. Second, the governor might not have a majority in the legislature and therefore subsist with a divided government, in which the legislative branch can more likely block her agenda. In this sense, fragmentation refers to the number of potential political veto players (Tsebelis 2002). Fragmentation has two crucial effects on the democratic game. On the one hand, it can obstruct policy enaction and implementation, and undermine the incumbent. On the other hand, it also keeps the incumbent in check so that she does not abuse her power.

The level of fragmentation within the cabinet depends on its configuration. Parties which gain access to power without the support of a coalition can govern alone. Those that reach office with a multiparty coalition can either dispense cabinet seats in proportion to each party's electoral or legislative contribution or alternatively tilt the balance toward the leading party. Either scenario can conjure different governance problems. On the one hand, there might be less internal disputes and more decisiveness if most cabinet members belong to a single party. However, this distribution might make the other partners less willing to support the administration in adverse times. On the other hand, a more balanced cabinet might better satisfy all partners but could also delay policy implementation or increase policy incoherence. Although fragmentation is usually measured as a continuous variable (or index), my main interest is to contrast broad patterns across different administrations. Therefore, I will classify cases as having low fragmentation when there are no divisions within the cabinet and when the incumbent has a legislative majority, and as high fragmentation otherwise.

Turnover and fragmentation can certainly covary. A more fragmented scenario, where the opposition has greater power, might increase the probability of turnover in the upcoming election. The lack of turnover, by contrast, might decrease fragmentation as an entrenched incumbent increases her strength and coopts the opposition or rival parties become less competitive. However, this covariation is not necessary. Even in dominant party settings where there is no turnover between parties, such as Santa Fe (Chapter 4) and Buenos Aires (Chapter 5), rivalries may form between intraparty factions. The combination of these two variables, I argue, establishes how far and in what direction politicians can affect the autonomy of their police.

Police Autonomy

Police autonomy refers to the police's capacity to "exercise control over their internal governance and external operations" without significant political supervision or interference (Stepan 1988, 93).[12] *Internal governance* refers to the different procedures that allow police to function as an organization, such as incorporation, training, promotion, transfer, internal discipline, displacement and so on. *External operations* are what police do with respect to citizens, that is, mainly crime prevention, repression and order maintenance (Wilson 1968). Politicians might seek to reduce police autonomy in either one or both dimensions, whether to promote democratic consolidation or protect their own electoral prospects (or both).

Most studies on bureaucratic politics rely on theoretical models imported from democracies with strong formal institutions, in which bureaucracies tend to exhibit meritocratic selection, tenure security, rule-based evaluation and relatively high administrative capacity (Polga-Hecimovich and Trelles 2016). In these contexts, bureaucrats' reputation for expertise and innovativeness enables them to build autonomy from their political masters (Carpenter 2001). Politicians, in turn, have stronger incentives to grant discretion to these agencies rather than intrude in bureaucratic affairs (Huber and Shipan 2002).

---

[12] Although Stepan's definition alluded to civil–military relations following redemocratization, the analogy is pertinent given that the police are also an armed bureaucracy, which can potentially destabilize democratic governments.

In contrast, bureaucracies in democracies with weak formal institutions often exhibit the opposite traits. Bureaucrats' recruitment, job security and promotion often depends on personal ties or electoral results rather than formal rules or objective performance indicators (Spiller et al. 2007). Unsurprisingly, these bureaucracies have fostered poor reputations due to systematic inefficiency, arbitrariness and corruption (Rauch and Evans 2000). Elected officials in developing democracies thus have stronger incentives to *restrict* bureaucratic autonomy and fewer inducements to invest in the professionalization of bureaucratic agencies.

These deficiencies are common among most police forces in Latin America. Even its most highly professionalized police forces, such as those in Chile or Colombia (Dammert 2009; Bergman 2018), are frequently involved in human rights abuses, political espionage and corruption scandals. Most police forces in the region did not undergo democratic reform processes until the 2000s, if then (Bailey and Dammert 2006). Their internal procedures, including their incorporation, training and promotion criteria, remain highly secretive and discretionary. Innovation is foreign to most police departments, whether in terms of technology for crime prevention or updated human rights training. Although more women have joined police forces in the last decades, most remain highly chauvinistic organizations, with little openness to gender equality. Not surprisingly, Latin American police are generally perceived by the public as corrupt or even complicit with criminals (Cruz 2009; Muggah and Tobón 2018).

Even more than in many other bureaucracies, high police autonomy carries serious risks in how they conduct their external operations, including human rights violations, fatal shootings and widespread corruption. High police autonomy can involve deficiencies in capacity and accountability, which are likely to increase police violence and corruption. In terms of capacity, autonomous police are more likely to preserve outdated norms and militarized practices, which are poorly fit to deal with complex crimes and powerful criminal organizations. Highly autonomous police are also likely to maintain arbitrary norms governing their recruitment, training and promotion procedures, which increases the appeal of material exchanges to curry favor with gatekeepers in the force. These practices downgrade human resources in police agencies. Officers who lack proper training, equipment and operational guidelines are more likely to either kill or be killed in clashes with criminals, especially in the highly stressful and dangerous situations that characterize police work in Latin America.

Additionally, autonomous police are unlikely to have strong internal or external accountability mechanisms. Monitoring and accountability offices lack prestige within police organizations and can rarely count on officers' cooperation when investigating fellow officers. Furthermore, accountability offices often reproduce predominant organizational norms, which may tolerate (or even promote) violence against certain social or ethnic groups or corruption to supplement meager salaries. Internal disciplinary measures thus often amount to mild reprimands: officers involved in fatal shootings may only be temporarily sidelined or transferred to other stations.[13] Furthermore, when police investigate shootings involving other officers, they are prone to tamper with forensic evidence, intimidate or even kill witnesses to protect their colleagues (Denyer Willis 2015). This lack of accountability can also foster a sense of impunity, leading police to believe they can apply lethal force or engage in corrupt dealings without significant consequences (Brinks 2008).

Unlike their counterparts in developed democracies, police in developing democracies emerged from authoritarian regimes without ever being responsive to elected politicians (Hinton and Newburn 2009). By contrast, they had served their autocratic superiors well. In Latin America, police and military forces applied the National Security Doctrine (promoted by US governments), by which they imprisoned, tortured, killed and disappeared thousands of citizens in multiple countries (Huggins 1998). Police in many countries also joined or constituted informal death squads to eliminate social "undesirables" and inhibit land invasions in urban informal neighborhoods or rural areas (Perlman 1979). Subsequently, after democratization, police did not need to forge their autonomy from elected politicians but rather to defend it to maintain their jobs and corporate privileges. High police autonomy, consequently, can result in rampant police corruption and indiscriminate police violence, which, in turn, shape uncoordinated crime regulation regimes.

Professionalization versus Politicization

In the preceding sections, I have argued that politicians have important incentives to reduce police autonomy. Here I explain how they might do so. Politicians may attempt to reduce police autonomy through formal or informal means. Formal instruments include statutory provisions (laws, decrees, resolutions, etc.) that place police internal governance processes

---

[13] Conversely, commanding officers might take advantage of vague disciplinary criteria to expel officers they dislike.

under political supervision, establish crime control strategies, tactics and procedures or select specific neighborhoods for police interventions.[14] One major subset of formal changes is "police reforms", which alter the force's organization and functions to make police more accountable to the rule of law and responsive to citizens (Bayley 2006, 23). Starting in the 1980s, governments in transitional democracies aimed to transform police forces tainted by their participation in authoritarian regimes. Thus, they placed police under political leadership, eliminated military functions and discourse, changed training modules, set up civilian boards to oversee appointments or promotion, created internal or external accountability offices and established guidelines to monitor police use of lethal force.[15]

However, politicians might also reduce police autonomy through *informal* means. Incumbents can resort to massive purges or individual appointments, promotions and transfers to remove dissidents and promote loyalists within the force. Elected officials may also protect corrupt officers from disciplinary sanctions or judicial prosecution. Protected police are then in politicians' debt, which makes them subservient to their demands. Consequently, police autonomy diminishes even though the police are no more closely aligned with the rule of law.

The reduction of police autonomy through formal means induces police professionalization, while informal means are conducive to politicization. Professionalization introduces more objective criteria to dictate police internal procedures and external operations. It implies that politicians increase the police's organizational capacity and hold them increasingly accountable to the rule of law. Politicization, by contrast, entails that the police serve the whims of political incumbents rather than impersonal norms. In this case, politicians promote, transfer, or displace officers primarily according to their personal preferences or political brokerages, regardless of officers' performance in reducing crime or improving citizen safety. When politicization occurs, police commanders know that to keep their jobs or gain promotion they need to cater to governing politicians, which might not necessarily imply serving the public or enforcing the law. Meanwhile, police organizational capacity might stagnate or decrease, as governing officials do not invest in the force but rather grant individual privileges to commanders. Furthermore, accountability deteriorates as police internal monitoring offices become irrelevant while political hacks

---

[14] See Frühling (2003, 15–16).   [15] See Pereira and Ungar (2004) and Ungar (2011, 5).

fill external overseeing positions. These distinct routes for reducing police autonomy have important consequences for how police regulate drug trafficking and other illicit markets.

As the case chapters will show, the degree to which political power is relatively stable (or fluctuates with turnover) and concentrated (or fragmented) influences whether and how politicians will reduce police autonomy. The resulting outcomes (i.e., high autonomy, professionalization or politicization) will affect how police interact with drug dealers and informally regulate drug markets.

Regulation

The regulation of any economic activity requires setting rules that govern those activities and monitoring the compliance with such rules, usually through a public agency (Baldwin et al. 2012). In the case of drug trafficking, the principal public agency in charge of monitoring and promoting compliance is the police. Officers are the "street-level bureaucrats" (Lipsky 2010) in most direct, frequent contact with drug dealers and the first responders to reports of crimes connected with this activity.

Formal rules to regulate drug trafficking include statutes that restrict the distribution, possession or consumption of different illicit substances. Most national governments have signed international frameworks prohibiting drug trafficking and enacted domestic policies in accordance with these prescriptions.[16] Police enforce these rules through drug busts, arrests and sometimes, armed confrontation with drug dealers. Many scholars have focused on the repressive side of the fight against drug trafficking, generally to show the failures of the prohibitionist paradigm known as the "war on drugs," whether in Latin America or in the United States (Bertram et al. 1996; Tokatlian 2019; Alexander 2020).[17]

However, state responses to drug trafficking also involve *informal* regulation, which is "unwritten, created, communicated and enforced outside of officially sanctioned channels" (Helmke and Levitsky 2004, 727). Besides prescribing formal norms, policymakers can also convey informal guidelines to state law enforcement agencies. Informal rules are

---

[16] The main international frameworks governing drug trafficking are the Single Convention on Narcotic Drugs (1961, amended by the 1972 protocol), the Convention on Psychotropic Substances (1971) and the United Nations Convention against Illicit Traffic and Narcotic Drugs (1988).

[17] See Angélica Durán-Martínez's extensive review and discussion of this literature (2017).

not necessarily illicit or corrupt. All police departments have informal instruments for dealing with crime. For example, police forces might allow certain drug dealers to operate while collecting sufficient evidence to arrest them or focus on one criminal organization to the neglect of others, due to resource constraints or intended media impact. Similarly, narcotics officers tend to overlook minor felonies committed by their informants, who are usually criminals (Reuter 1982; Skolnick 2011). However, in weak institutional contexts, informal regulatory techniques constitute a greater share of state responses to criminal markets and tread more frequently into illicit territory, what Trejo and Ley (2020) refer to as "the gray zone of criminality." Police officers' main informal regulatory instruments are varying types and dosages of corruption and violence. Meanwhile, their regulation targets the structure of drug markets and the violence they generate.

Regulatory Instruments: Police Corruption and Violence
State corruption implies that public authorities use the power of their office to extract money or favors from another individual or collective actor for private benefit (Rose-Ackerman and Palifka 2016). In the case of the police, corruption entails the discretionary use of their authority to enforce the law. It can imply receiving a reward for something they are supposed to do anyway or that they should not do or employing illegal means to achieve approved ends (Punch 2009). In this book, I distinguish between four main types of corrupt activities by police in relation to drug trafficking: **toleration, protection, predation** and **criminal entrepreneurship.**[18]

Police may *tolerate* certain types and levels of drug dealing at given times or locations by simply ignoring this illicit activity. While these actions certainly deviate from officers' law enforcement obligations, they are not necessarily profit-driven but rather often intended to maintain the peace in their turf (see Chapter 6). In this sense, toleration resembles Alisha Holland's concept of forbearance, which implies that politicians and bureaucrats intentionally opt to not enforce the law (Holland 2017). Politicians might explicitly or implicitly order police to tolerate certain types of illegal activities because it is politically costly to repress them or because they benefit their constituencies with jobs or access to consumer goods (see Dewey 2015). To families involved in retail drug distribution,

---

[18] These types condense the nine categories in the typology of corruption provided by Roebuck and Barker (1974).

generally poor and without steady employment, it often represents a nonnegligible income. Like forbearance, toleration involves capacity, intentionality and revocability (Holland 2017, 14): State actors must choose to exercise it when, given their resources, they could repress the crime, and they must maintain a credible threat to shift their response to repression at any time. Additionally, police tolerance does not necessarily benefit a specific group over its market competitors. When tolerating drug dealing, police are using illegal means to serve approved ends.

Protection implies that police actively provide favorable conditions to a specific criminal organization in return for monetary or nonmonetary compensation (see Chapters 4 and 5). Protection is selective and relational: if police are protecting group X, they rarely can simultaneously protect group Y, at least while maintaining their credibility as protectors (Snyder and Durán-Martínez 2009). More likely they will crack down on one group at the behest of the latter. Police protection constitutes a racket because they protect their clients (criminals) both from other objective threats (rival gangs or other law enforcement agencies) as much as from the threat posed by police themselves (Tilly 1985). Such protection may take place at various stages of the law enforcement process. Criminals may pay police a tax to carry out their operations with little interference, which implies that police refrain from arresting dealers in that neighborhood or avoid patrolling the area altogether. Police may also supply gangs with information about upcoming raids by other law enforcement agencies or invasions by rival criminal groups. Officers may shift ongoing criminal investigations away from certain individuals or organizations. Police officers might also enforce the law, for example, arrest members of a drug gang, but only after receiving payoffs from the gang's competitors. Protection might require police to occasionally seize the gang's drugs, money or weapons and even arrest a few underlings to keep up appearances before inquisitive politicians, prosecutors, judges, journalists or civil society. Most dealers will happily comply to keep receiving favorable treatment and assistance from the police. In short, in contrast with toleration, protection relies on private, selective and material exchanges, whose benefits are appropriated by the police or their political superiors.

A third type of police response is *predation*, which implies that the police seek to exploit criminal actors to capture rents from their activities without affording them protection from law enforcement or rival gangs (see Chapters 3 and 4). Predatory police may intimidate, kidnap, torture or even kill traffickers to extract rents from them. Just like criminals can use violence to lower the price of bribes, police can resort to violence to raise the price of "protection" (Dal Bó et al. 2006; Lessing 2017). They can also plant or fabricate evidence to incriminate dealers or torture individuals to extract confessions and/or payments. Unlike in the previous arrangement, criminals do not usually benefit from police protection but generally suffer police violence as a means to extract payoffs; hence, predation increases the possibility of confrontation with organized criminal actors. In other words, predatory police resemble Olson's "roving bandits," who plunder gains from civilians' economic activities without increasing their safety, well-being or future investments (Olson 1993; Bates 2008).

A final type of corruption, *criminal entrepreneurship*, occurs when police officers carry out illicit economic activities themselves. In this scenario, a clique of police officers handles the transportation, storage, safety and even distribution of illicit drugs; police cut out traffickers and assume the role of drug dealers themselves. Since this modality of corruption eliminates the interaction between police and drug dealers, it is beyond the scope of this book.

In addition to corruption, the other major instrument used by police to regulate drug trafficking is violence. As sociologist Egon Bittner stated, "The use of force is the essence of the police role" (Bittner 1970). Police officers routinely use force to subdue suspects or criminals and to protect citizens or themselves. These actions vary in the severity of physical harm imposed on the suspect, the extreme being the use of lethal force.[19] That police use of force implies violence may be obvious to the persons directly or indirectly affected by them, but not necessarily to the officers involved (Fassin 2013, 127). I focus on police *lethal* violence, the use of physical force which results in the death of another person/s, although my case narratives also include references to nonlethal violence, such as torture and intimidation.[20]

---

[19] Scholars specializing in the police refer to this as the "continuum of police use of force" (Alpert and Dunham 2004).

[20] Broadly speaking, deaths due to police intervention can be accidental or intentional, although it is often difficult to empirically distinguish between them. Accidental deaths involve police inappropriately discharging their weapon due to fear, adrenaline or lack of preparation, as well as when stray bullets fired at criminals strike innocent bystanders. Intentional deaths, by contrast, imply that police officers have the motivation to inflict deadly harm on other individuals. Intentional deaths may also be deemed legitimate, at least in the eyes of the law, when police are judged to have applied reasonable and proportional force to address the threat at hand.

There are several reasons why police use deadly force against actual or suspected criminals. This book does not engage with more critical perspectives regarding the repressive role police play in society (Simon 2007; Wacquant 2009; Fassin 2013; Seigel 2018). My interest is rather to unwrap how police use lethal violence to affect the dynamics of illicit markets, particularly drug trafficking. Police's informal regulation of drug trafficking involves continuous interactions with potentially violent individuals. Correspondingly, the logic of police lethal violence often resembles that of organized criminal actors and is frequently intertwined with police corruption (Lessing 2017).

Police may use violence to tax criminals, which can make their enforcement more credible, or to protect criminal groups by attacking competing organizations. Alternatively, violence might become a tool for predation, as when officers intimidate, torture, or even kill individuals to extract rents from them or their associates without any credible promise of protection attached. Police may also kill to retaliate against an individual or group who has killed or injured a fellow officer. Finally, the police might employ violence to discipline drug dealers that have violated the implicit or explicit terms of their agreement. Violence and corruption in the regulation of drug trafficking are not mutually exclusive but often intrinsically linked.

The uses of violence presented above are predominantly instrumental and selective. Nonetheless, police might also apply violence "irrationally" and indiscriminately. When confronting criminals, police officers can fire their weapons aimlessly, wounding or killing any civilian who happens to be there. These "irrational" uses of violence are also likely to condition criminals' behavior. If criminals perceive that they are dealing with trigger-happy police, they will be more predisposed to use violence to preempt police attacks or have less regard for maintaining order in their turf, since they assume police will respond violently anyway. This leads us to discuss two interrelated objects of police regulation: criminal violence and the structure of illicit markets.[21]

Objects of Regulation: Drug Markets and Criminal Violence

Drug trafficking is an enormously profitable transnational crime involving the production, trafficking and commercialization, both wholesale

---

[21] Like other citizens, police officers can also resort to violence to resolve interpersonal disputes of sentimental or monetary nature. The difference is that police have ready access to firearms and can then hide behind the power of their uniform to avoid the consequences of such actions.

and retail, of restricted substances.[22] This book centers on *retail* drug distribution in urban areas, that is, the sale of narcotics to individual consumers, as well as the activities undertaken by criminal actors to prepare for (e.g., storage, fractioning) or safeguard these operations. The reason for this truncation is that storage and retail distribution are the stages in which dealers are most exposed to subnational law enforcement, since they require relatively fixed locations to stash, fraction, refine ("cut") and sell illicit drugs. States usually are more present in the urban areas where drugs are sold than in the rural areas where drugs are cultivated. Additionally, urban areas concentrate most of developing countries' population (and voters), which gives politicians greater electoral incentives to prevent violent crime from spiraling out of control. Hence, state regulators will seek to maintain low or at least tolerable levels of violence associated with this illicit market.

State regulation affects two crucial factors: market fragmentation and stability. Criminal markets can be either concentrated – in the extreme, monopolized – or fragmented. In the case of concentration, a given criminal group controls the largest market share of different phases (e.g., production, transport, wholesale or retail distribution) in the illicit economy and is capable of disciplining its members when they break the group's peacekeeping norms. By contrast, in fragmented markets different criminal groups coexist in the same territory and compete for routes, consumers and state protection. The natural supposition is that fragmented markets are inherently more violent than concentrated ones (Snyder and Durán-Martínez 2009). Nonetheless, fragmented markets might be stable if no player seeks to alter the existing equilibrium and take over their competitors' market share. Conversely, centralized markets may unravel if the dominant group splits or if a challenger disputes the incumbent's supremacy. Market players might achieve stability through a collective agreement or third-party enforcement, in other words, state intervention. While state actors might prefer to negotiate with concentrated market players, they can also enforce informal regulations in fragmented markets given their power asymmetry with respect to drug dealing groups.

Police interventions may either stabilize or destabilize illicit markets. For instance, if police arrest the members of an organization, other groups will be enticed to take over its turf or market share; by seizing drugs,

---

[22] See www.unodc.org/unodc/en/drug-trafficking/index.html.

weapons or cash of a given group, police can also deplete an organization's resources and indirectly fortify their rivals. While credible protection by police of a given group should maintain a stable market and raise entry barriers for potential rivals, noncredible protection will incite challengers and destabilize the market. Additionally, compacts between police and a dominant gang may motivate other criminal groups to challenge such dominance. However, this cohesion might last only until the dominant group is removed, after which temporary allies will become rivals once more. In short, uncoordinated informal regulatory arrangements may alter the structure of a given market, which is likely to be reflected in the prevailing dynamics of violence.

Drug trafficking, like other illicit markets, does not necessarily entail violence, yet some of its features favor this outcome. Illicit markets require the use, or threat of, violence to resolve competitive disputes, which criminologists Paul Goldstein and Peter Reuter refer to as the systemic nexus between drugs and violence (1985; 2009). Drug dealing groups typically resort to violence to defend their turf against rival gangs or the state or invade the territory of other organizations to increase their market share.[23] A street dealer may kill a customer who shirks on a debt or a rival who threatens to take over his corner. These actions can incite retaliation, whether by other gangs or the police, triggering prolonged spirals of violence.

Violence is also a common method to resolve internal *succession* struggles within organized criminal groups (Reuter 2009). State policies can dramatically fuel this type of violence. When the state kills or jails the leader of a criminal organization, his most ambitious lieutenants are likely to wage bloody struggles to lay claim to the post. This type of confrontation was common in the Neapolitan Camorra, in Mexican cartels whose leaders were taken out during President Calderón's war on drugs and in the Medellín cartel following the death of Pablo Escobar (Saviano 2010; Calderon et al. 2015; Durán-Martínez 2017).

Additionally, the state can also disrupt the interpersonal trust criminals need to carry out their operations. When group members cooperate with the police or are suspected of doing so, they will suffer harsh punishments, in part to maintain the group's internal cohesion and to disincentivize further defections (Martínez 2016; Vargas 2016). Criminals can also use violence to punish civilians suspected of collaborating with the state as informants (Durán-Martínez 2017, 48).

---

[23] (See Papachristos et al. 2013; Lessing 2015)

Finally, criminal actors who control specific territories may also use violence to dispense justice within that locale, often as part of their tacit agreement with the state. Oftentimes, state officials delegate to criminals the responsibility of maintaining "social control" by punishing robberies, rapes or other types of unacceptable behavior in either of these settings. This control can be part of the agreement that enables criminals to carry out their most profitable activities, such as drug dealing. Hence, criminals are likely to punish those who violate coexistence norms in their turf, whether it be in a prison or marginalized neighborhood (Skarbek 2014; Arias 2017).

Illicit markets can generate violence in other ways. Often, being associated with a certain criminal network, in other words, hanging out in the "wrong crowd," makes individuals much more likely to kill or be killed (Papachristos et al. 2013). Furthermore, different forms of violence are often concatenated (Tilly 2003). As Auyero and Berti (2015) point out in their ethnographic study of violence in Argentinean informal neighborhoods, violent incidents involving drug dealers' disputes for turf, money or status can spillover into domestic violence between spouses, siblings or by parents against children, such as when a mother beats her child who has stolen from her in order to buy drugs. This overlap makes it empirically difficult, and theoretically problematic, to differentiate between the primary motives of individual acts of violence, even when just considering homicides with potential links to drug trafficking.

Of course, not all state interventions will affect these types of violence. However, police corruption or violence can fuel or contain criminal violence, depending on the coordination and frequency of these responses. Figure 2.2 summarizes the relationship between police regulation of drug markets, market concentration and stability and the different modalities of resulting criminal violence.

Here, I elaborate the dynamics of this argument. I first explain how changes in political competition, namely turnover and fragmentation, shape police autonomy and, consequently, how police regulate drug trafficking in metropolitan areas.

DYNAMICS

As Adam Przeworski famously stated, democracies are political regimes in which parties lose elections. Not only must political incumbents vacate government buildings after their term expires, but new occupants might also have to share power with political associates or rivals. Nonelected officials and government bureaucrats, including police, are also aware of

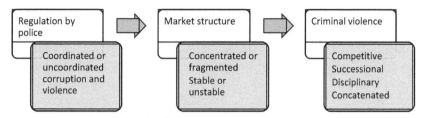

FIGURE 2.2. The relationship between police regulation, market structure and criminal violence
Source: Author's elaboration.

these elementary rules of democratic competition and tend to act according to their assessment of the government's strength or weakness. I borrow from scholarly analyses of how political competition affects processes like market and state reform to illustrate how it shapes police autonomy. Politicians' control of police will then affect how officers control drug trafficking and its associated violence.

How Political Turnover and Fragmentation Affect Police Autonomy

Political turnover refers to whether the same party (or faction) remains in power at the state-level executive from one electoral term to the next (Grzymala-Busse 2003). *High turnover* increases police autonomy through two mechanisms. First, it undermines policy stability. When a new party takes power, incumbents are likely to change security policies, political authorities and police commanders to signal their differences with the preceding administration and satisfy their electorate and activists. These changes not only run counter to bureaucratic inertia in police but can also foster dissent within the force, as different officer cohorts are either promoted, neglected or retired, leading the losing groups to resist political incumbents' encroachment on their autonomy.

Second, electoral alternation carries transition costs. When a new administration arrives, incumbents have to learn the ropes of their jobs and start relationships with the police anew, which can delay policy implementation and obstruct coordination (Post 2014). Before new incumbents can acquire the necessary expertise to manage the police, there might be changes in political leadership or in the policy orientation of the administration. Thus, under high turnover, politicians are hard-pressed to reduce police autonomy.

Political fragmentation refers to the dispersal of power during a given term, whether through cabinets made up of several parties or factions, or in the legislative arena as divided government. In a context of high turnover, high fragmentation can further hinder efforts to reduce police autonomy. Higher legislative fragmentation can obstruct policy enactment and implementation because it gives police more potential allies to resist such initiatives. Meanwhile, heterogeneous cabinets often lack policy coherence, which can erode police compliance with gubernatorial decisions. Finally, high fragmentation may entice police to supply rents to the incumbent's rivals, who may have greater future influence on their career trajectories.

In a context of high turnover, *low fragmentation* is insufficient to reduce police autonomy beyond a single administration. While incumbents may enact statutes to professionalize police or make informal attempts to politicize the force, successors from a different party or faction are likely to erode or reverse these measures upon gaining power. High turnover thus increases police autonomy, regardless of fragmentation.

In contrast, *low turnover* decreases police autonomy through two mechanisms. First, it increases policy stability. Statutory changes or informal arrangements are more likely to stick since incumbents will probably maintain policies implemented by themselves or their own party. Second, police commanders are more inclined to perceive entrenched incumbents as "the only game in town" and comply with their decisions. When commanders discount that the incumbent – or her party or faction – will remain in power, they will seek to gain favor with her to ensure their career advancement. In short, turnover dictates *whether* politicians can reduce police autonomy, yet political fragmentation influences *how* they do so.

With *low turnover* and *high fragmentation*, governing politicians are more likely to professionalize the police. A key aspect of professionalization is the restriction of police corruption by governing officials. Higher fragmentation can lead politicians to adopt this stance for one of two reasons, depending on the inclination of the opposition. First, stronger rent-seeking political rivals might want to appropriate these illicit funds for themselves, which threatens incumbents' capacity to maintain order, as dispersed protection pacts undermine peacekeeping agreements with criminal actors and exacerbate conflict (Snyder and Durán-Martínez 2009; Durán-Martínez 2017). Second, a stronger reformist opposition can expose corruption schemes and denounce the incumbent in the legislature, the media, or the courts, weakening her chances in the upcoming election. A stronger opposition might also exercise greater control of police corruption through congressional committees and oversight offices, which makes it more difficult for incumbents to ensure immunity from prosecution to their police allies. Greater fragmentation therefore precludes incumbents from monopolizing patronage, graft or, in this case, police rents from crime (Geddes 1994; Grzymala-Busse 2003). Similarly, greater fragmentation might strengthen accountability mechanisms to keep police violence in check. In short, whether to prevent rivals from capturing illicit rents or to avoid political scrutiny, politicians facing higher fragmentation will tend to restrain police corruption.

By contrast, entrenched parties with *low fragmentation* have greater incentives and opportunities to politicize the police and appropriate its rents from crime. First, political incumbents are subject to weaker horizontal accountability. Legislative proposals from the opposition to keep police and incumbents under control are less likely to pass. Oversight offices might be filled by party activists and exist only in name. Second, police commanders have weaker incentives to broker deals with politicians from marginalized opposition parties or factions, as these cannot grant them credible protection or influence their career prospects. Overall, governments with low turnover and low fragmentation can "politicize the state, capture resources ... and privilege themselves unchallenged," including in their control of police (Grzymala-Busse 2003, 1130–31).

To summarize, low turnover is necessary to reduce police autonomy in weak institutional contexts, where changes in the administration typically lead to serial policy replacement (Levitsky and Murillo 2013). Meanwhile, under low turnover, high fragmentation can motivate incumbents to restrict police corruption and promote professionalization, while low fragmentation favors politicization and the political appropriation of police rents from crime.

How Police Autonomy Shapes Drug Trafficking Regulatory Regimes

The degree and form of police autonomy conditions how police employ violence and corruption to regulate drug dealing, in turn shaping the structure of the drug market and levels of criminal violence. This section delineates the theoretical pathways between variants of police autonomy and drug trafficking regulatory regimes. I first explain how greater police autonomy results in *uncoordinated regimes* – particularistic confrontation and negotiation – and then how reduced police autonomy generates *coordinated regimes* – which vary depending on whether politicians reduce police autonomy through politicization (protection rackets) or professionalization (coordinated coexistence).

Particularistic Confrontation

Particularistic confrontation is the paradigmatic uncoordinated regulatory regime, consisting of a generalized predatory approach by the police. In this scenario, police carry out disjointed violent actions against criminal actors, often in defiance of political authorities. Additionally, while police corruption is also rampant, politicians do not restrict or centralize the sizable rents police collect from illicit activities. Violations of the law are not isolated events carried out by a few rogue cops. By contrast, this regime involves systematic violent attacks by police units against confirmed or suspected dealers and traffickers.

High autonomy lies behind the unrestrained use of lethal force by the police, which confront drug trafficking – and other forms of crime – with techniques and practices incubated during authoritarian regimes. Due to their militarized training, police officers conceive themselves as fighting a war where criminals in general, and drug dealers in particular, are enemies to be annihilated. This organizational predisposition entails little or no acknowledgment of due process or the protection of human rights. Tortures, disappearances and summary executions are common and justified, even cheered. At the same time, high police autonomy implies that there are few existing – much less effective – internal or external monitoring agencies that oversee police use of lethal force. Consequently, punishment for police lethal intervention is unlikely, which further motivates officers to engage in violent behavior. As we will observe in the cases of Rio de Janeiro (Chapter 3) and Buenos Aires (Chapter 5), some administrations have even offered bonuses or promotions to officers who engaged in "brave" acts of public service, including shootings of criminals.

High police autonomy results not only in high but also arbitrary and indiscriminate violence. Autonomous police lack clear directives that define their objectives and the methods to achieve them. Therefore, officers carry out haphazard raids that raise the probability of armed confrontation with criminals and incite retaliation. Officers may seek revenge against a given individual – criminal or not – for personal reasons or attack a neighborhood to convey a message to the local gang. Not only are these actions rarely coordinated within the police, but they often disobey political orders.

Another feature of particularistic confrontation is its rampant police corruption. Due to the lack of relevant objective criteria to govern their internal procedures, police are more likely to seek illicit rents for career advancement, organizational advantages and personal enrichment. Furthermore, spasmodic political attempts to reform the police foster

internal dissent and reduce commanders' time horizons, inciting opportunistic behavior. Police corruption thus becomes fragmented as each
squad attempts to run its own protection racket. The collected funds flow
in multiple directions instead of through a single chain of command.
Governing politicians neither restrict nor centrally appropriate these
rents. Because of high political fragmentation, multiple political actors
vie for the proceeds of police corruption while police are less likely to
contribute rents to incumbents who cannot credibly influence their career
advancement or ensure them impunity from criminal prosecution.

This uncoordinated corruption increases anarchic violence by both the
state and criminal actors for three main reasons. First, police apply
violence to extort criminals into paying larger rents or punish those that
refuse to pay for protection. Criminals are likely to retaliate, triggering
spirals of violent exchanges with police, with civilians caught in the
crossfire. Second, uncoordinated police crackdowns might splinter
existing drug dealing groups, resulting in succession struggles or invasions
by other gangs. This may inhibit the consolidation of organized criminal
groups and the stabilization of illicit markets. After a police raid, traffickers might also attack members of their own communities to punish (or
dissuade) citizen cooperation with the police. Finally, decentralized rent
extraction prevents police from offering credible protection to drug traffickers, whether from other law enforcement units or criminal rivals.
Protection agreements are fleeting at best: the officers who protected a
dealer today might apprehend or kill him tomorrow. This uncertainty
may motivate criminals to preemptively attack the police. Preparing for
the state's onslaught, criminals will arm themselves to repel state aggression, for which they will need to expand their market share, which implies
conquering other territories and thus spurs more violence. In short,
particularistic confrontation intensifies criminal violence, especially in
the marginalized neighborhoods where drug gangs run their operations.

Particularistic Negotiation
Particularistic negotiations are a less extreme uncoordinated regulatory
regime, in which different police units extract and appropriate drug
trafficking rents for themselves. The central feature of this regulatory
regime is its high and disorganized police corruption, as various police
divisions and territorial precincts broker separate deals with drug gangs,
with the promise of protection in return for rents. However, this rent
extraction is uncoordinated both within the police and between police
and political authorities. These failed negotiations are also likely to

increase criminal violence, although police violence is lower than in particularistic confrontations.

In this arrangement, politicians neither professionalize nor politicize the police. The failure to professionalize the police perpetuates corruption, while the lack of politicization disperses the rents it generates. As political sociologist Peter Evans stated, "a protection racket whose triggermen cut individual deals at the first opportunity does not last very long, and the larger the coercive apparatus involved, the more difficult the problem" (Evans 1989, 565).

When multiple police units broker inchoate deals with criminal actors this destabilizes the drug market and increases criminal violence. As more low-level police offer protection at a reduced cost (since less people benefit from the rents), barriers to entry will decrease and more small-time dealers will start to sell their product. Without credible protection from the police, dealers have greater incentives to steal each other's merchandise and territory. Not only do police fail to deter this competition but they often promote it. A given police unit might sell out its present clients to higher bidders or stand idly by as their clients shoot up another neighborhood. This dynamic generates turf wars and retaliatory violence between drug trafficking groups – with ordinary citizens once again suffering the consequences.

This highly fragmented market structure also accounts for the lower police violence than the one we find in particularistic confrontation. Being dealers aware of their power asymmetry with respect to the police, they are unlikely to resort to violence against officers. Police violence against drug dealers is also less probable since police can extract rents from criminals without fearing retribution and hence rely less on arbitrary brutality.

The main police response in particularistic confrontation and negotiation is predation: Police extract rents from criminals without offering credible protection. What happens when police and criminals *can* enter into credible agreements? Either protection or toleration will prevail, in either one of two types of coordinated regimes: protection rackets and coexistence.

Protection Rackets

The first variant of coordinated regimes, *protection rackets*, implies that state actors shield specific criminals from law enforcement in exchange for material benefits (Snyder and Durán Martínez 2009). Protection rackets are characterized by their high yet organized corruption and relatively low violence. In terms of police autonomy, politicians control their police mainly through informal mechanisms. Incumbents eschew professionalizing reforms. They promote loyalists, remove obstructionists, debilitate accountability mechanisms and assure impunity to their accomplices. The successful appropriation of police rents by politicians organizes police corruption in three ways. First, it extends time horizons for police engaged in corruption: since political protection makes it harder to arrest and prosecute corrupt officers, they have less need to engage in opportunistic predation of dealers. Second, it compels lower-level units to channel rents to commanders, who can credibly influence their subordinates' career trajectories due to their linkages with political authorities. Third, it generates repeated interactions between police and criminals, fostering stable bargains. Not only do both parties benefit from the illicit compact, but they have strong incentives to prevent its unilateral dismantling.

Due to their high yet coordinated corruption, protection rackets also exhibit lower criminal violence. Police owe it to their political superiors to maintain acceptable levels of order in their district or otherwise risk losing their corporate privileges, including their capacity to collect illicit rents, or even their jobs. Therefore, police are more likely to pressure criminals to maintain peace in their turf. Criminals, meanwhile, are more likely to comply because otherwise the police can credibly shut down their operations. Furthermore, police protection deters invasions by other criminal groups – or law enforcement agents – and internal succession struggles, as the group's leadership is more likely to remain in place. This regulatory regime also prevents violent clashes from deteriorating into prolonged chains of violence, given that criminals want to preserve their police protection. Furthermore, police can credibly limit drug groups' expansion, which reduces their capacity to retaliate against the state. Since police can obtain regular rents without resorting to violence, police lethality will also decrease. In sum, protection rackets show that corrupt states can also be effective in achieving certain outcomes, such as relative peace (Darden 2008, 36).

Coordinated Coexistence

The final type of regulatory arrangement is *coordinated coexistence*, which consists of implicit or explicit agreements to restrain armed confrontation between the state and organized criminal actors. This regime does not rule out violent clashes between police and criminals, but rather implies that "neither side makes a total attempt to destroy the other" and that "violence ... follows the implicit rules of engagement about what is and is not acceptable to each side" (Staniland 2012, 251). While police do not abstain entirely from their law enforcement responsibility, they will attempt to avoid the escalation of conflict with drug traffickers. In terms of how they impact drug markets, police will refrain from advancing on criminals' territory or depleting their resources, seeking to maintain rather than alter the existing balance of power. Therefore, this regulatory regime presents lower and more stable state and criminal violence.

Police professionalization is necessary for this regime to occur. As we have seen in the previous regimes, police predation strangles criminals' economic profitability and motivates them to confront other criminal groups to obtain territorial control, a larger market share and more revenues. Police corruption can incite criminals to attack the state to lower the price of the bribes they are willing to pay. It also risks retaliation by criminals against corrupt police officers, followed by subsequent police reprisals and so on. Therefore, because corruption can frequently spur violence, police should moderate their illicit rent extraction.

Police violence should also abate for this arrangement to subsist. When police lethal actions are restricted, police are less likely to disrupt criminal organizations and incite retaliatory, territorial, successional or disciplinary violence. Of course, confrontation between state and criminal actors is still possible, but this should manifest as sporadic peaks rather than sustained climbs. Furthermore, both state and criminal actors should seek to contain rather than fuel spirals of violence when confrontation occurs. A more tolerant state enables illicit businesses to thrive, with less violence by both regulators and regulated.

For these conditions to materialize, politicians should improve the capacity and accountability of police organizations. Reducing police corruption and violence requires, among other things, better recruitment and training, modern crime prevention approaches, rigorous political directives and functioning accountability mechanisms to punish excesses. Politicians should not make officers and commanders kick back rents from crime in exchange for personal or corporate favors. Additionally, lower-ranking officers should perceive that corruption is not commonplace among commanders and that it is not the best strategy for career advancement. Of course, police (and political) corruption will still exist, but it should be lower and more fragmented than in the other types of regimes.

Coordinated coexistence exhibits greater formality than the other regulatory regimes. Police professionalization involves clearly delineated crime prevention strategies and functioning police accountability mechanisms, which are embodied in formal decrees and public documents. Nonetheless, in this scenario, police can still resort to informal covenants with drug dealers to regulate this activity. On the one hand, crime prevention strategies might focus on reducing violence while implicitly tolerating other, non-violent crimes, such as drug dealing. On the other hand, in territories where criminal actors exhibit either governance capabilities and/or willingness to retaliate against the state, police officers might prefer to neglect or tolerate their behavior to avoid violent escalation.

One might argue that coordinated coexistence is more likely where there is a single major drug trafficking organization since centralized criminal actors are more capable of restraining lower-level members. Likewise, police are more likely to limit their extortion or violence against criminals who have greater retaliatory power. However, police regulation can also shape the evolution of the drug market and consolidate criminal groups. For example, while arresting or killing criminal leaders can lead to violent succession struggles or invasions by rival organizations, avoidance of such actions will help stabilize and consolidate the drug market.

CONCLUSION

In this chapter, I explained why elected politicians in weakly institutionalized democracies may want to control the police. I outlined that political turnover and fragmentation are the main factors that condition their capacity to do so and whether such control occurred through professionalization or politicization. The importance of political competition underscores that the police are more likely to comply with incumbents who wield – or are perceived to wield – greater political power. I then explained how police autonomy affects whether the *informal* regulation of illicit markets through state corruption and violence is coordinated or uncoordinated, resulting in four types of regulatory regimes – particularistic confrontations, particularistic negotiations, coordinated protection rackets and coordinated coexistence. In short, political competition and police autonomy yield different regulatory arrangements embodying diverse police informal responses to drug markets in metropolitan areas.

The next four chapters will show how these regimes emerged, developed and, in some cases, collapsed over time. I illustrate the relationship between political competition, police autonomy and drug trafficking regulatory regimes in four cities in Argentina and Brazil since redemocratization in the 1980s. I begin with the two types of uncoordinated regimes – particularistic confrontation and negotiation – examined through the cases of Rio de Janeiro and Rosario, and then turn to the two coordinated types – protection rackets and coordinated coexistence – analyzed by the cases of Buenos Aires and São Paulo, respectively.

3

Particularistic Confrontation

The Persistent War between Gangs and Police in Rio de Janeiro

OVERVIEW

For most of the period since the return of democracy in the 1980s, the state of Rio de Janeiro lived through something close to a drug war. The Capital City is home to some of the most violent drug gangs in the country and was one of the most dangerous places in Brazil during the 1990s, with homicide rates above 60 per 100,000 inhabitants. Policing in Rio is a deadly occupation, for both citizens and police officers themselves: Between 1998 and 2019, police killed close to 20,000 people while suffering over 2,500 casualties. Many of these deaths resulted from the dispersed, uncoordinated attacks carried out by Rio's Military Police (*Polícia Militar*, PM) against traffickers operating in the city's sprawling favelas (informal neighborhoods). The PM also violently extorted dealers for protection that rarely materialized and brokered short-lasting arrangements (*arregos*) with them. In other words, the police regulated drug trafficking through *particularistic confrontations*. This predatory tactic spurred more violence by traffickers not only against police, but also against rival gangs and average citizens. Most state-level governments have been unable or unwilling to modify this regulatory regime.

After the renewal of open state elections in 1982, several state governments in Rio de Janeiro attempted to reform the state police to restrict its human rights abuses. However, high political turnover and fragmentation prevented governments from implementing these reforms or ensuring their continuity. Between 1983 and 2006, no party managed to remain in power in Rio de Janeiro from one term to the next (see Table 3.1). Each new administration shifted security staff, policies and police commanders,

TABLE 3.1. *State executive elections in Rio de Janeiro, 1982–2014*

Election year	Governor	Governors' party	Governor's vote share (margin of victory, percent)[a]
1982	Leonel Brizola	PDT	34.2 (3.6)
1986	Wellington Moreira Franco	PMDB	49.4 (13.5)
1990	Leonel Brizola	PDT	61 (43.2)
1994	Marcello Alencar	PSDB	37.2 (12.2) *
1998	Anthony Garotinho/ Benedita da Silva	PDT	46.9 (16) *
2002	Rosinha Garotinho	PSB	51.3 (26.9)
2006	Sérgio Cabral	PMDB	41.4 (37) *
2010	Sérgio Cabral/ Luiz Pezão	PMDB	66.1 (45.4)
2014	Luiz Pezão	PMDB	40 (11) *
2018	Wilson Witzel	PSC	41.3*

[a] (*) Indicates that the governor won the election in a runoff. Numbers in parentheses reflect the margin of victory in the second round.
Source: Author's elaboration from TSE, ISP and NEV/USP

fostering dissent within the police and tensions with the government. To make matters worse, reformist center-left governments, like that of Leonel Brizola of the Workers' Democratic Party (*Partido Democrático Trabalhista*, PDT), were succeeded by conservative politicians who undid reforms and unleashed police to raid favelas and attack gangs, such as Moreira Franco and Marcello Alencar, from the Party of the Brazilian Democratic Movement (*Partido do Movimento Democrático Brasileiro*, PMDB) and the Brazilian Social Democracy Party (*Partido da Social Democracia Brasileira*, PSDB) respectively. These last two governors' plans backfired as criminal violence increased in the city and state of Rio de Janeiro.

Rio's fragmented political landscape also hindered the government's capacity to implement police reforms or capture police rent extraction. No state government in Rio had a legislative majority. The share of legislative seats controlled by the governor's party was never higher than 35 percent, in 1982, and as low as 13 percent in 1998 (see Figure 3.1).[1] Governors thus needed to form heterogeneous – and thus often unreliable – coalitions to rule, which obstructed consensus on police

---

[1] Rio's unicameral state legislature renews itself entirely every four years.

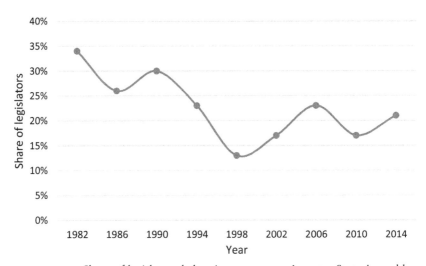

FIGURE 3.1. Share of legislators belonging to governor's party, State Assembly of Rio de Janeiro (1982–2014)
Source: Author's elaboration from Tribunal Superior Eleitoral (TSE, High Electoral Court).

governance. This high fragmentation also gave police multiple political allies with whom to oppose reform initiatives and various clients for their rent extraction from different illicit activities. Finally, rarely did the same party control the state government *and* the municipality of the City of Rio. This certainly affected the implementation of police reforms as mayors, typically more conservative than the governor, decried these initiatives (Hinton 2006). However, I will show that the main tensions usually occurred within the governor's own coalition, which failed to provide sufficient coherence and stability for security policies to shape police behavior.

Without a dominant party to centralize rent extraction, the police preyed upon drug traffickers and other criminals to extract rents for itself or at most shared them with different state and local politicians. The police's illicit revenue collection was uncoordinated not only with the state government but also within the police itself, which prevented it from brokering credible coexistence pacts with powerful drug gangs. The resulting regulatory regime consisted of segmented, violent and corrupt exchanges between police and drug gangs, including extortive kidnappings and sporadic raids by police, to which traffickers retaliated in kind.

TABLE 3.2. *Political turnover, fragmentation, police autonomy and drug trafficking regulatory regime in Rio de Janeiro, 1983–2014*

Period	Turnover	Fragmentation	Police autonomy	Drug trafficking regulatory regime
1983–2007	*High* No reelection of party or faction	*High* Divided cabinets and minority legislatures	*High* No reform No political control of police rent extraction	*Particularistic confrontation* High violence by police and criminals High and anarchic police corruption
2008–2014	*Low* Continuity in power of PMDB	*High* Divided cabinets and minority legislatures	*Low* Professionalization Political restriction of police rent extraction	*Coordinated coexistence* Reduced violence by police and criminals Less (and more organized?) police corruption

Source: Author's elaboration

This regulatory regime persisted until the implementation of the Pacification (or UPP) program in 2008,[2] in which the government instructed the police to occupy certain favelas in the City of Rio and focus on retaking territory and seizing weapons rather than confiscating drugs. This program reduced police autonomy, professionalized the police and briefly shifted the regulatory regime toward *coordinated coexistence*, as the state and drug gangs restrained their mutual confrontation. Coherence within the PMDB's administration enabled this policy to emerge while the entrenchment of the PMDB, which won three consecutive elections between 2006 and 2014, provided the policy stability required for this program to persist. At least during its first years, the UPP program managed to significantly reduce police and criminal violence in the Rio de Janeiro metropolitan area. Table 3.2 summarizes this temporal variation.

---

[2] Pacification refers to the Police Pacification Units (UPP) program. Through this chapter, I use both terms interchangeably.

The next section provides a brief historical introduction to policing and drug trafficking in Rio de Janeiro before redemocratization in 1982. The chapter follows by showing how high turnover and fragmentation increased police autonomy and shaped particularistic confrontation as the main drug trafficking regulatory regime between 1982 and 2007. I continue by centering on the implementation of the Pacification program during the Cabral and Pezão administrations (2008–2014) and discussing the government's relative success in reducing police autonomy and regulating drug trafficking through coordinated coexistence. I conclude by discussing the decline of the UPP program and the subsequent implications for security policy in Rio.

Alternative Explanations

Unstable and violent drug markets in Rio de Janeiro seem at first glance overdetermined. The state's metropolitan area features multiple competing drug gangs that control drug outposts in favelas neglected and abused by the state, making the drug market a unique system for illicit rent extraction by police (Misse 2007). Overpopulated favelas lacking basic infrastructure are surrounded by some of the wealthiest neighborhoods in Brazil, which supply dealers with troves of wealthy customers, a grotesque representation of social inequality. In these favelas, many young, typically black and brown men lacking opportunities for social mobility, craving the respect brought by wielding guns and earning fast money find drug trafficking gangs an appealing job prospect (Goldstein 2003; Dowdney 2004). Military police, meanwhile, are imbued with a "warrior ethos" inherited from the dictatorship, in which violence is the default response to crime, and see traffickers as an updated version of political insurgents (Pinheiro 1997). Indeed, traffickers have often portrayed themselves as revolutionaries and popular bandits in an effort to project greater legitimacy (Amorim 1993), which probably further enervated police officers. One could point to any of these factors to explain the police's generally truculent response to Rio's burgeoning drug market.

However, as this chapter will show, these factors do not completely account for the police's anarchically violent regulation of drug trafficking, which I denote *particularistic confrontation*, nor its dampening during the first years of the Pacification program. Most of these explanations underplay the role of political competition in obstructing police reforms since redemocratization. Scholars have focused on the tensions between state-level and local-level incumbents, the interactions between political leaders or social networks within favelas and elected officials (Arias 2006; McCann 2014) and the relation between dealers and the state at the neighborhood level (Arias 2013; Magaloni et al. 2020), yet most underplay the role of political instability and internal fragmentation at the state-level in determining police autonomy and its subsequent regulation of drug trafficking. While I acknowledge differences at the micro-level in terms of violence and criminal governance, this chapter (and subsequent ones) will concentrate on the state-level patterns exhibited by this regulatory regime.

Focusing on the relation between politicians and police helps understand the fact that Rio's drug market is fragmented, to a large extent, due to a political decision to confront the main drug gang, the Red Command (CV), in the late 1980s and most administrations' inability or unwillingness to professionalize the police, which has led police to prey on dealers as an organizational reflex to its high autonomy. This explanation is leveraged by the contrast with the other cases in this book. In São Paulo (see Chapter 6), which exhibits similar levels of social and racial inequality as Rio, the regulation of illicit markets unfolded in a sharply divergent manner, especially since the mid-1990s. The Argentine metropolitan areas I examine also display pervasive corruption in the political system and the police department yet regulate drug trafficking in a more coordinated manner (see Buenos Aires, Chapter 5, and the first part of Santa Fe, Chapter 4).

Finally, within case variation in Rio over time undercuts alternative explanations centered on structural factors like inequality, the lure of drug markets – for both young men and corrupt police – and the police's "essential" warrior ethos. Rio's Pacification program constituted a brief but significant shift in drug market regulation, derived from the government's ability to implement certain aspects of police professionalization. This transformation is not simply attributable to progressive administrations, social pressure or international events. One would hardly label the PMDB, a centrist, pragmatist party, as progressive beyond its original stance against the dictatorship in the late 1970s and early 1980s. While Rio is rife with social movements that have historically demanded police reform and alternative approaches of violence prevention, these burst into the scene in the 1990s, when police regulation through particularistic confrontation was at its peak and were unable to curb this arrangement for more than a decade. Finally, although the city's hosting of the 2014 World Cup and the 2016 Olympics undoubtedly motivated politicians to find alternative ways to reduce intolerable levels of criminal violence, they neither determined the course the government would take nor guaranteed its success. I will show that changes in political competition and police autonomy are central to understanding the brief but significant drop in police violence during the early years of the UPP, signaling an unequivocal change of drug market regulation in Rio.

POLICE RACKETS AND THE RISE OF THE CV BEFORE DEMOCRATIZATION

The state's regulation of organized crime through corruption and violence preceded the return of democracy in Rio de Janeiro. The state's Military Police has a long history of violent, illegal repression, especially of the poor (Holloway 1993). During the last Brazilian dictatorship (1964–1983), the state government formed the elite squad BOPE, considered one of the most highly trained and ruthless in the world,[3] to conduct operations against guerrilla groups and other armed actors. At the same time, active and retired police officers established informal death squads, often sanctioned by political authorities, that terrorized residents of poor neighborhoods in the urban periphery to deter land invasions (Perlman 1979).

Until the 1970s, the main organized criminal actors were involved primarily in clandestine gambling, running a numbers game called *jogo do bicho* (Misse 2007). The protection rents collected by police then fed political machines such as that of former Governor Antônio Chagas Freitas (1979–1982).[4] *Jogo do bicho* rarely incited violent confrontations between police and *bicheiros* (Lessing 2017, 170). Drug trafficking was not yet a relevant source of rents for police or politicians. However, starting in the 1970s there would be significant shifts in illicit markets and in the leading characters of organized crime.

The gangs that would later control drug trafficking in Rio de Janeiro were born in the Ilha Grande prison during the 1970s. Following the military regime's enactment of the National Security Law of 1969,[5] the state government mixed common criminals with political prisoners, who passed their greater organizational skills to the former (Amorim 1993; Gay 2005, 55). Subsequently, the incarcerated groups formed the Falange Vermelha (Red Phalanx) to defend themselves against the then-dominant prison gang, the Jacarés. The Falange would then become the Comando

---

[3] See Soares et al. (2008).   [4] See Motta (2000, 94).
[5] Lei de Segurança Nacional (National Security Law), esp. decree article 27.

Vermelho (Red Command, CV), Rio's most powerful *facção criminosa* (criminal faction), which monopolized drug trafficking in the city until the late 1980s.

In the 1980s, a further change took place in the international drug trafficking market. Until then, cocaine was foreign to most Brazilians. Marijuana was the prevailing consumption drug (Dowdney 2004, 25–28). However, the development of cocaine refinement labs run by Colombian cartels in the Amazon made Brazil a relevant player in the international drug economy. Colombian traffickers started to move drugs through Brazil to export them to Europe through the country's ports. In the process, they paid Brazilian traffickers with a share of the product (Gay 2015). This development reduced the price of cocaine, previously only available for upper-class Brazilians. Drug trafficking increasingly became the main source of income for criminal gangs, which had previously concentrated on bank robberies or kidnappings (Amorim 1993, 142).

Buoyed by the economic growth of the 1970s, Rio de Janeiro developed into a prominent cocaine consumption market. Former Civil Police Chief Hélio Luz famously said that Ipanema – the chic Southern Zone neighborhood in the City of Rio de Janeiro – "glowed at night," due to the amount of cocaine that circulated there. The posh neighborhoods got the high-quality, white powder cocaine while the city's favelas got the cheap, highly addictive and destructive crack. The city's favelas became strategic locations in which to stash and distribute drugs to the rest of the city or ship them overseas from ports in the Guanabara or Sepetiba Bays (Evangelista 2003, 46).

As the military regime began its democratic opening in the late 1970s, Rio de Janeiro held direct elections for governor in November 1982. The election of center-leftist candidate Leonel Brizola heralded a major transformation in the state's management of the police and its conduct toward the poor. However, it would be the first of many failed attempts to reduce the autonomy of the Military Police.

FRAGILE POLICIES, AUTONOMOUS POLICE AND
PARTICULARISTIC CONFRONTATION, 1983–2007

From Defending Human Rights to Rewarding Police Lethality: Reform Cycles and High Police Autonomy, 1983–2006

Partisan turnover and policy instability began with the recovery of Rio's democracy. Marking the end of authoritarianism, progressive governor

Leonel Brizola (PDT, 1982–1986) announced major changes to reduce police autonomy. Along with Colonel Magno Nazareth Cerqueira, the visionary commander of the PM, Brizola advocated for a citizen – rather than military – police (Cerqueira 2001). To this end, he dissolved the secretary of security, which had been under control of the army, and instituted a new training module regulating police use of force (Hollanda 2005, 81–82). Brizola and Cerqueira also eliminated promotions for *bravura*, which rewarded police for arrests and confirmed kills. Finally, they tried to restrict the Military Police's invasive *pé na porta* ("foot in the door") policy, used to harass and abuse favela residents (Carrion Jr. 1989, 57; Sento-Sé 1999, 288; cf. McCann 2014, 39).

However, both reformists faced intense opposition from politicians and police. Brizola lacked a legislative majority and had trouble forming a governing coalition. He had run against the conservative political machine parties – the PMDB and the Partido Democrático Social (Democratic Social Party, PDS) – but once elected needed their support in the legislature, which generated dissent within his own administration (Sento-Sé 1999, 253). Conservative political elites then turned against Brizola, attributing the rising violence to the government's "soft on crime" approach and supporting police protests (Sento-Sé 1999, 289). At the same time, Brizola failed to garner stable support from the political left, including the Workers' Party (PT), which saw him as a populist trying to gain national prominence (McCann 2014, 9, 34).[6]

Meanwhile, internal dissent within the Military Police obstructed Cerqueira's community policing approach. According to a former BOPE official, "Cerqueira had a visionary proposal, but … it was a vision outside of what the police wanted; there was a lot of resistance, and Cerqueira was not a charismatic leader. He spoke better to those outside of the force than those in it."[7] Street-level police resisted either by allowing crimes to occur – claiming that "with the governor's human rights policy, we cannot do anything" – or engaging in excessive use of force to undermine the government (Hollanda 2005, 132–35).

---

[6] Interview by author with current PM colonel, Rio de Janeiro, September 1, 2014. Brizola's political project of "brown socialism" (*socialismo moreno*) rejected the class cleavages drawn by the Workers' Party (PT) and appealed to the nonorganized, informal poor.

[7] Interviews by author with former BOPE officer, Rio de Janeiro, September 1, 2014, and former PM colonel, Rio de Janeiro, September 4, 2014. A nonminor issue was Cerqueira being the first Afro-Brazilian person to command the Military Police. For divisions within the police, see also Hollanda (2005, 139).

The increase in violent crime and police lethality at the end of Brizola's administration contributed to the 1986 election of PMDB candidate, Wellington Moreira Franco, a conservative politician whose stance on policing and security contrasted dramatically with that of his predecessor.[8] This partisan turnover triggered a significant increase in police autonomy. Moreira Franco promised to end criminal violence within six months and, once in office, let the police loose to "reclaim" the favelas, ordering a major crackdown against the CV (Arias 2017, 67).[9] The resulting surge in police and criminal violence – homicides increased by 39 percent during his term[10] – made him one of the most unpopular governors in Brazil and facilitated Brizola's landslide win in the 1990 election.

The reform cycle restarted upon Brizola's return to office. Brizola and Colonel Cerqueira relaunched their community policing initiatives. But even though Brizola won the election with 60 percent of the vote, he still lacked a legislative majority and the support of most political parties. As two leading security experts described, his administration thoughtlessly repeated the proposals of his first term and his party was weakened by the exit of two of its main leaders, Cesar Maia and Marcello Alencar, who would run on the PSDB ticket in the ensuing election (Soares and Sento-Sé 2000, 17). Once again, internal political fragmentation stalled his efforts to reduce the autonomy of the police and he "did not have the time to consolidate his reform," according to a police commander who supported the initiative. After Brizola left office to run (unsuccessfully) for the presidency in 1994, he was replaced by Vice-governor Nilo Batista, who suffered numerous police protests. Due to the increase in violence in the city, Batista was forced to accept the federal government's military intervention, codenamed Operation Rio, at the end of 1994 (Resende 1995). Meanwhile, resentment in the Military Police against Cerqueira got so bad that he was murdered in 1999 by a police officer, presumably in retribution for his tough stance against corruption in the force.[11] Once again, a reformist, center-left administration had failed to reduce police autonomy.

---

[8] See Moreira Franco (1991, 155–57).

[9] For crackdown on CV see "Vicious 'Red Command': The gang that taught terror to Rio." *Los Angeles Times*, Aug. 5, 1989.

[10] Source: www.metropoles.com/brasil/acabar-com-o-crime-no-rio-uma-velha-promessa/amp.

[11] "Estranha eficiência," *Isto é*, September 22, 1999.

The 1994 election produced another drastic shift in security policy. The new governor, Marcello Alencar, of the Partido da Social Democracia Brasileira (Brazilian Social Democratic Party, or PSDB), a former Brizola protégé who then parted ways with his mentor, reestablished the secretary of security and, contrary to Brizola, brought a former Army General to head it. The new secretary general, Nilton Cerqueira, instituted *Faroeste* – "Wild West" – a bonus for "fearless" police actions, reinstalling the promotion for bravery that Brizola had abolished (Cavallaro and Manuel 1997, 34–38). As a former Military Police Captain told me:

[Faroeste] rewarded the police force's repressive actions: seizures, arrests and confrontations, even if it resulted in the death of the criminal; it substantially increased police salaries. I had someone in my class who was a Lieutenant, like I was, and got promoted to Captain after a large seizure. That really mobilized the military police apparatus, where the value of promotions is huge, and job prospects are greater than in the Civil Police. Many police were promoted by this logic and many also received a bonus.[12]

In part because of this initiative, police fatal shootings amounted to more than 10 percent of all homicides in Rio de Janeiro.

A new instance of turnover in 1998 triggered another, even briefer, reform cycle. Anthony Garotinho, a charismatic young politician who rose up the ranks of Brizola's PDT, won the election and initially promoted a major reform. During the campaign, he and his top security advisor, anthropologist Luiz Eduardo Soares, had published a book containing seven proposals to improve security in Rio, including an overhaul of both the Military and Civil Police (Garotinho and Soares 1998, 145–49). During their first months in office, they renovated Civil Police stations and implemented a community-policing program, the GPAE,[13] which many consider a predecessor of the UPP (Riccio et al. 2013; Lessing 2017). Like Pacification after it, GPAE focused on reducing criminal violence rather than drug trafficking and curbing lethal interventions by the police. Unlike Pacification, the government implemented GPAE only in one favela in the city.

---

[12] Interview by author with former Military Police captain, Rio de Janeiro, September 4, 2014. Also, interview by author with current Military Police colonel, Rio de Janeiro, September 1, 2014.

[13] GPAE stands for *Grupos de Policiamento de Áreas Especiais* (Police Group for Special Areas).

To a large extent, fragmentation within the administration diminished its coherence in implementing the reform. The security office was split between two groups: Soares and other progressive intellectuals, backed by the *Partido dos Trabalhadores* (PT, Workers' Party) and the pro status quo hardliners, headed by former army generals Siqueira and Quintal de Oliveira.[14] Leaning toward the latter, Garotinho fired Soares in mid-2000 and broke his alliance with the PT soon afterward.[15] Soares claimed that Garotinho then made a deal with a heavily corrupt and violent police faction to halt reform so as not to endanger his bid for the presidency in 2002. Soares eventually escaped to the United States in a self-imposed temporary exile after several threats on his life.[16] While Garotinho held that Soares had been "an inexperienced administrator" without the patience to see the reforms implemented, the reform effectively ended after Soares and his collaborators resigned. The administration even shut down the GPAE program, after Rio's mayor accused it of protecting drug traffickers. The reform briefly reignited during the nine-month tenure by Garotinho's vice-governor, PT politician Benedita da Silva, who appointed a progressive law professor as security secretary and promoted intelligence operations to arrest drug traffickers (Maggessi 2006), but it ended with Benedita's electoral defeat in October 2002 by Rosângela Assed Barros Matheus de Oliveira ("Rosinha Garotinho"), Anthony Garotinho's wife.

The ensuing gubernatorial period is another case of high political turnover and fragmentation resulting in increased police autonomy. Rosinha rapidly stopped and reversed Benedita's reformist initiatives, initially restoring hardliner Josias Quintal as secretary of public security. Garotinho himself took over as secretary of public security in April 2003. The Garotinhos not only disregarded reform but attempted to centralize police rent extraction to build their political machine, in part through territorial networks involving drug dealers (Arias 2013, 270). However, in a highly fragmented political scenario, they competed for these rents with politicians from other parties, especially Rio's mayor Cesar Maia (Arias 2017, 68). Having left the PDT in opposition to Brizola, the proportion of state deputies and local mayors loyal to the Garotinhos was minimal. Three interviewees explicitly singled this period as the one

---

[14] See Soares' depiction of his tenure as deputy security secretary (Soares 2000).
[15] The motive was allowing a filmmaker to pay a drug trafficker to make a movie about his life, which both Soares *and* the public security secretary had approved.
[16] "He fought the Law and…" *Los Angeles Times*, June 12, 2000.

with the highest level of "political interference" with respect to the police, not only by the governor but also by state deputies and municipal mayors in determining police appointments.

Overall, high political turnover and fragmentation derailed most government efforts to reduce police autonomy following the return of democracy in Rio de Janeiro (1983–2007). Policy instability hindered the capacity of several administrations to reduce police autonomy through reforms, producing what Lessing refers to as a "political pendulum" (Lessing 2017, 180–88). Furthermore, the lack of coordination between police and political authorities and the force's own internal divisions – between commanders like Colonel Cerqueira who advocated for community policing programs and those who favored a more traditional, violent approach to crime control – impeded politicians from centralizing police rents from crime and precluded stable deals with drug trafficking gangs. Violent and erratic confrontation with drug gangs became the default course of action. Professor João Trajano Sento-Sé, an expert on crime from the State University of Rio de Janeiro, summarized the state's political challenges and policy failures during this period:

The PMERJ had since the 1980s had some experiences of community policing, especially in favelas. The problem was that none of them ever had effective political support; they ended up being solely decisions of some sectors of the military police, with timid political support by the executive, [which] did not invest accordingly, did not take care of the program as a strategy. It had great resistance from the PM, and skepticism from public opinion. That's why they were short-lived and had no continuity.[17]

Particularistic Confrontation: The Persistent and Fragmented "War on Drugs" in Rio de Janeiro

Rampant Police Violence: "We Entered Favelas at Night and Killed Traffickers"

During this period (1983–2007), Rio's Military Police regulated drug trafficking through dispersed corruption and uncoordinated attacks. Police officers repeatedly engaged in intimidation, torture and summary executions, for two main reasons. On the one hand, conservative administrations, like those of Moreira Franco and Alencar, gave the police explicit directives and incentives to crack down on criminal gangs. On the other hand, when centrist or progressive administrations, like those of

---

[17] Interview by author with João Trajano Sento-Sé, Rio de Janeiro, September 9, 2014.

Brizola or initially Garotinho, sought to curtail their autonomy, the police often engaged in arbitrary, indiscriminate violence to destabilize the administration.

An example of the first mechanism is Moreira Franco's order to raid favelas occupied by the Comando Vermelho (CV). These invasions affected the drug trafficking market and its associated violence in two ways. First, they ended the CV's monopoly rule, motivating other gangs to invade their turf.[18] Officials in the Moreira Franco administration claimed to have reduced the CV's control of drug trafficking in the city from 90 to 25 percent of the market, as well as its power in the state's prisons.[19] However, two other criminal factions – Friends of Friends (ADA) and Third Command (TC) – would take up this market share and increasingly compete against the once hegemonic drug gang.

Second, the police's irregular confrontation motivated drug gangs to acquire increasingly sophisticated weapons to defend themselves against invasions from police and other gangs. While previous gang members had only had handguns to fight the police, during the 1990s they progressively purchased automatic rifles (AR-15s, AK-47s, etc.) and even grenade launchers and bazookas to take down police helicopters (Misse 2011).

The implementation of *Faroeste* by Security Secretary Nílton Cerqueira, during Marcello Alencar's administration (1995–1998) also illustrates how increases in police autonomy affected police violence and drug trafficking regulation. Faroeste provoked an immediate rise in police killings, which accounted for almost one out of every ten homicides in the City of Rio de Janeiro in 1995 (Garotinho and Soares 1998, 76–77). As the second column in Table 3.3 shows, police killed 220 presumed opponents in 1994, Brizola's last year in office, but 358 in 1995, during Alencar's first year in government. By contrast, the number of injured people (third column) barely increased from 126 to 131, which hints that police were increasingly applying lethal force as a first response. Between January 1993 and May 1995, the monthly average of civilian casualties in confrontations with police doubled from 16 to 32 (Cano 1997, 40). The number of murdered police also increased. While there were 31 police officers killed between 1992 and 1994, there were 90 between 1995 and 1997 (Garotinho and Soares 1998, 77). Higher police autonomy increased violence both by and against the police.

---

[18] Maggessi 2006, 140.
[19] "He fought the Law and..." *Los Angeles Times*, June 12, 2000.

TABLE 3.3. *Victims of police intervention in Rio de Janeiro, 1993–1995*

Year	Opponents killed	Opponents injured	Accidental civilian deaths	Accidental civilian injuries	Police killed	Police injured
1993	155	103	7	48	5	33
1994	220	126	8	80	6	25
1995	358	131	10	91	10	40

Source: Cano (1997)

Police resorted to violence as the default course of action to control drug trafficking, regardless of the government in charge. Lacking (or disregarding) political strategies to control crime, police frequently lashed out against traffickers and civilians in informal neighborhoods. As the former BOPE captain cited in the introduction of this book lamented, "There was no security policy, either for the BOPE or the Military Police Battalions (*Batalhões da Polícia Militar*, BPM). We simply entered favelas at night, killed two or three traffickers, seized a couple of weapons, and that was our measure of success. I realized we were just *enxugando gelo* [not achieving anything]."[20] While these actions might have pleased conservative administrations, they certainly undermined the authority of politicians who intended to reform the police.

A Military Police colonel also explained the relation between the absence of security policies and the police force's violent actions:

If there is a declared state of war, there can't be a security policy; if there isn't a policy, you don't change the police and only produce violent and brutal police, [who are] only prepared for war. Police need to be tough, brutes, beasts, otherwise they don't survive. The violent cop is the only one that is useful for this system. You have to be inside a Caveirão – the BOPE's armored car – looking out as bullets bounce against the steel. Few can endure that. Then only the borderline cop, the one who's between law and illegality, is the useful one.[21]

This phrase clearly illustrates the type of training that Military Police recruits received for most of this period. The Military Police are prepared to fight. Given that initial mindset, and the dire situations they often encountered, it makes sense that short-term initiatives to implement alternative policing strategies did not gain traction within most of the force.

[20] Interview by author with former BOPE Captain Rodrigo Pimentel, Rio de Janeiro, September 8, 2014.
[21] Interview by author with Miltary Police colonel, Rio de Janeiro, September 1, 2014.

Police responses following the deaths of fellow officers were especially brutal. The most egregious example took place during Brizola's second administration, when, following deaths of police officers at the hands of traffickers, PM squads murdered eight street children outside the Candelária church and gunned down twenty-one persons in the favela of Vigário Geral within a couple of months. During Batista's short tenure, the Military Police also invaded various favelas without political or judicial authorization, in order to "prove their worth" before the federal army's intervention in Operation Rio (Resende 1995, 78). Many *cariocas* (as Rio citizens are known), in fact, celebrated the military's arrival because they perceived it as less corrupt and violent than the police.

The high autonomy of Rio's Military Police, whether granted by politicians or wrestled against their wishes, resulted in police applying unmitigated violence to regulate drug trafficking. The other main instrument of regulation – police corruption – was not so much an alternative as a complement to the violence police exercised.

Dispersed Corruption: "Police Always Extorted the Criminals"
Police corruption, resulting from high police autonomy, was the other central instrument of the state's regulatory strategy toward drug trafficking. Corruption within the force was massive. In 1994, the state security secretary publicly admitted that up to nine out of ten police officers were involved in corruption (Resende 1995, 75–76).[22] However, police did not coordinate their corruption either internally or with politicians. Its decentralized nature inhibited prolonged ceasefires between police and dealers. Police tenure insecurity – derived from the high rotation of political superiors, police commanders, statutory policies and procedural guidelines due to political turnover – heightened the appeal of collecting rents to advance in their careers, earn an additional income, or simply get things done within the organization, such as fixing their patrol cars, obtaining extra ammunition or taking days off (Gudel 2009). Drug dealing gangs proved an attractive source of such rents.

The Military Police continuously resorted to violent predatory techniques and extortion against traffickers and dealers in favelas to extract these rents. One former trafficker I interviewed described his exchanges

---

[22] As a former colonel in charge of overseeing the Military Police (PM) told me, these corrupt practices were more widespread in the PM than in the Civil Police (PC), because PM officers are on the street, while PC officers only take bribes not to investigate crimes once these are denounced in the police station.

with the police in crude terms, "The police always came into [the favela] and extorted the bandits." He recounted how, after he had already done time in prison, "The police picked me up and told me to give them what I had; the battalion commander said that if he saw me there again he would kill me."[23] Another former trafficker told me how police threatened to open an *inquérito* (formal inquiry) against her, unless she paid them off. She said, "When you are the leader in the community, if there was a robbery, a carjacking, or whatever, near the neighborhood, police say that you are responsible and open an investigation."[24]

Corruption is often seen as a key ingredient in deals struck between police and criminals to inhibit confrontation. However, this prolific rent extraction did not produce sustainable peacekeeping agreements. As Professor Michel Misse, an expert on drug trafficking from the Federal University of Rio de Janeiro (UFERJ) told me, "Here in Rio there is not a pact but an *arregro* [arrangement]. Police extort money but do not provide protection."[25] On the contrary, corruption and violence were mutually reinforcing. When traffickers failed to pay their dues, police invaded the favelas, expropriated bandits, or even carried out summary executions. This exacerbated traffickers' willingness to retaliate against police (Lessing 2017, 184). A current Military Police colonel also illustrated the link between violence and corruption on the part of the police, "[The police officer] who's capable of killing is capable of kidnapping and extorting a trafficker. If you strike at violence, you lower police corruption. This [high corruption] is another consequence of war."[26]

Police did not coordinate their illicit rent extraction with political authorities either. While clientelistic networks connecting traffickers, resident association leaders, police and local politicians proliferated (Leeds 1996; Arias 2006a, 2006b), no politician or party established a centralized racket or political machine. For instance, the Garotinhos tried to consolidate an illicit rent extraction network with police but failed. Moreover, during his wife Rosinha's mandate, former Governor Anthony Garotinho was indicted for heading a crime racket with the head of the Civil Police, Alvaro Lins, and other officers. While Garotinho was exonerated, Lins was sentenced to twenty-eight years in prison, which suggests that there was no political protection for high-ranking police commanders, a key feature of protection rackets.

---

[23] Interview by author with former trafficker I, Rio de Janeiro, September 16, 2014.
[24] Interview by author with former trafficker III, Rio de Janeiro, September 18, 2014.
[25] Interview by author with Michel Misse, Rio de Janeiro, September 3, 2014.
[26] Interview by author with Military Police colonel, Rio de Janeiro, September 1, 2014.

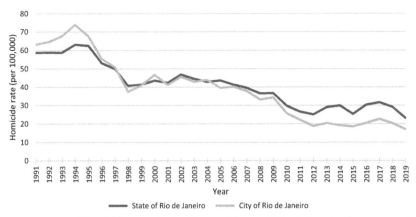

FIGURE 3.2. Homicide rates in the City and State of Rio de Janeiro (1991–2019)
Source: Author's elaboration from Instituto de Segurança Pública – Rio de Janeiro (Institute of Public Security of Rio de Janeiro).

These corruption schemes, while probably providing vast funds for those involved, failed to contain criminal violence in Rio de Janeiro, signaling that governments facing high political competition find it harder to utilize the police to obtain rents from crime as well as to produce peaceful orders.

Criminal Violence: "You Either Won or Lost"

The state's regulation of drug trafficking through particularistic confrontation increased criminal violence, due to frequent clashes between drug traffickers and police, between rival trafficking gangs, and by traffickers or police against civilians in favelas.[27] Criminal violence in Rio de Janeiro fluctuated at elevated levels in line with each administration's capacity to control the police.

As Figure 3.2 shows, criminal violence often follows political cycles. Homicide rates peaked during Brizola's second administration (1991–1994), coinciding with a new failed attempt to reform the police. Criminal violence decreased in the Alencar administration (1995–1998) and increased again following the brief reform attempt by Soares during Garotinho's administration, and the subsequent unraveling of the police, between 1999 and 2003. Homicide rates would decrease significantly following the implementation of the Pacification program in 2008, particularly in the City of Rio de Janeiro, only to increase again after the

---

[27] An estimated 57.3 percent of homicides in 1992 were related to drug trafficking (Soares 1996).

program started to wane in 2014. The state trend in violence usually follows that of the Capital City and greater metropolitan region of Rio de Janeiro, which is home to 65 percent of the state's population.[28] This region also has the largest concentration of favelas, many of which are controlled by trafficking gangs, and where police violence and corruption are more likely to prevail.[29] The widening gap between the State and City murder rates in the 2010s relates to the initial success in the UPP and the deteriorating conditions in the Metropolitan periphery, especially the Baixada Fluminense, where several favelas are controlled by militia groups.

In a regime of particularistic confrontation, not only is violence high, but also indiscriminately applied by state and criminal actors. A former trafficker, describing his time spent selling drugs in the favela, used bellicose terms similarly to the officers cited in the previous section, "We lived in a time of war. You either won or lost. When police came in, you either killed or were killed. I had some weapons training and could fire a few shots, but others shot at will and all over the place, not thinking at whom they were shooting, if they were another faction, police, or the community."[30] This lack of firing skill is not surprising given the high number of young men and women who participated in drug trafficking gangs (Dowdney 2004), many of whom also consumed drugs or alcohol. A former high-ranking BOPE officer expressed a similar perception, "The BOPE had to intervene because [regular] military police did not know how to shoot, and neither did the traffickers, so this resulted in a lot of killings."[31]

Police raids on favelas, whether to arrest or kill traffickers, reinforced violence both within the gang and in the community, for multiple reasons. First, typically a new leader would seek to occupy the place of the arrested or killed chief and would have strong incentives to use ostensible violence to establish a reputation and consolidate his control (Goldstein 2003; Gay 2005; Penglase 2014).[32] Second, police raids encouraged rival factions to

---

[28] Source: 2014 census.
[29] Within the Capital City of Rio de Janeiro, homicide rates are particularly concentrated in some of the city's favelas (Rodrigues and Rivero 2012; Zaluar and Barcellos 2013, 28). Violence is much higher in the Northern Zone favelas, closer to the airport, ports and the City's main corridor (Avenida Brasil), than in rich Southern neighborhoods like Copacabana or Ipanema, where many middle or upper-class individuals buy drugs.
[30] Interview by author with former trafficker I, Rio de Janeiro, September 16, 2014.
[31] Interview by author with former BOPE officer, Rio de Janeiro, September 1, 2014.
[32] Often, leading drug traffickers (*donos*) remained in charge of distribution in their respective favela even after being imprisoned (Gay 2005, 2015).

invade the territory (Maggessi 2006, 175).[33] High police autonomy thus exacerbated violence by destabilizing drug markets.

Traffickers also unleashed violence against citizens in their neighborhoods, usually with two countervailing purposes. On the one hand, they sought to maintain order and monitor public space in their territories, punishing those who committed crimes – particularly rapes – against other favela residents (Arias 2017, 128). As a former trafficker told me, "We [traffickers] took care that nothing happened in the community. You can see that there are many more rapes now. Before, if we had rapists, if we had thieves in the community, we killed them, we took care of it. Even if we were of different factions and fought each other, we all had the same rules as to what was tolerated or not in the community."[34] At the same time, gang leaders gained legitimacy by offering protection to residents who did not trust the state (Wolff 2015, 22). On the other hand, criminals also punished those suspected of collaborating with the police to set an example for the rest of the community (Leeds 1996; Goldstein 2003; Arias 2006b).

In short, this period (1983–2007) is characterized by constant alternation in the governorship, as well as incoherent administrations with little legislative support. It certainly did not help that the City of Rio was governed by political rivals who often undermined the implementation of reforms. The pattern of high turnover and fragmentation resulted in rapid, reiterated shifts in security policies, as incumbents pursued and then abandoned reformist initiatives, even when factions within the police supported them. Consequently, the police retained their high autonomy, and regulated drug trafficking through indiscriminate repression and corruption, resulting in high criminal violence. Starting in 2008, the installation of Police Pacification Units (UPPs) in several favelas implied a temporary and partial transition to a coordinated coexistence regulatory arrangement.

PACIFICATION: A TEMPORARY COORDINATED COEXISTENCE, 2008–2014

After a period characterized by high turnover and fragmentation, which resulted in high police autonomy and regulation of drug trafficking via particularistic confrontations, Rio de Janeiro's government shifted

---

[33] In a similar vein, Lessing argues that nonselective, or indiscriminate, confrontation by the state generated incentives for traffickers to respond violently to state repression (Lessing 2015).

[34] Interview by author with former trafficker IV, Rio de Janeiro, September 18, 2014.

toward a coordinated coexistence regime between 2008 and 2014. This change did not occur immediately following the inauguration of the new administration in 2007. In fact, the newly elected governor of Rio de Janeiro, Sérgio Cabral (PMDB, 2006–2013), began by following the security policy playbook of his predecessors. His campaign proposal did not focus on police reform but on renewing the force's vehicle fleet, setting up control towers over the main highways and increasing Military police battalions and police personnel.[35] During his first year in office, the government maintained the reactive logic police had always used (Beltrame 2014, 103) and authorized violent police operations, particularly in the massive favela complex Alemão. Consequently, the number of deaths resulting from police interventions reached a record high 1,330 in 2007. Total homicides also hovered at an alarming rate of 40 per 100,000. With several international events which would draw the world's attention to Rio de Janeiro over the following years, the government needed a change in its security policy and its regulation of drug trafficking to lower criminal violence.

In December 2008, the state government of Rio de Janeiro began to install Police Pacification Units (UPP) in various favelas of the Capital City. After a couple of haphazard interventions, the administration designed a formal strategy that prioritized regaining territorial control of gang-ridden favelas over cracking down on the gangs or confiscating drugs. The government began to announce invasions in advance instead of letting police arbitrarily raid marginalized neighborhoods (Lessing 2017, 193). The administration also targeted other areas of police autonomy such as its training and discretionary use of force to stock the UPPs with better qualified officers. In this section, I assess how political turnover and fragmentation led to the UPP program's emergence, and more importantly, its persistence for more than eight years, which distinguishes it from most previous alternative policing strategies, and only lasted a few years at most. This section highlights the within-case variation of regulatory regimes in Rio de Janeiro and how decreased political competition can reduce police autonomy even in an extremely dire setting, marred by repeated failures in its recent history.

Unlike the informal rules that drove particularistic confrontation, Pacification featured explicit and transparent guidelines. Officials from the secretary of security specified how police should intervene in favelas

---

[35] "Confira as propostas de Sérgio Cabral para o governo," *O Globo*, September 29, 2006.

and alerted drug dealers to flee to avoid confrontation. However, I still classify this period as a partially informal regulatory regime, for several reasons. First, police still maintained high discretion in their interaction with drug dealers in the favela, even when abiding with the overall spirit of the program; in fact, several allege that the standard police (mis) treatment of favela residents persisted. Second, various officers also took advantage of the calm wrought by Pacification to broker protection deals with traffickers. Third, the program also affected the way in which traffickers, who are not guided by formal rules, approached the police and rival gangs, and maintained order in the favela. While police professionalization, the precondition for coexistence, implies a greater presence of formal elements, a large part of police regulation of drug markets continues to be based on informal rules.

"Police Are an Organ of the Executive": Reducing Police Autonomy in Rio

Sérgio Cabral's administration needed to reduce violence in the city in preparation for the international events it would host over the following years: the 2007 Pan-American games; the 2013 Global Youth Encounter – which brought Pope Francis to Rio; the 2014 FIFA Soccer World Cup; and the 2016 Olympic Games. Undoubtedly, these global events strongly influenced governing politicians' decisions: promoting Rio as a city safe for foreign visitors would clearly not hurt Cabral or his party's electoral chances in 2010. However, this international incentive does not entirely explain how his administration managed to maintain this initiative during the entire period (2008–2015), while all other prior efforts to reduce police autonomy dissolved in less than a gubernatorial term. The entrenchment of the PMDB and the high fragmentation it faced explains this evolution.

Like his predecessors, Governor Cabral encountered a highly fragmented political scenario. Without a majority in the first round, Cabral won the runoff election. He also headed a broad, heterogeneous coalition and lacked a majority in the state legislature. However, he implemented the UPP by building different political alliances and bolstering his security secretary, José Mariano Beltrame, gradually reducing police autonomy in the process.[36]

---

[36] Beltrame, as well as his team, were former Federal Police officers and thus relatively insulated from Rio's internal politics.

Low turnover, or the PMDB's entrenchment in office, accounted for the persistence of the UPP program over time. Cabral became the first Rio governor to win reelection in 2010 and his vice-governor, Luiz Fernando Pezão, carried on after him in 2014.[37] More importantly, Security Secretary Beltrame and most members of his team remained in their posts through this entire period, ensuring the persistence of this policy.

The state government inaugurated the first UPP in the Dona Marta favela in December 2008. A key factor in installing subsequent units was coordination with the government of the City of Rio, which had elected Eduardo Paes, also from the PMDB, as mayor in October 2008. It was the first time since 1986 that the same party governed both the State and the City of Rio de Janeiro, which houses close to 40 percent of the state's population and most of its gang-controlled favelas. The city government invested close to R $30 million to pay bonuses for the UPP police (R $500 per month per officer initially[38] and R $750 since 2012[39]). This coordination between state and local governments provided the political and financial support necessary to implement and sustain the program: All but the first UPP were installed after Paes' term began on January 1, 2009 (see Appendix 2). In his memoir, Security Secretary Beltrame reflected:

It's impossible to not register the daily feedback that Governor Sérgio Cabral, and, starting in January 2009, Mayor Eduardo Paes gave me about the provisions taken [on the UPPs]. They saw the opportunity of change way before the more conservative police sectors. When we reflect on the success or failure of public policies, we can say that, without an alignment from top to bottom, nothing will work. (Beltrame 2014, 111)

Lacking a partisan majority in the state legislature, Cabral used his party's coalition with the Workers' Party (PT) at the national, state and local level to build programmatic support for the UPP. This ensured the partisan left would not veto the state government's security proposals, preventing clashes like those between Brizola and the PT in the early 1980s or between Soares and Garotinho in the late 1990s. The federal government provided fiscal resources and military troops for

---

[37] Pezão had already stepped in for Cabral in July 2014, after the governor resigned to run for the national senate.

[38] Established by state decree 41.653/2009 (January 22, 2009). USD equivalent: $213.

[39] "Policiais militares de UPPs receberão aumento na gratificação," *Imprensa RJ*, July 25, 2012. (USD equivalent: $368). Also, interview by author with state security secretary (SESEG) mid-level official, Rio de Janeiro, September 19, 2014.

interventions in problematic favelas,[40] like the Complexo da Maré, which gave the program political credibility among center-left state deputies and councilmen – or at least dissuaded them from criticizing the program outright. As a PT councilman told me, "We understood that, for [PT Presidents] Dilma and Lula, governing Brazil depended in a way on the PMDB, because it was the largest party in the National Congress ... hence in Rio we have a national, state and local alliance [with the government]."[41] In fact, a PT state deputy introduced the first bill regulating the implementation of the UPP in late 2010 (Cano et al. 2012, 17).[42]

The state's high political fragmentation also compelled the governor to insulate Secretary Beltrame from external political influence that could manipulate the Pacification program. Thus, the administration averted a particularistic give and take with other state or local politicians, and restricted political opponents from using the police to run protection rackets. Beltrame narrates how, early in Cabral's administration, a mayor from an important city came into his office seeking the appointment of a given police commander and was bluntly dismissed (Beltrame 2014, 96).[43] A former BOPE officer also stated that, in contrast with other administrations (especially Garotinho's), there was not as much political interference in determining promotions during Cabral's tenure:

Not today, Cabral did not get involved in that [i.e., police appointments]. For instance, during Garotinho's time, commanders of battalions and stations were determined by the influence of state deputies, especially in the areas further from the center, like the Baixada Fluminense, the Western Zone, etc. To get promoted, especially to colonel, you needed a good relationship with the command and the security secretary; otherwise, you got stuck at Lieutenant. Technically, there is a commission that evaluates both objective and subjective criteria, but the objective ones are always left aside.[44]

The entrenchment of the PMDB in the state government ensured the stability of Cabral's security staff and policy, and the consequent

---

[40] For example, state police and municipal guards received training courses and housing credits, among other things, through the Programa Nacional de Segurança com Cidadania (PRONASCI, National program of Security with Citizenship).

[41] Interview by author with PT councilmember Reimont, Rio de Janeiro, September 4, 2014.

[42] This law was regulated by decree N. 42.787, sanctioned on January 6, 2011.

[43] See also Alves and Evanson (2011, 202) and the autobiography of former Security Secretary Márcio Colmerauer (Colmerauer 2014, 37).

[44] Interview by author with former BOPE officer, Rio de Janeiro, September 1, 2014.

reduction of police autonomy. Beltrame persisted as security secretary for more than nine years (2007–2016), while the average tenure for his ten predecessors between 1995 and 2006 had been less than fifteen months.[45] Moreover, he outlasted five different heads of the Military Police and four Civil Police chiefs. Former PM Colonel Jorge da Silva, a critic of the administration, explicitly mentioned this matter during our conversation:

Q: Everything the police do is decided by the government?

A: The police are an organ of the executive. When the governor decides he will concentrate all the staff in the UPP, what is the PM commander going to do? He has to obey; if not, he's out. You know how many PM commanders passed with Beltrame? Five.[46]

A key episode shows how the governor's political support of his secretary shaped the relationship between the administration and the police. At the end of Cabral's first year in office (2007), a group of Military Police colonels protested in demand of higher wages and better working conditions for their troops (Coronel Paúl 2011, 29–40). The administration, which perceived the protest as an illegitimate attempt by police commanders to pressure the new governor, rejected the demands and dismissed the PM commander general, who had condoned the protests. Forty-one PM officials responded by demanding Beltrame's resignation and their commander's restitution.[47] Cabral declared that, "Those few [colonels] that are looking for trouble and disorder will not manage to destabilize the [administration]," and stood by Beltrame.[48] The secretary then expelled eight high-ranking commanders, transferred other intransigent colonels to irrelevant positions and promoted the remaining protesters to coopt them.[49] Following this crisis, there were no more police rebellions. The government's unity and its subsequent political stability gave the police stronger incentives to collaborate with the administration, even if it meant

---

[45] Beginning with the reestablishment of the secretary within the government in 1995, during Marcello Alencar's administration. See Table A.1.

[46] Interview by author with former PM Colonel Jorge da Silva, Niterói, September 19, 2014. Da Silva, who had been commander of the PM during Garotinho's administration, was one of his advisers during the latter's campaign.

[47] "Exoneração de Ubiratan provoca crise na segurança," *Jornal do Brasil*, January 30, 2008.

[48] "Apoio a coronel exonerado divide PM e abre crise na segurança do Rio," *Jornal do Brasil*, January 30, 2008.

[49] One of the colonels initially leading the protest became the next commanding general of the Military Police. The resistant colonel was transferred to "the freezer" – an irrelevant bureaucratic post – and then expelled from the force (Coronel Paúl 2011).

a reduction in its autonomy. Like one of the leaders of the original protest told me, "after [us – the protesting colonels], no one in the Military Police said 'no' to the government."[50]

The perceived success of the initial twelve UPPs aided Cabral's landslide reelection in 2010: He obtained 66 percent of the vote in the first round, 45 points over his closest contender. Naturally, the father of the UPP, Security Secretary Beltrame, remained in his post as well, while the program persisted and expanded: By the end of 2014, thirty-eight UPPs were in place.[51] Partisan continuity over the next two administrations (Cabral-Pezão 2010–2014, and Pezão 2014–2018) enabled the implementation and persistence of the UPP and other initiatives that reduced police autonomy and shaped a distinct regulatory regime of drug trafficking, at least in the City of Rio de Janeiro.

Designing and Implementing the UPPs: Reducing Police Autonomy
The UPP program entailed a reduction of police autonomy in at least two ways, relating to their internal governance and external operations. First, the program modified police training and appointment procedures. All Military Police recruits received preparation in community policing, conflict mediation, human rights, gradual use of force and so on. Additionally, all new recruits were initially assigned to the UPPs before being transferred to PM battalions to avoid being "contaminated" by the corrupt practices of their older peers.[52]

Second, the UPPs also modified the logic by which police intervened in favelas. While police previously invaded marginalized neighborhoods without political (or judicial) authorization, the security secretariat planned and supervised Pacification operations (Beltrame 2014). Governor Cabral's order was that "No one enters a community without a planned and well-thought-out action, something that is not altogether clear to the public" (Alves and Evanson 2011, 209). The elite squad, BOPE, would usually lead the invasion and once the favela was secure, the Military Police would set up the UPP. Often this amounted to offices and locker rooms in makeshift containers, like in the Rocinha UPP I visited in November 2014 (see Figure 3.3). Other units were significantly more advanced, like the Nova

---

[50] Interview by author with Colonel Paúl, Rio de Janeiro, August 25, 2014.

[51] Cabral resigned in July 2014 and left his vice-governor (Luiz Fernando de Souza) Pezão to finish his term. Pezão won his own election in 2014.

[52] Interview by author with public official in the secretary of security office, Rio de Janeiro, September 19, 2014.

FIGURE 3.3. Police Pacification Unit in Rocinha favela (November 2014)
Source: Photographed by the author.

FIGURE 3.4. Police Pacification Unit in Nova Brasília favela, Alemão Complex
(November 2014)
Source: Photographed by the author.

Brasília UPP in the Alemão Complex (Figure 3.4), which I visited in the same fieldwork trip. The administration also announced the occupations beforehand, allowing the traffickers to leave the favela to avoid bloodshed, a decision criticized by conservative politicians, who claimed it allowed criminals to move to the periphery and increased crime there.[53]

This superior planning with respect to previous interventions does not imply that the UPP program was devoid of improvisation. In recalling the implementation process, a former UPP commander-in-chief stated,

---

[53] See, for instance, the account of the peaceful occupation of the São Carlos favela. "Polícia faz operação no Complexo de São Carlos para instalação de unidades de polícia," *O Globo*, February 6, 2011.

"I improvised a bit, selecting police that I thought would be enthusiastic about the idea, but there wasn't, despite the good will, a systematic effort to create an institutional structure. I feel the same way with the secretary [Beltrame]. I don't doubt the good will, but I think there have not been structures to maintain these changes."[54] This concern presaged Pacification's upcoming challenges and its ultimate failure. Furthermore, the administration selected some areas for UPP interventions in response to specific criminal events, such as the killing of two journalists by militias in the favela of Batam. This was the only favela controlled by militias in which the administration set up a UPP. Nonetheless, compared with the dearth of policy directives in previous administrations, the UPP effort represented a major progress in terms of security policy planning and implementation (see also Denyer Willis and Mota Prado 2014).

In addition to the UPPs, Cabral's administration employed other actions to reduce human rights abuses by police. Contrary to Alencar's Faroeste policy, the administration rewarded police for achieving a *lower* number of civilian casualties. To this end, the administration created a system for monitoring certain strategic security indicators in 2009,[55] as well as *Autos de Resistência* (deaths resulting from police intervention) since 2011.[56] Additionally, the government monitored police officers' actions through cameras on their persons and vehicles. In the words of a municipal guard, "Before, the police had a certain liberty because nothing was recorded. Today, when they enter a community, they are more careful in [respecting] the resident's human rights in case they make a complaint, and you end up with an administrative process."[57]

Notwithstanding its merits, Pacification was not a comprehensive police reform. It did not alter the organizational structure and core functions of Rio's military and civil police. Furthermore, the administration did not rattle other areas of police governance. It made few discernible improvements in the institutions designed to control the Civil and Military Police – the *Corregedorias* (Internal Affairs unit), external *Ouvidorias* (Auditing agencies) or the Public Ministry.[58]

---

[54] Interview by author with former PM colonel and UPP commander-in-chief, Rio de Janeiro, September 16, 2014.

[55] Executive Decree No. 41.931/2009.

[56] Executive Decree No. 42.780/2011. See also "From hero to villain in Rio," *The Economist*, September 14, 2013.

[57] Interview by author with municipal guard of the City of Rio de Janeiro, Rio de Janeiro, September 3, 2014.

[58] Interview by author with Luciana Boiteux, State Penitentiary Council, Rio de Janeiro, September 9, 2014.

Nonetheless, Pacification represented the most important (and effective) effort to date by state-level governments in Rio to reduce police autonomy since democratization.

"Before We Shot Each Other and Got Out. Now We Stay." The Implementation of Coordinated Coexistence in the Rio Metropolitan Area

In an interview with the British newspaper, *The Guardian*, Security Secretary Beltrame summarized the UPPs' main goal, "We cannot guarantee the end of drug trafficking nor is it our intention. What we want to end is the paradigm of territorial control by armed drug traffickers."[59] This vision was also explicitly articulated in the UPP's official website, "It is not the objective of the UPPs to end drug trafficking or criminality. It is to retake territories occupied by heavily armed criminal factions."[60] These quotes summarize how Pacification differs from the particularistic confrontation that characterized Rio de Janeiro's regulation of drug trafficking during the previous two decades. As a current PM colonel put it, "Before the UPP, we went in, shot each other and got out. Now we stay."[61]

The UPPs constitute an alternative regulatory regime, *coordinated coexistence*, in other words, an implicit agreement between state and criminals to refrain from continuous confrontation. This regulatory regime springs from the reduced autonomy of Rio's police. The UPPs decreased police officers' indiscriminate violence and uncoordinated extortion against traffickers and other favela residents. Political officials instructed police to forego drug seizures in favor of confiscating weapons, implicitly tolerating drug dealing in favelas. At the same time, traffickers also sought to avoid confrontation with the police, at least temporarily. Consequently, this period exhibits lower police and criminal violence, and (paradoxically) more coordinated police corruption, although many of the problems inherent in the previous regulatory regime remain.

Decreasing Police Violence

After the implementation of the UPPs, state-driven violence has clearly declined. As Figure 3.5 shows, police homicides increased sharply between 1999 and 2007, when they reached a record 1,330, a rate of

---

[59] "Rio de Janeiro police occupy slums as city fights back against drug gangs," *The Guardian*, April 12, 2010.

[60] Source: UPP website, www.upprj.com/index.php/faq.

[61] Interview by author with current Military Police colonel, Rio de Janeiro, September 1, 2014.

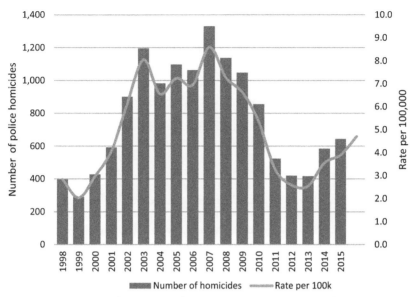

FIGURE 3.5. Homicides resulting from police intervention, Rio de Janeiro,
1998–2015
Source: Author's elaboration from Instituto de Segurança Pública do Rio de Janeiro (ISP-RJ).

8.6 homicides per 100,000 individuals. By contrast, police homicide rates
dropped continuously between 2008 and 2013, reaching a minimum of
400 cases – 2.5 per 100,000. This pattern illustrates a clear shift toward a
less confrontational police force during Pacification's early years.

The UPPs reduced police violence significantly. According to
Magaloni et al. (2020), police killings in favelas would have been
60 percent higher without the UPP intervention.[62] This decrease partly
stems from the differential training for rookie police officers, greater
monitoring of police actions and the system of performance metrics that
rewarded police for lower casualty rates. However, the decrease also
reflected the emergence of an alternative regulatory regime, as police
steered away from indiscriminate favela invasions and were tacitly, if
not explicitly, instructed by the government to tolerate drug trafficking
in the favela.[63]

---

[62] See also Ferraz and Vaz (2013).
[63] This explanation coincides with Lessing's claim that Pacification implied a shift toward
conditional repression by the state, with criminals adopting a hide-and-bribe strategy
toward police.

Police were no longer sporadically invading favelas or avenging killings of officers by traffickers. The number of killed police also decreased. Comparing the dynamics of violence between past programs and the UPP's regulatory effort, a former commander of the Military Police explained how Pacification precluded traffickers' retaliation while also reducing the probability of invasion by drug gangs:

> Police always place fixed control points in places where there are few police, and when there is a problem – you have a criminal that everybody knows is there, so police have to arrest him; police want to seize drugs; [or] you have group A fighting with group B – then police go there. Then, every time police come in with a larger group, you have a reaction by the traffickers, and it increases the insecurity of the place. The result: criminals and police dead and injured .... As police occupy that space [with the UPP] neither of those two things will happen: police will not enter (because they are already there) nor will you have an invasion by a rival gang.[64]

Notwithstanding the initial success of Pacification, ingrained police violence is difficult to eradicate. In this sense, not everybody praised the program or found it significantly different from past police practices.[65] A former BOPE captain explained:

> The UPP proposed community police, proximity police, younger, more educated, more prepared police, trained for a better relationship with the community. But that police officer belongs to the same police force that combats, the police of the BOPE, the Tropa de Elite. He is also a truculent police officer, who hits the [favela] resident in the face, who rapes the women. Unfortunately, if you ask them whether they prefer to be UPP or BOPE, they want to shoot; they don't want to go to the UPP and be a proximity police, they want to be a combat police. Trafficking resists in the main communities and confronts the UPP .... Then the UPP police officer has already taken a position of war, being more aggressive, he hates trafficking and traffickers. That's very dangerous.[66]

A specific case, the disappearance and murder of Rocinha stoneworker Amarildo in 2013, symbolized the endurance of the PM's vices despite, or rather because of, the UPP program. The commander of the Rocinha UPP – a former BOPE high-ranking officer – had received information that Amarildo was a major local drug dealer and sent a unit to arrest and interrogate him. Amarildo was tortured and his body was missing for

---

[64] Interview by author with Colonel Ubiratan, Rio de Janeiro, September 4, 2014.
[65] For an insightful criticism of Pacification, see the ethnographic work by Stefanie Israel de Souza (2019a; 2019b).
[66] Interview by author with former BOPE Captain Rodrigo Pimentel, Rio de Janeiro, September 8, 2014.

days, only turning up after several street protests,[67] and his family's meeting with Governor Cabral.[68] The commander and several members of his unit were arrested and charged. Multiple interviewees – and not only human rights activists – spontaneously brought up this case. The new commander at Rocinha, when I interviewed him, admitted that this episode tarnished the image the UPP intended to project.[69] According to one of the investigating officers, Secretary Beltrame did not want to grant the Civil Police green light to investigate the case so as not to further damage the UPP's credibility. The investigating officer was sacked from his precinct and forced to retire.[70]

Leftist politicians and social movement activists also contended that the UPP was merely "window dressing," while police officers' abuses of favela residents continued.[71] Nonetheless, practically all candidates in the 2014 gubernatorial election promised to maintain the UPPs, whose greatest impact had been in the reduction of police lethal violence.[72]

Persistent Police Corruption

It is difficult to say if, and how, Pacification changed the level and form of police corruption in Rio de Janeiro. On the one hand, the new training given to military police officers before entering the UPP intended to reduce corruption by separating new recruits from "contaminated" officers. On the other hand, it is doubtful that extended police corruption can significantly decrease in the short or medium term, even by offering a bonus to UPP officers. Most interviewees responded that corruption had not varied much with respect to previous patterns, even though police were making greater efforts to prevent and punish it.

In comparison to the previous period (1983–2007), there are two main changes with respect to police corruption. First, larger groups of police

[67] The only positive aspect of Amarildo's disappearance is that it revealed society's decreased tolerance for police abuses, even when they affected favela residents.

[68] Interview by author with national newspaper journalist, Rio de Janeiro, September 10, 2014. The protests regarding Amarildo's disappearance coalesced with opposition to the government's increases in bus fares, which also stirred major riots in São Paulo.

[69] Interview by author with Military Police Captain, commander of Rocinha UPP, December 2, 2014.

[70] Interview by author with former Civil Police investigator, Rio de Janeiro, September 8, 2014.

[71] Interviews by author with NGO representatives, Rio de Janeiro, September 5, 2014; Judge Rubens Casara, Rio de Janeiro, September 9, 2014; and Truth Commission representative, Rio de Janeiro, September 4, 2014.

[72] "Ataques entre candidatos marcam primeiro debate no Rio," *O Globo*, August 20, 2014.

have been found running protection rackets with traffickers, showing a higher degree of internal collusion than before. For example, in 2011, the PM arrested thirty officers from the Fallet UPP who received over R $50,000 in bribes.[73] Second, higher-level commanding officers from both the PM and the PC appear more frequently connected to these rackets. In addition to the case mentioned here, in February 2011, a Federal Police investigation arrested 38 police officers, including the second-highest ranking officer of the Civil Police, for participating in a drug trafficking protection racket.[74]

The more frequent interaction between police and traffickers in favelas with UPPs also incentivized corruption to avoid continuous confrontation. As Professor Michel Misse told me, "As police are very corrupt, within the UPP drug trafficking still goes on, only more discreetly and [by] paying bribes to police".[75] This signals a change in the modality rather than the scale of corruption: from police extorting traffickers through violence to granting dealers protection in exchange for rents and mutual nonaggression.

As before, governing politicians have not been linked to illicit rent extraction from drug trafficking – except in the Garotinho administration. Despite the PMDB's known involvement in corruption scandals such as the Petrolão,[76] the opposition politicians I interviewed did not denounce corruption among its top state officials, in sharp contrast with those in Buenos Aires, the paradigmatic site of coordinated protection regimes (see Chapter 5). Meanwhile, politicians from different parties have been involved in protection rackets with militias that control several favelas in the Western Zone and the urban periphery (Albarracín 2018). While the government brought down several militia leaders as the result of a legislative inquiry in 2007, these groups still control various favelas and have deep political connections.

In short, the UPPs diminished police incentives to resort to violent extortion to extract rents from trafficking. Nonetheless, bribes and other protection schemes might have become more frequent as the police increased their interaction with traffickers in favelas. While some officers

---

[73] "Beltrame nega crise em UPP e reforça que policiais corruptos serão expulsos," *O Dia*, September 12, 2011.

[74] "38 arrested for police corruption in Rio," *The Rio Times*, February 15, 2011.

[75] Interview by author with Michel Misse, Rio de Janeiro, September 3, 2014.

[76] The *Petrolão* refers to the judicial investigation on corrupt procurement processes by the state oil company, Petrobras.

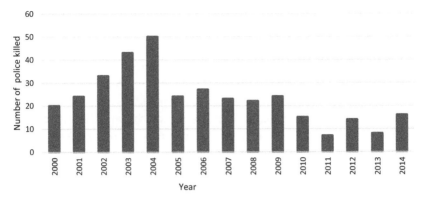

FIGURE 3.6. Police officers killed on duty in Rio de Janeiro, 2000–2014
Source: Author's elaboration from ISP-RJ.

might simply broker peacekeeping agreements, others might take the opportunity to set up their own protection rackets.

Reducing Criminal Violence

The regulation of drug trafficking via coordinated coexistence substantially decreased criminal violence. Between 2008 and 2014, homicide rates decreased by 40 percent in the City of Rio de Janeiro and by 20 percent in the state overall, reaching their lowest point in this entire period (1991–2019, refer back to Figure 3.2).

Coordinated coexistence also disrupted spirals of violence between police and criminals. Traffickers in favelas restrained their aggression against police inside the favelas. While 50 police officers were killed in 2004, there were only 8 fatal victims in 2013 (Figure 3.6).[77] As the former PM commander interviewed in the previous section stated, since police permanently occupy spaces formerly controlled by traffickers, there is no need for police units to invade favelas, and rival gangs will stay out to avoid clashes with the police.

The former traffickers I interviewed acknowledged that drug gangs did not confront the police as much as they used to, although they also warned that criminal factions were dormant, ready to pounce on the state whenever they sensed the opportunity. As one of them told me, "If they haven't, it was because they did not want to have problems."[78] While this regulatory

[77] Unfortunately, the Institute of Public Security (ISP) stopped publishing the number of police killed *off duty* – which has always been larger than that of police killed on duty – after 2007.

[78] Interview by author with former trafficker IV, Rio de Janeiro, September 18, 2014.

regime diminished traffickers' confrontation with police, it did not eliminate drug traffickers' presence in, and sometimes control of, favelas.

During my fieldwork, I conducted two separate visits to Rocinha, one of the largest favelas in Rio de Janeiro, where I spoke with several residents, municipal state representatives and the top police officials. All community residents agreed that the Rocinha UPP – installed in 2011 – had not changed anything, at least not for the better. They stated that while previously they could turn to "the power" (i.e., traffickers) to resolve disputes and maintain order in the favela (Arias 2017, 128), now disorder prevailed.[79] Residents also asserted that confrontation between the gangs and the state persisted, although it was less frequent than before. A local Civil Police delegate corroborated this perspective, suggesting that "[Traffickers] took advantage of the Amarildo case and increased their resistance."[80] In short, while Rocinha residents considered that the UPP had not established an alternative governance to that of traffickers in the favela, they recognized that it did restrain confrontation between traffickers and the police.

Many interviewees also perceived that the program fragmented trafficking and enabled less experienced criminals to take over neighborhood gangs. As a former BOPE Captain told me, "Before, police used to detain seven teenagers per day; today they catch around thirty-five a day. It is a signal that in [the favelas of] Alemão, Mangueira, Rocinha, the first generation of traffickers (18–26 years old) are in prison and the younger generation rises. They are younger, more violent and with the benefit of impunity."[81] A UPP commander also stated that, "Trafficking was clearly weakened by the UPP; they no longer show off weapons but there are crossfires . . .. It changed [things] in that more minors are used, and smaller quantities of drugs are sold. The market is more fragmented."[82] This increasing fragmentation, coupled with drug gangs' decreased social control within favelas, were worrying signs regarding the stability of the Pacification program and the coordinated coexistence regulatory arrangement.

To summarize, the implementation of the UPPs reduced police autonomy and altered the regulation of drug trafficking in the metropolitan

---

[79] From 2006 to 2011, when ADA trafficker Nem was *dono* (boss) of Rocinha, the gang refrained from violence against the state or civilians to protect their business (Glenny 2016). Rocinha had, therefore, relative order *before* the state's intervention.

[80] Interview by author with Rocinha Civil Police delegate, Rio de Janeiro, December 4, 2014.

[81] Interview by author with Rodrigo Pimentel, Rio de Janeiro, September 8, 2014.

[82] Interview by author with UPP commander, Rio de Janeiro, December 2, 2014.

area of Rio de Janeiro, which shifted from particularistic confrontation to coordinated coexistence between 2008 and 2014. Important reductions in police and criminal violence notwithstanding, remnants of particularistic confrontation lingered. Police still repeatedly violated human rights, and civilians still perceived them as extremely corrupt. While Pacification aspired to eradicate corruption, it might have facilitated it by placing the police in permanent contact with drug traffickers, thus motivating police to broker corrupt exchanges with dealers to avoid confrontation.

EPILOGUE: POST GLOBAL EVENTS, FISCAL CRISIS AND RETURN TO "NORMAL"

In Rio de Janeiro since redemocratization, high political turnover and fragmentation increased police autonomy and shaped particularistic confrontation as the predominant drug trafficking regulatory regime. Incumbents' initiatives to reform and control their police forces rapidly collapsed if they got off the ground at all. Unrestrained police units engaged in dispersed attacks and fragmented, unstable deals with drug traffickers, piling up bodies on both sides. In short, competitive politics and autonomous policing turned Rio de Janeiro into one of the most violent cities in Latin America during the 1990s and early 2000s.

The combination of greater internal coherence and decreasing turnover since 2008 enabled the government to reduce police autonomy via the Pacification program, and transition to a different, more tolerant regulatory regime – coordinated coexistence. However, Pacification has failed to eliminate the police force's entrenched corruption and violence, or to replace drug traffickers' governance in marginalized neighborhoods.

As the 2014 World Cup and the 2016 Rio Olympics games ended and the glitter of international events subsided, the political, fiscal and security boon of the previous years faded as well. The state's political leaders were uniformly involved in major corruption scandals: All living former governors of Rio are either in prison or on trial.[83] The state and city sank into a deep fiscal crisis, barely able to pay its public employees, including its police officers.[84] The troubles in Rio echoed the political turmoil at the national level in Brazil, which combined an economic recession, a lambasted political class that included one impeached president (Dilma

---

[83] Source: www.bbc.com/news/world-latin-america-46384397.

[84] Source: www.valor.com.br/international/news/6437139/city-rio-officials-halt-all-payments-financial-crisis-worsens?print=1.

Rousseff) and two convicted former presidents (Lula da Silva and Michel Temer), and incendiary levels of insecurity.

Enthusiasm for the UPP program had waned as well. Rio's violence entered a recrudescence phase (Lessing 2017, 164, 197–99).[85] Beltrame left his post in October 2016. His successors called for reducing the number of UPPs from thirty-eight to twenty, and nine UPPs were shut down by the end of 2018.[86] Homicides increased between 2016 and 2018 and although they decreased the following year, police lethal interventions surged dramatically.

Riding the punitive wave led by new President Jair Bolsonaro, Rio's new governor, Wilson Witzel, a political newcomer from the Social Christian Party (PSC)[87], recently urged to restore the UPPs.[88] However, he also called on police to "shoot criminals in the head." His tolerance of, and enthusiasm for, police brutality certainly contributed to the new rise in police lethal interventions. The rate of police homicides in 2019 was 9 deaths per 100,000 people, larger than the total homicide rate of most countries. Attempts to professionalize the police made during the previous administrations have withered. Once again, the state is embroiled in the policy instability and improvisation that characterized most of the democratic period.

While Rio de Janeiro illustrates the impact of high political competition and police autonomy on drug trafficking regulation, other cases in Latin America exhibit similar albeit less extreme patterns. The next chapter considers a less bellicose scenario of uncoordinated regulatory regimes: the metropolitan area of Rosario, located in the Argentine province of Santa Fe. While exhibiting high criminal violence, especially for Argentine standards, unlike in Rio de Janeiro, the state police has not engaged in dispersed attacks but in fragmented and corrupt deals with traffickers.

---

[85] Source: http://agenciabrasil.ebc.com.br/geral/noticia/2017-07/apos-sucesso-nos-jogos-olim picos-seguranca-publica-no-rio-vive-crise.

[86] Source: http://agenciabrasil.ebc.com.br/geral/noticia/2018-02/policia-militar-estuda-reduzir-numero-de-upps-no-rio-de-janeiro.

[87] Mr. Witzel has, for instance, equated criminals to terrorists and Nazis and advocated for snipers from helicopters to shoot them dead: www.reuters.com/article/us-brazil-polit ics-witzel/rio-governor-says-only-a-matter-of-time-before-he-becomes-brazil-presi dent-idUSKCN1UB2WE.

[88] Source: https://agenciabrasil.ebc.com.br/geral/noticia/2019-07/pm-quer-retomar-programa-de-unidades-de-policia-pacificadora-no-rio.

4

Particularistic Negotiation

The Decentralization of Police Corruption and Increase in Violence in Rosario, Santa Fe

OVERVIEW

On the evening of October 11, 2013, Santa Fe governor, Antonio Bonfatti, was watching the Argentina–Perú qualifying match for the 2014 Football World Cup when fourteen bullets pierced through his private home. Miraculously, he and his wife escaped unscathed. The ensuing investigation revealed that it was not a drug gang – on which the administration had started to crack down – but members of the provincial police,[1] themselves involved in drug trafficking, who carried out the attack.

Important sections of the Santa Fe provincial police have been embroiled in organized crime since the return of democracy in 1983. However, in previous years, they surely would not have confronted an elected official in this way. This chapter shows how increasing political competition in Santa Fe made politicians lose their grip on the provincial police, which brokered dispersed pacts with drug dealers, resulting in a substantial increase in criminal violence, especially in Rosario, the province's most important city.[2]

The province of Santa Fe evolved from a regulatory regime of coordinated protection rackets to one of *particularistic negotiation*, in other

---

[1] I use "provincial" as the equivalent of "state-level."

[2] Situated on the coast of the Paraná River, Rosario is the main outlet for Argentine agricultural exports, especially grains, many of them harvested in the province. Rosario has also historically been a key transshipment port of copious quantities of illicit substances to and from Argentina but did not become a major internal consumption and distribution market until the 2000s.

TABLE 4.1. *Political turnover, fragmentation, police autonomy and drug trafficking regulatory regimes in Santa Fe, 1983–2015*

Period	Turnover	Fragmentation	Police autonomy	Drug trafficking regulatory regimes
1983–1996	*Low* Peronist continuity in power	*Low* Peronism has united factions in cabinet and legislative majority	*Low* *Politicization* No reform and appropriation of police illicit rents	*Protection rackets* High and centralized police corruption Low police and criminal violence
1997–2015	*High* Alternation between Peronist factions and with Socialist party (2007)	*High* Fractured cabinets (Socialism) Divided government (Peronism)	*High* No consolidated reform No informal control, i.e., centralization of rents (esp. in Socialism)	*Particularistic negotiation* High and anarchic police corruption Low police violence High criminal violence

Source: Author's elaboration

words, dispersed deals with drug dealing gangs, which destabilized the drug market and increased criminal violence in the province's main metropolitan areas (see Table 4.1). Following democratization, the Peronist party governed the province uninterruptedly for 24 years (1983–2007). Facing little competition – low turnover and low fragmentation – Peronist administrations politicized the police and appropriated its rents from various criminal activities. In turn, police regulated drug trafficking and other illicit markets through protection rackets with low levels of violence. However, factional disputes within Peronism during the late 1990s and, especially, the victory of the Socialist party in 2007, increased turnover and fragmentation and, consequently, the autonomy of the police through successive reform cycles between administrations, as well as policy obstruction and incoherent policymaking within each administration. The police began to regulate the expanding drug market through particularistic negotiations. Each unit ran its own racket, collecting rents for itself rather than kicking them up to commanders or governing politicians. As the drug market splintered, violence escalated due to conflicts between drug dealing gangs, while the police were no less corrupt than before.

Alternative Explanations

The violent unraveling of Rosario's drug market shocked many Argentine politicians and analysts, who, in typical sensationalistic fashion, started referring to the city as the "Argentine Medellín" (Cavanagh 2014). I argue that the prevailing regulatory regime – *particularistic negotiation* – with its alarming rise in criminal violence, resulted from greater police autonomy fueled by political competition in the province. Nonetheless, other geographical and political factors could also explain the drug market's trajectory in this metropolitan area.

Geographically, Rosario has a prime location in Argentina's drug distribution network. It is the primary port for Argentina's agricultural exports, especially soy and its derivatives. It lies on the banks of the Paraná River, one of the main transport routes for drugs pouring into Argentina from Paraguay and other Latin American countries on ships that are rarely checked (Stevens 2017). It is also a key stop in National Route no. 34, one of the main thoroughfares for drugs crossing from the northeastern Bolivian border. However, these conditions also existed during previous years when the provincial police regulated the drug market in Rosario in a much more coordinated fashion, in other words, through protection rackets with political acquiescence. While one could correctly argue that Argentina's drug boom is more recent, Buenos Aires – another central distribution hub – had a markedly different trajectory to that of Rosario and maintained an ordered drug market through this period, as I will show in Chapter 5.

Meanwhile, other analyses could agree with my theory's emphasis on the political conditions that explain drug regulatory regimes but disagree on the specific factors. On the one hand, some could argue that the province's police anarchy and drug market cataclysm is largely attributable to the Socialist party's naïveté and incompetence at the governorship. On the other hand, others could counter that the fact that the local and provincial government was governed by an opposition party motivated the federal government – headed by Peronist Cristina Fernández de Kirchner – to withhold necessary collaboration that could have stemmed the bloodshed. Even while these explanations have some merit, they are hardly the most relevant story.

First, as this chapter shows, police governance began to unravel as a consequence of multiple reform cycles during the late 1990s and early

2000s, in which alternating Peronist factions were in power. During this period, police corruption was rampant and its association with the burgeoning drug market was evident. An important difference is that there was more political participation in police illicit rent extraction than under the Socialists. While this does not absolve the Socialist party from its incapacity to control the police, the provincial security force was still far from a professionalized department when the Socialists took office in 2007.

Second, it is true that the federal and provincial government clashed repeatedly during this period. A notorious example was when a national legislator from Kirchner's party referred to the provincial government as "narco-socialist."[3] However, this tension hardly accounts for the uncoordinated drug market regulation that prevailed in Rosario. Despite its animosity, the federal government had no role in administering the provincial police. While not being able to prosecute criminals for drug trafficking, the state judiciary had sufficient legal tools to go after the main drug gangs and their associates for other crimes, especially homicides. One could argue that the federal government could have sent in troops to help stem the violence, as the presidential administration of Mauricio Macri did once he took office in 2016 (Sweigart 2017). However, as the increase in violence in subsequent years showed, this was at best a temporary solution that did not address the main problem facing the province and its main metropolitan areas: police corruption and its acquiescence by elected politicians.

POLICE AND POLITICAL INSTITUTIONAL LEGACIES IN SANTA FE

Like with most police forces in Argentina, the newly elected democratic government of Santa Fe in 1983 had good reasons to distrust the provincial police and seek to control it. The Santa Fe provincial police had actively participated in the last dictatorship (1976–1983), managing one of the main clandestine detention centers outside of Buenos Aires. This authoritarian legacy would tarnish the police for many years after the democratic transition. Furthermore, some police commanders during the dictatorship were not just involved in gross human rights violations but

---

[3] "Larroque habló de 'narcosocialismo' y encendió la furia opositora," *Perfil*, November 1, 2011.

also smuggled Bolivian cocaine into the province (Del Frade 2000), an early sign of the department's connection with drug trafficking.

The institutional context for police reform was, a priori, unfavorable. Santa Fe's political institutions generate high political turnover and fragmentation by design. Unlike the other cases in this book, the province never reformed its constitution to allow for the governor's reelection. Therefore, each term necessarily brings with it a new incumbent. Furthermore, governors need only a plurality to win elections, which lowers the threshold needed to reach executive office.

The other distinctive political institution of Santa Fe is the *Ley de Lemas*, or double simultaneous vote (DSV), which was in place between 1990 and 2004.[4] Through this system, each party could present as many lists (*sublemas*) within the party label (*lema*) as it wanted for each electoral position at stake (governor, legislators, mayors, etc.). The votes from each intraparty list would then count towards that party's total votes.

The Ley de Lemas increased intraparty fragmentation while ultimately reducing turnover, at least temporarily. Factions could compete in the general election while remaining in the party. This system distorted electoral results. While gubernatorial candidates from the Radical Civic Union (*Unión Cívica Radical*, UCR) or the Socialist party received more votes in three of the four elections under this system, the combination of votes of different *sublemas* enabled the Peronist party, which contained several factions of various ideological inclinations, to emerge victorious (see Table 4.2). Finally, in 2004, Peronist governor, Obeid, abolished the Ley de Lemas, a decision that would have major consequences for political competition in the province.[5]

In the legislative realm, although the electoral system exhibits clear majoritarian biases it has not impeded fragmentation due to factionalism. The province renews its two legislative chambers entirely every four years, in concurrence with gubernatorial elections. The lower chamber elects fifty deputies with the whole province as the electoral district and grants an automatic majority of twenty-eight to the list with the most votes. Nonetheless, many governments have struggled to maintain a legislative majority due to conflicts between coalitional parties or intraparty factions. Meanwhile, the provincial Senate is composed of nineteen senators, one for each electoral district, chosen by plurality vote, which has

[4] Law 10.524 (1990).
[5] "La legislatura de Santa Fe derogó la polémica Ley de Lemas," *La Nación*, December 1, 2004.

TABLE 4.2. *Governors of the Province of Santa Fe, 1983–2015*

Election year	Governor[a]	Party/ Coalition	Governors' vote share (margin of victory, percent)	Election under Ley de Lemas[b]
1983	José M. Vernet	PJ	41.4 (1.1)	No
1987	Víctor Reviglio	PJ	44.1 (16.1)	No
1991	Carlos Reutemann	PJ	46.8 (6.3)	Yes**
1995	Jorge Obeid	PJ	50.7 (3.4)	Yes**
1999	Carlos Reutemann*	PJ	57.6 (16.2)	Yes
2003	Jorge Obeid*	PJ	51 (5.8)	Yes**
2007	Hermes Binner*	PS-FPCS	52.7 (10.7)	No
2011	Antonio Bonfatti	PS-FPCS	39.7 (3.6)	No
2015	Miguel Lifschitz	PS-FPCS	31.7 (0.1)	No

[a] (*) Indicates that the new governor is from a different party or faction than predecessor, or, high turnover.
[b] (**)Indicates that the governor was not the most voted candidate but won due to the aggregation of votes of his party, because of the Ley de Lemas.
Source: Author's elaboration based on Andy Tow Electoral Blog

benefited conservative Peronist from over-represented districts in the interior and made them a powerful veto player in both Socialist and Peronist administrations. This high fragmentation would hamper reform attempts during the late 1990s and hinder police governance during the years of Socialist mandate.

PERONIST DOMINANCE AND POLICE POLITICIZATION, 1983–1996

Between 1983 and 2007, the Peronist party (PJ) governed the province uninterruptedly. During the first part of this period, low turnover and low fragmentation prevailed in the province, as there was one dominant faction in power. This combination allowed Peronist administrations to sideline police reform and appropriate rents from police corruption.

The low political fragmentation is evident in the Peronists' control over both legislative chambers during this period. The party obtained a majority in the chamber of deputies in all but one election between 1983 and 2007 and often controlled over 70 percent of the senate. Nonetheless, this dominance eclipses differences between rivaling Peronist factions, especially since the mid-1990s (see Figure 4.1).

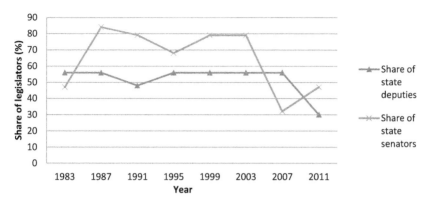

FIGURE 4.1. Share of provincial deputies and senators belonging to governor's party, Santa Fe (1983–2011)
Source: Author's elaboration from Andy Tow's Electoral Blog and Santa Fe Electoral Court.

During the 1980s, the Peronists won two consecutive elections, maintained their cohesion and faced little external opposition. In the 1983 elections, Jose María Vernet, the candidate of the orthodox faction, won the governorship, making Santa Fe the largest territory controlled by Peronism at the time.[6] After his arrival in office, Vernet set up the "Peronist Cooperative," an informal alliance between different party leaders to distribute cabinet positions and patronage jobs and preserve party unity. From this group Víctor Reviglio, who had initially served in the administration as minister of health, emerged as the chosen successor for the 1987 election, which he won by a 16 percent margin over the UCR candidate. Political corruption scandals involving Reviglio's vice-governor and the Peronist mayor of Santa Fe clouded this administration and jeopardized the PJ's chances in the 1991 election.[7] Two game-changing decisions resulted. One was Peronist President Carlos Menem's promotion of a political outsider, Carlos Reutemann – a former high-speed racing driver – as the next candidate for governor.[8] The other was the enactment of the Ley de Lemas to preserve party unity. This combination ensured Reutemann's electoral victory in 1991: Although he

---

[6] The UCR had won the presidency as well as the provinces of Buenos Aires and Córdoba.
[7] See "Vernet and Reviglio, con pasados polémicos," *La Nación*, December 30, 2001, and "El regreso del Trucha," *Pagina12*, January 10, 2005.
[8] Menem brought several famous political outsiders as candidates for top position in the party, including Reutemann, popular singer Ramón "Palito" Ortega and boat-racing champion Daniel Scioli, who would then become governor of Buenos Aires (see Chapter 6).

received fewer individual votes than the UCR candidate, he won by pooling the votes of all the other *sublemas* within the PJ.

The PJ remained unified and in power in 1995 as Reutemann designated Jorge Obeid, then mayor of the Capital, as his successor (Damianovich 2001, 33–42). However, this election would be the last moment of party unity. The two leaders parted paths and alternated in office. Reutemann returned to the governorship in 1999, while Obeid, running against Reutemann's handpicked successor, won again in 2003.

The two governors embodied the often-contradictory tendencies that characterize Peronism. Reutemann, a political outsider, represented the center-right fraction of the party, was aligned with the national governments of Menem (1989–1999) and Duhalde (2002–2003), and even had various individuals who had participated in the dictatorship in his cabinet. Obeid, by contrast, had participated in the Peronist youth movement during the 1970s, and been detained during the dictatorship. He became one of the main representatives of the center-left Peronist faction, closely aligned with the governments of Néstor and Cristina Kirchner (2003–2015). The increasing competition between Reutemann and Obeid hindered the latter's attempts to reform the police during his two terms.

The Double Pact with The Police: Absence of Reform and Collection of Illicit Rents

Until 1997, Peronist governments did not attempt to reform the police or otherwise professionalize it. At the same time, the party's entrenchment and low fragmentation for most of this period enabled it to capture rents from police corruption, thus reducing police autonomy through politicization. As the secretary of public security of the Socialist administration told me, "In Santa Fe, the political decision [in the 1990s] to control the police was to tax it. In other words, the police had to give the political authority a certain amount of money each month. *That is strategically a way of controlling the police – illegally, but a way of control.*"[9] While this view can be biased by partisanship, a federal prosecutor of left-leaning Peronist sympathies similarly suggested that Peronist governments allowed police corruption but also limited it:

---

[9] Interview by author with Security Secretary Matías Drivet (emphasis added), Santa Fe City, November 15, 2013.

[The police structure] did not change during the administrations of governors Vernet, Reviglio, Reutemann, Obeid, etc., but the PJ always had a very particular relationship with the police. I think they were always conscious about placing strict limits, establishing very concretely what could and could not be done.[10]

As this prosecutor stated, Peronist governments since the 1980s refrained from democratizing the police. Governor Vernet maintained the police structure inherited from the dictatorship, along with several officers who participated in human rights abuses.[11] He also enacted a new Provincial Personnel law, which made it harder to dismiss state officials under investigation, including police officers suspected of corruption or other misconduct.[12] Reviglio's government (1987–1991) did not introduce legal changes to the police's internal governance and external operations either.

Reutemann maintained this accommodation with the police. During his two administrations, he bestowed the police with material and institutional resources, proclaimed iron fist policies and even encouraged human rights abuses (González 2007, 157). His policies elicited support from the police leadership. When I asked the provincial police chief during his first term to evaluate Reutemann's security policy, he said, "[It was] perfect, because he trusted us, and he gave us the resources we needed. For instance, one day I went to tell the governor I needed a helicopter and he told me the only one he had was his own, but that I could take it …. When a governor suspects you, you can't work in the same way."[13]

This informal accommodation with, and control of, the police by Peronist governments enabled police to run various protection rackets while simultaneously containing criminal violence.

Coordinated Protection Rackets

During the first two decades after the return of democracy, protection rackets were the main informal regime by which the police regulated illicit

---

[10] Interview by author with federal prosecutor of Santa Fe, Juan Murray, Rosario, November 12, 2013.

[11] The most recent police organization law dated from 1975, one year before the military regime took power.

[12] "Santa Fe tiene 400 policías que están procesados y siguen en actividad," *Clarín*, May 11, 2001.

[13] Interview by author with former provincial chief of police, Mariano Savia, Rosario, November 11, 2013.

markets in Santa Fe. Police collected rents from various organized criminal activities, including the incipient drug market, with political acquiescence and even involvement. These rent extraction activities persisted
without substantial increases in criminal violence.

"How Many Campaigns Have the Police Funded?" Police and Political Corruption

Before the 2000s, drug trafficking in Santa Fe was not yet the primary
source of police rents or the security concern of later years. Nonetheless,
several interviewees confirmed that the police managed other rackets,
primarily clandestine gambling and prostitution. The secretary of complex crimes for the Socialist government, a former officer herself, commented on the force's association with these illicit markets:

I entered the police in 1987. [Drug trafficking] then was not a problem. The issues
of police connivance in that period were clandestine gambling, prostitution: the
classic stuff. Drug trafficking did not exist, it was not even perceived as a business.
Obviously, that has changed. I wish we could return to clandestine gambling.[14]

Another former police officer and current union delegate went further,
asserting that politicians benefited from police rent extraction:

A: There was corruption, but it was focused on the command, mostly.
Q: The regional command?
A: Yes, from there on up. But there was always a direct connivance
   with politicians in power. That's clear. There was a chief of police
   that in 1986 – I think – said in the main newspaper, "How many
   campaigns have been paid with money from clandestine gambling."
   Check out how things have changed now.[15]

Secondary sources confirm these allegations of police association with
illicit markets, with active participation by politicians. Toward the end of
Reutemann's first administration in April 1995, a group of officers released
a communiqué stating that the incumbent undersecretary of public security
implemented a collection scheme that auctioned police precincts to the
highest bidders. Similarly, a former precinct boss publicly stated in 1998
that, "The Provincial Chief of Police, the Police chief in the City of Santa
Fe, and the Minister of Government collected the money from illegal

[14] Interview by author with former Secretary of Complex Crimes Ana Viglione, Santa Fe,
November 15, 2013.
[15] Interview by author with the former police officer and current union delegate, Rosario,
November 7, 2013.

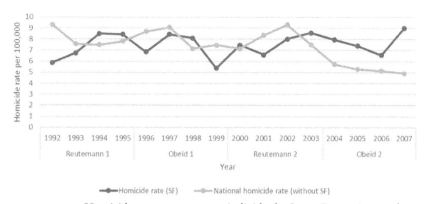

FIGURE 4.2. Homicide rates per 100,000 individuals, Santa Fe province and national average (without Santa Fe), 1991–2007
Source: Sistema Nacional de Información Criminal (SNIC, National Crime Information System), National Justice Ministry.

gambling" (Del Frade 2000, 128). While there were no direct accusations of governors themselves, it seems unlikely that they ignored these rackets.

Police and politicians were also involved in the protection of the incipient drug market. One of the most resounding cases occurred in 1993. A lower court judge was investigating six police officers and other civilians involved in a drug ring. Suddenly, she was promoted to the Higher Court of Appeals, most likely to take her off the investigation. Unsurprisingly, the officers were acquitted (Del Frade 2000, 156–61). The same judge would go on to denounce an entire regional police unit in 2007 for its presumed involvement in drug trafficking. Once again, her investigation did not get far.

"Police Controlled the Street": Containment of Criminal Violence
Police retributed politicians' tolerance of their illicit rent extraction not only with a share of the funds but also with an effective control of criminal violence. In the words of a former police captain and current union delegate, "Police controlled the street. If something happened, it was minimal, *or it had a license to happen*."[16]

The evolution of homicides in the province during this period lends some credit to his affirmation. Between 1983 and 2007, provincial homicide rates (darker line in Figure 4.2) mostly remained below the national

---

[16] Interview by author with police union delegate, Rosario, November 7, 2013, emphasis added.

average (lighter line), especially until 2000. This tendency shifted during the second half of this period. The last year of Obeid's second term in office (2007) marked the end of a three-year decrease in homicide rates that had begun in 2003, coinciding with Argentina's economic recovery due to the commodity boom of which the province of Santa Fe was a primary driver. While homicides rates decreased more slowly in Santa Fe than in the rest of the country, in 2007, the gulf between the state and the country quickly widened. The provincial homicide rate was almost twice the national average and nearly double Santa Fe's rate in 1991: It had increased from five to nine homicides per hundred thousand individuals. Over the following years, the increase would be even larger.

PERONIST FACTIONALISM AND POLICE REFORM CYCLES, 1997–2007

In contrast with his predecessors, who had sidelined police reform and harnessed police rent extraction, Governor Obeid (1995–1999; 2003–2007) proposed a major reform to reduce police autonomy.[17] Although Obeid initially rose to power with Reutemann's blessing, this reform pitted the two leaders and their factions against each other, igniting fragmentation within the party.

Obeid's administration passed a law that dismissed police involved in the dictatorship,[18] modified the force's recruitment and training procedures, dissolved the Robberies and Burglaries division – whose torture and murder of a young detainee had accelerated the reform[19] – and created the first Internal Affairs Office to monitor the force (Palmieri et al. 2001; Sozzo 2005).[20] However, growing fragmentation within the PJ impeded the full enforcement of these initiatives. Although the Peronists had a nominal majority in the legislature, they were split between pro-Obeid and pro-Reutemann blocs, which obstructed the reform (González 2007, 159; Damianovich 2001). As a former high-ranking member of Obeid's two administrations, told me, "We sent a reform project to the legislature in 1997–1998, but it got stuck in the chamber; neither the pro-government

---

[17] See also Rosúa (1998) and González (2007).   [18] Law 11.511 (November 6, 1997).
[19] "Los policías que no tienen destino," *Pagina12*, July 5, 1998.
[20] Decree 1359 (August 22, 1997). Later, the government introduced a new decree (626/98) placing the external affairs division directly under the political office of security.

nor opposition legislators promoted it because it directly eliminated the provincial police chief and centralized control in political hands."[21]

Police commanders benefited from this fragmentation, operating with opposing Peronist factions to resist the reform. This same official told me that the police chief, whom they had inherited from Reutemann's administration, challenged the government's policies in the provincial Senate, controlled by the rival Peronist faction.[22] This police chief, who had praised Reutemann effusively, expressed a symmetrical disgust for Obeid, "The other [governors] understood us perfectly well and trusted what we said. That's why we had a good police force. But Obeid was really a person who was on a different path. [He] was terrible."[23]

This fragmented political scenario allowed the police to drag their feet, weakening an unfriendly government and counting on its replacement by a more favorable administration. Reutemann granted their wishes as he took office for a second time in December 1999. A few days after his inauguration, the new government and justice minister announced, "The previous reform project is buried."[24] Reutemann made other significant changes in security staff, for example, appointing a former National Intelligence Agency officer, notorious for his role in the dictatorship, as secretary of public security, in other words, the person directly in charge of the police. Rosúa provided another example of the impact of this instance of turnover:

During Obeid's first government, we made an agreement with the European Union in which they would contribute to the police's technical training. We signed the deal, which took a lot of work, but at the time of implementing it, Obeid was no longer in government and Reutemann was in office. A French consulting firm had won the bid; the French were already here; all that was needed was a law to approve this agreement. Reutemann sent it to the legislature, the legislature voted for it, but Reutemann vetoed it, and it was a major blow to the process of police reform.[25]

[21] Interview by author with Fernando Rosúa, Rosario, November 7, 2013. This reform intended to establish a new law regulating the police organization – the existing one dated from the 1970s – and condense the three laws that regulated the provincial police at that point into one.

[22] Interview by author with Fernando Rosúa, Rosario, November 7, 2013. The police chief, Mariano Savia, corroborated this account in our interview.

[23] Interview by author with Mariano Savia, Rosario, November 11, 2013.

[24] Cited in Sozzo (2005, 51).

[25] Interview by author with Fernando Rosúa, Rosario, November 7, 2013.

In contrast with Obeid's attempt to promote the respect of human rights in the police, Reutemann and his top security officials stimulated police violence through their discourse and actions. In 2000, the secretary of public security declared, "We are not here to protect the rights of criminals"[26] and then rewarded an officer involved in two controversial fatal shootings. The number of casualties from police intervention nearly doubled between 1999 and 2000, jumping from 26 to 48 dead, and from 116 to 233 wounded (Sozzo 2005, 29).[27] The epitome of police violence occurred in response to the social protests which took place during the December 2001 crisis. Reutemann fueled the repression by refusing to negotiate with social protestors and ordering police to use live ammunition instead of rubber bullets to repress the protests (Pandolfo 2010, 203). Santa Fe police killed seven social activists in two days, the most casualties in all of Argentina's provinces. While there were hardly any attempts to professionalize the police, for most of this period, they were responsive to the government; in other words, politicization prevailed as the main form of governmental control of the force.

Obeid replaced Reutemann as governor again in 2003 and began another reform to reduce police autonomy. He placed the former head of Internal Affairs as the force's first female chief, created the Institute of Public Security (ISEP), in which civilians would jointly supervise police training,[28] and, having become the dominant faction, managed to get the legislature to approve a new Police Personnel law in 2006.[29] Among other changes, it established boards with political and civil society representatives to decide police promotions, depriving police commanders of their prerogative in this matter.[30] A member of the Socialist administration explained how this system worked in the past:

Before, selection committees were like this: you were an under-officer that wanted to become an officer; ok, aha, well, this will be $10 thousand pesos, you can pay it in two, three months. If you can't pay it now, when you get promoted and have a new division, it gets deducted. I participated in one of these boards with Tognoli,

---

[26] Sozzo (2005, 51).
[27] Máximo Sozzo, a local security expert, compared this transition with that between Duhalde and Ruckauf in Buenos Aires in 1999 (see Chapter 5). Interview by author with Máximo Sozzo, Santa Fe, November 18, 2013. See also "Arturo Cruz será el nuevo jefe de la Policía," *El Litoral*, December 15, 1999.
[28] Law 12.333 (approved on September 2, 2004).
[29] Law 12.521 (approved on April 6, 2006).
[30] Several government officials in the subsequent Socialist administrations recognized the importance of this feature, as well as the resistance it generated from the force.

Sola [the provincial chief and vice-chief until October 2012], another politician and three former bosses. The guys came and crossed out names, without any selection criteria other than what we already knew. You didn't see it directly, but you knew how it happened.[31]

However, Obeid's administration was again unable to enforce these changes. The ISEP ended up combining civilian and police training staff and loosening educational requirements to recruit more personnel. Furthermore, neither him nor the succeeding Socialist administrations implemented the civilian boards regulating police promotions.[32] While Obeid might have had the numbers to promote his reforms in the legislature, the deterioration of these policies in the upcoming Socialist administration shows that legislative majorities are insufficient to professionalize the police in a context of high turnover marked by policy instability and high transition costs.

Despite the absence of sustained police reforms, former police interviewees concurred that Peronists exercised greater control of police corruption than the Socialist governments in power since 2007. A high-ranking official described Obeid's personal control of police corruption:

I think Obeid was very tough and very positive in controlling the force, because anyone who wanted to get involved in a corrupt deed knew that if he were caught, he would immediately lose his job and his career. He was very tough, very rigid, even pressuring the people in Internal Affairs so that they did their job correctly and punished those who did not adjust to the government's directives.[33]

In short, most Peronist administrations managed to control police rent extraction, either restricting or appropriating it. This situation would shift in 2007. With a new party in government and greater dispersal of political power both within and between the parties, police corruption became rampant and more damaging to the government and the province.

SOCIALIST ADMINISTRATIONS: POLICE ANARCHY AND PARTICULARISTIC NEGOTIATIONS, 2007–2015

On December 10, 2007, for the first time since the return of democracy in 1983, a non-Peronist government took power in the province of Santa Fe.

---

[31] Interview by author with Undersecretary of Provincial Security Ministry Diego Poretti, Santa Fe, November 14, 2013.
[32] During this interval, the Socialist government suspended this provision by decree and only implemented it in 2014.
[33] Interview by author with former high-ranking police officer from the Rosario department, Rosario, November 12, 2013.

Hermes Binner, the former mayor of Rosario and one of the founders of the provincial Socialist party, was sworn in as the head of a coalition – the Progressive, Civic and Social Front (FPCS) – that included the Radical Civic Union (UCR) and other non-Peronist parties. Of these, the Socialists were the most important party, having governed the province's largest city (Rosario) continuously since 1989.[34] The election of 2007 was the first conducted without the Ley de Lemas (DSV) since 1987, which undoubtedly facilitated Binner's victory given the fragmentation in the Peronist field. During the Socialist administrations, police exploited both the instance of partisan turnover in 2007 and the subsequent fragmentation in the cabinet and the legislature to resist the government's timid encroachments on their autonomy.

"There Are No Precise Orders": Increased Police Autonomy

While they inherited a police force that remained unreformed after twenty-four years, the Progressive Front administrations did not manage to reduce police autonomy either. Socialist governors proclaimed that they would build a different relationship with the force than the Peronists, whom they accused of benefiting from police corruption. However, the Socialists did not attempt to strengthen the political control over the police or subordinate it to the rule of law through encompassing reforms. Although they did not pocket police rents from crime, they did not restrict police corruption either.

Part of the Socialists' inability to transform the police derived from high transition costs and problems inherited from the preceding administration. During the first Socialist administration, Binner implemented certain changes to reduce police autonomy, such as the creation of the ministry of security. Binner's first security minister, Daniel Cuenca, a criminal law jurist and university professor, also created a secretariat of control of the police to monitor the force. However, this would not be enough, as Cuenca himself related, "In setting up a ministry from scratch, I wasted a lot of time on administrative issues such as [approving] promotions, locations, prisoner custody, etc., and had less time for daily

---

[34] The Radicals had been the second largest party since 1983 – having gained more votes than Peronist individual candidates in 1991 and 1999 – but lost their prominence after the failure of De la Rúa's presidency (1999–2001).

operations" or broader reformist initiatives.[35] Moreover, he inherited a chaotic administrative situation from the previous government, "Debts, lack of [signed] promotions, no staff, not even a desk."[36] Cuenca rapidly encountered police resistance to his command, which fluctuated from passive disobedience, "Some get in line, others pretend to," he said, to active intimidation. For example, he found notes in his office that read: "Get out, usurper," and eventually decided to bring in his own meals to the ministry for fear that the officers who worked there might taint the cafeteria food. The stress eventually took its toll. He suffered a near heart attack while in office and resigned in December 2009.

The tenure of Cuenca's replacement, Álvaro Gaviola – the former director of the Civil Registry, with no prior experience in security – illustrated how high fragmentation within the cabinet can increase police autonomy. Gaviola's appointment stirred conflict with the Socialists' coalition partners, who wanted a different candidate and complained of Binner's unilateral decision.[37] Furthermore, as soon as Gaviola took office, he appointed a former police commander as secretary of security – the second most important position in the ministry – but had to reverse his decision immediately after several reformist cabinet members, appointed by Cuenca, threatened to resign.[38] As these officials, who had participated in the initial reformist attempts, gradually left the cabinet, the administration relinquished control over the police.[39] As a legislator from the opposition told me, "Instead of politicians driving things, they were allowing police sectors to come into the government to run the force."[40]

Although the Socialist retained the governorship in 2011, their political capital decreased substantially. Binner's successor, Socialist leader Antonio Bonfatti, benefited from Peronism's split between the center-left Front for Victory (FPV) and the right-leaning Unión PRO, yet the Progressive Front's vote share fell from 52.7 percent in 2007 to 40 percent

[35] Interview by author with former Security Minister Daniel Cuenca, Rosario, November 20, 2013.
[36] Interview by author with former Security Minister Daniel Cuenca, Rosario, November 20, 2013.
[37] "El mal humor de los radicales," *Pagina12*, December 4, 2009.
[38] "Superti subió a Giacometti y lo debió bajar por la rebelión de los secretarios," *La Capital*, December 4, 2009.
[39] Interview by author with a former mid-level political official in the first Socialist Administration, Rosario, November 20, 2013.
[40] Interview by author with FPV state deputy, Eduardo Toniolli, Rosario, November 12, 2013. Also mentioned in interview with Fernando Rosúa.

in 2011. Furthermore, the Progressives lost their majority in the lower chamber, and remained a minority in the Provincial senate, controlled by the Peronists.

Bonfatti appointed the former secretary of penitentiary affairs, Leandro Corti, as his first security minister in December 2011. Like Cuenca, Corti was a lawyer and academic with no partisan affiliation with the government. He intended to assert greater control of the police, particularly in his informal interactions with the force's commanders, but did not receive enough political support. He crudely recounted that to control the police, "First you need not to take money from the police, even if it sounds elementary. Second, you need to have a lot of political support, because you will not be making too many friends. Hitting these guys on the head implies having a pretty big dick, so to speak."[41] He also commented on the difficulties of being security minister, beyond the usual bureaucratic and administrative problems, "You have no personal life, and the cops know everything: if you take drugs, if you're gay, if you are a womanizer, if you have kids, if you are separated, everything."

Corti resigned in June 2012, after Governor Bonfatti undercut his decision not to hold a football match in Santa Fe for security reasons.[42] Subsequently, Bonfatti appointed long-time Socialist state deputy, Raúl Lamberto, as security minister. It was the first appointment of a security minister from the party ranks and proved to be the most stable as Lamberto remained in place until the end of Bonfatti's administration in December 2015. Lamberto aimed to reach a consensus with the commanders, while at the same time gradually increasing the government's control of the police. As he told me:

You define political power with political decisions. The decision to educate, to train [the police] is very important. The decision to establish administrative control is very important. Now, it must be done in a framework: it's a boat that you have to fix as it sails along, because this is the police you have, and you don't have the chance to say, "OK, I'll stop, fix it and move on." For that, you need political decisions, a plan and consensus that you reach with dialogue, with comprehension, by delineating that the old structures did not work.[43]

[41] Interview by author with former Provincial Security Minister Leandro Corti, Santa Fe, November 14, 2013.
[42] "Por el partido de Central renunció al Ministerio de Seguridad Leandro Corti," *La Capital*, June 6, 2012.
[43] Interview by author with current Security Minister Raúl Lamberto, Rosario, November 19, 2013.

However, this ministerial shift did not reduce the autonomy of the police. Many criticized Lamberto's approach, arguing that tough decisions rather than consensus were the way to deal with the police. For instance, former minister Corti stated, "The [Socialists] have an absolutely naïve, comfortable and even irresponsible position. I know that Lamberto is not corrupt, but he has this political thing of winging it, surfing [muddling] through, and here you need someone to make determinations and political decisions with support."[44]

In October 2012, four months into his tenure, Lamberto faced a major crisis that illustrated how autonomous police were from political control: the arrest of Police Chief Hugo Tognoli.[45] A federal investigation revealed that Tognoli protected at least two major local drug traffickers. After a few days on the run, the former chief turned himself in to the province's Elite Squad. Both Socialist administrations had promoted Tognoli because of his "impeccable record": Under Binner he had been made head of the Narcotics Division, and Bonfatti placed him in charge of the entire police force in December 2011. This case supported the opposition's claim that police commanders managed and filtered promotions for political authorities. Also revealing is that a federal agency, the Airport Security Police (*Policía de Seguridad Aeroportuaria*, PSA), conducted the surveillance that led to Tognoli's arrest. After this incident, the government could no longer ignore the need to clean up the force. As one high-ranking political official in the security ministry expressed, "This helped reflect that we needed a structural change and this idea became shared by most sectors within the police, who understood we needed strong transformations in training and in the force's operational capacity."[46] Although the government worked on a project to decentralize the police structure and reduce the power of the top commanders, even this limited reform was not fully implemented.[47] To some extent, it is

[44] Interview by author with former Provincial Security Minister Leandro Corti, Santa Fe, November 14, 2013.

[45] "Tognoli se entregó y quedó detenido en Santa Fe," *La Nación*, Oct. 23, 2012. See also "Ousting of police chief highlights Argentina's vulnerability to organized crime," *InsightCrime*, October 31, 2012.

[46] Interview by author with Security Minister Lamberto, Santa Fe, November 19, 2013. Also interview by author with Undersecretary of Public Security Diego Poretti, Santa Fe, November 14, 2013.

[47] Interview by author with member of the Center for Municipal and Provincial Studies (CEMUPRO) team in charge of developing a reform plan. See also "El gobierno inicia la reforma policial," *El Litoral*, February 9, 2013 and "Idas y vueltas de la reforma policial," *El Litoral*, August 31, 2014.

telling that former Peronist Governor Obeid had introduced the most important change the Socialists intended (but failed) to enforce – civilian boards to approve police promotions.[48]

The internal fragmentation and instability within the Socialist cabinet generated other policy implementation problems. Political rivals and police alike pointed to the administration's "lack of coherent messages" to the police – partly a consequence of the government's high internal fragmentation – as a root cause of its failure to control the institution. An example is the following dialogue I had with a police union delegate:

Q: What are the main problems or conflicts the police have with the political leadership?
A: First, that there are no precise orders. It's all improvised, day-by-day. According to where the conflict is, we see how we resolve it. Today there is [one secretary of security], but tomorrow you come along with other ideas and modify everything.[49]

The police exploited these internal divisions and the Socialists' loss of their majority in the lower chamber during Bonfatti's term (2011–2015) to increase their autonomy. A legislator from the Progressive Front claimed that police "operated with legislators, to change the course of policies, to obstruct the new selection and promotion mechanisms."[50] The provincial public defender, not aligned with the administration, confirmed that, "The police were much more active in operating politically than the government."[51] In other words, police took advantage of the province's political fragmentation to cooperate with the opposition to undermine the administrations' policies. Opposing politicians contributed to this resistance. The government complained that the legislative branch, in which they did not have a majority, repeatedly summoned members of its security cabinet to "ridiculous" proceedings to undermine the administration. As the secretary of complex crimes told me:

If you look at the entire history of this province, who has gone [to the legislature] as much as we have? [Security Minister] Lamberto went three times, I went once.

---

[48] Interview by author with Máximo Sozzo, Santa Fe, November 18, 2013.
[49] Interview by author with current police union delegate, Santa Fe, November 15, 2013.
[50] Interview by author with state deputy, Alicia Gutiérrez, Rosario, November 12, 2013.
[51] Interview by author with state public defender, Gabriel Ganon, Santa Fe, November 13, 2013.

They say a lot of things that muck up the playing field, and that take you out of the everyday management to respond to things that are stupid.[52]

As discussed earlier, there are contending perspectives as to whether Peronist governments limited police corruption or appropriated it. However, most interviewees agreed that Peronists were more effective in informally controlling police corruption, at least to prevent it from destabilizing the government. By contrast, the Socialists were less adamant in reducing police corruption through either formal or informal mechanisms. Former Minister Corti hinted at this difference between the two parties:

You have to be rational in the sense of having some criteria of justice, not cracking heads whenever you feel like it, but giving clear signals that this is the line and that if you step out of line, the political leadership will [use] the stick. This is the Socialist administration's main Achilles' heel [but] they don't see it that way. Whether it's because of fear, style, political culture, I think that, in this regard, Peronism has been much more realistic.[53]

The Socialist administration, nonetheless, encountered significant resistance from sectors in the police against its limited encroachment. Many security ministers and high-level staff received multiple threats. The government also endured a police rebellion in December 2013, when officers refused to patrol the streets, demanding higher salaries and better working conditions.[54] The Bonfatti administration requested the federal government to send in the national military police to prevent lootings and riots and,[55] finally, raised police wages by decree, ending the crisis. A similar rebellion in Buenos Aires (Chapter 5) was rapidly suppressed, because the rebellious troops lacked the support of the higher-ranking officers against the administration.

The Socialists' arrival in government after twenty-four years of Peronist rule changed the relationship between incumbent politicians and the police. According to politicians from both the administration and the opposition, the Socialists severed the corrupt linkages with the police that had characterized previous administrations. However, due to

---

[52] Interview by author with former Secretary of Complex Crimes Ana Viglione, Santa Fe, November 15, 2013.

[53] Interview by author with former Provincial Security Minister Leandro Corti, Santa Fe, November 14, 2013.

[54] "Santa Fe: Se sublevó un gremio de policías y Bonfatti los denunció penalmente," *La Política Online*, December 5, 2013.

[55] "El gobierno envía 1500 gendarmes a Santa Fe por pedido de Antonio Bonfatti," *La Nación*, December 7, 2013.

high transition costs and policy instability resulting from high turnover and policy incoherence due to fragmentation within the cabinet and the legislature, the Socialists failed to reduce police autonomy. This decline in political control over the police would shape the force's subsequent regulation of drug trafficking in the province.

Particularistic Negotiations: Decentralized Corruption and High Criminal Violence in Santa Fe

High police autonomy in Santa Fe resulted in particularistic negotiations as the main drug trafficking regulatory regime, especially after 2007. Police engaged in dispersed deals with multiple criminal actors, without the control or coordination of political superiors. Consequently, criminal violence increased dramatically between 2008 and 2014, particularly in the metropolitan area of Rosario.

To be clear, drug trafficking and its associated violence preceded the Socialist government. During the early 2000s, *barras bravas* – cliques of hooligans – from the city of Rosario's main soccer clubs, Rosario Central and Newell's Old Boys, already embedded in illicit businesses like reselling game tickets and "protecting" parked cars during matches, became increasingly involved in street-level drug dealing, and fought for control of this market. These struggles soon turned fatal. In 2005, assassins gunned down the leader of the Newell's faction, one the city's main drug traffickers, after his former police associates apparently set him up for the hit (Federico 2008, 176–77). The police's involvement with traffickers, as well as this execution style assassination in Downtown Rosario, foreshadowed what was to come.

Admittedly, the Socialists faced a different scale of drug trafficking, which increased significantly in Santa Fe over the last decade. The number of drug seizures grew tenfold, from 105 in 2001 to 1,234 in 2012, the first year of Bonfatti's administration (Figure 4.3). There is a marked jump between 2008 and 2009, two years into the first Socialist administration of Governor Binner. Around 75 percent of these procedures were street controls as opposed to raids, an indication that the police found most drugs by chance rather than through criminal investigations. However, while drug trafficking grew in most Argentine provinces, none exhibited an increase in criminal violence as rapid or large as Santa Fe.

The volume of cocaine seizures increased consistently over time as well (see Figure 4.4). While the provincial police seized only 14kg of cocaine in 2001, a decade later this amount had grown to 490kg.

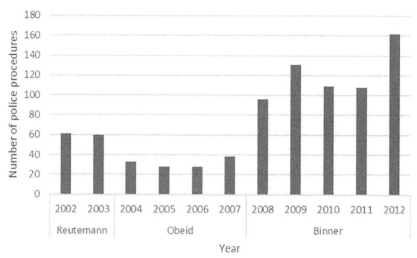

FIGURE 4.3. Number of drug seizures in Santa Fe (2001–2012)
Source: Author's elaboration from Santa Fe Ministry of Security.

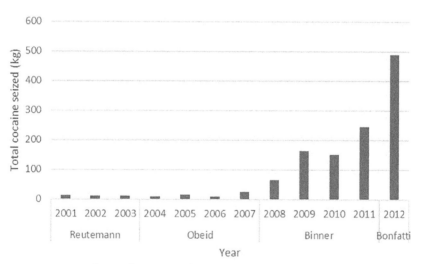

FIGURE 4.4. Volume of cocaine in kg seized in Santa Fe (2001–2012)
Source: Author's elaboration from Santa Fe Ministry of Security.

Finally, the number of individuals detained for drug-related offenses between 2009 and 2012 practically equaled the number of drug procedures. On most occasions, police arrested individuals for consumption or possession of drugs for retail distribution. Police in Santa Fe, as in most cities and countries, formally regulated drug trafficking by arresting the least powerful participants in the drug supply chain, while not disrupting this illegal business.

"Today, Even Corporal Cacho Asks You for Money": High and Decentralized Police Corruption

Although police connections with organized crime preceded the Socialist administrations, they expanded notoriously between 2007 and 2015. As we saw, the case epitomizing the entrenchment of corruption in the force was the arrest of provincial Police Chief Hugo Tognoli in October 2012.[56] Tognoli, along with subordinates from his tenure in the Narcotics division, had been involved in at least two cases of complicity with drug traffickers, including protecting a wholesale cocaine dealer in exchange for $30,000 pesos per month.[57]

The government's lack of coordination with the police in extracting rents from crime left these sectors without political protection, which facilitated their investigation and arrest by judicial authorities or federal forces. Tognoli was not the only high-ranking police officer arrested for protecting drug traffickers. The criminal investigation into one of the main drug gangs in Rosario – the Canteros, also known as "Los Monos" [The Monkeys] – convicted nine police officers for partnering with the gang (Santos and Lascano 2017). Multiple low-level police units engaged in dispersed protection deals with low-level traffickers. Many interviewees pointed out that, in Rosario, the main drug distribution mechanism was through "bunkers" – enclosed fortifications in marginalized neighborhoods – which operated in broad daylight, mostly with police authorization. The state judge who investigated the Canteros described the police's haphazard protection of drug trafficking, "[Police] sold immunity, protected the bunker, the transit and selling of the drugs . . .. We've even seen some regiments of police that robbed bunkers."[58] A federal judge conveyed the intensity of this regime, "The emblem of impunity is the way drugs were sold in Rosario, the bunker – a Rosarian invention – a fortress so that everybody knows. The only thing missing is a neon sign."[59]

While police corruption was certainly not a new phenomenon in Santa Fe, the Socialist administrations' lack of control over police rent extraction was. The sitting Socialist secretary of complex crimes admitted that,

[56] See "Renunció el jefe de la Policía de Santa Fe," *El Litoral*, October 19, 2012, and "Acusado de proteger al Narcotráfico renunció el jefe de policía de Santa Fe," *La Nación*, October 20, 2012.
[57] See "La larga saga de Hugo Tognoli," *Pagina12*, November 3, 2012.
[58] Interview by author with state judge, Juan Carlos Vienna, Rosario, June 25, 2014.
[59] Interview by author with federal judge, Héctor Vera Barros, Rosario, June 24, 2014.

while police corruption continued under their watch, it did not end up in governing politicians' pockets – hinting this was standard practice in previous administrations. She then explained how this change undermined police credibility to regulate illicit activities:

Some police officers are still collecting money, but they also know that it's not for any of us. That's a strong message because it says you [the police] can no longer guarantee impunity. You can charge but you can't guarantee protection [to criminals]. Because I don't warn you when I'm going to raid the place. Then you'll have to be accountable, but that's your problem.[60]

Police corruption lost its political protection but also became increasingly fragmented within the force itself, as everybody sought a piece of the action. A federal judge thoroughly described this transformation, "Drug trafficking in Rosario became scandalous because police protection, which always existed but was contained, became decentralized, so every police precinct ran three or four bunkers."[61] Former security minister Corti described the police force's decentralized corruption more graphically, "[Today] even corporal Cacho asks you for the money."[62]

Dispersed negotiations between police and drug dealers further decentralized the drug retail market, particularly in Rosario. According to one of the journalists most familiar with the local drug market, four gangs fought for control of the city's neighborhoods and distribution points.[63] The gangs then outsourced retail sales to individuals or families in poor neighborhoods.[64] A study by the National University of Rosario (UNR) found more than 400 retail points in the city, most of them peddling small quantities of drugs. Two decades earlier, the mayor at the time had asserted that there were only fifteen drug selling points in Rosario, another indicator of how much drug trafficking had grown in volume and number of sellers (Del Frade 2000, 107).

This market fragmentation further diminished the effective regulatory capacity of police, particularly in terms of containing criminal violence. A neighborhood social movement activist in Rosario poignantly explained the link between police autonomy, decentralized drug trafficking and criminal violence:

---

[60] Interview by author with former Secretary of Complex Crimes Ana Viglione, Santa Fe, November 15, 2013.

[61] Interview by author with federal judge, Vera Barros, Rosario, June 24, 2014.

[62] Interview by author with former Provincial Security Minister Leandro Corti, Santa Fe, November 14, 2013.

[63] Interview by author with journalist, Carlos del Frade, Buenos Aires, October 5, 2013.

[64] Interview by author with social movement activists, Rosario, November 7, 2013.

Today, what's happened with drug trafficking is a product of deregulation, of the de facto self-government of the police; the business has grown horizontally. Small and mid-size family companies have proliferated that devote themselves to drug trafficking without being heavyweight drug dealers. They are small families that mounted a kiosk [selling point] in a neighborhood and are in constant dispute with the police force. It is even becoming a problem for the police to regulate all this. There is a horizontal spread of violence. All kinds of conflicts, in most cases, are solved with guns. There is another point: another great corollary of police self-government is that the community has more access to firearms. In fact, it is illustrative that, if you run a statistical cross analysis, most homicides occur with guns that are police standard issue.[65]

This scale of police corruption was not unprecedented in Santa Fe. The previous regime of protection rackets, consisting of organized deals between politicians, police and criminals, featured as much (or even more) corruption but managed to contain criminal violence. However, this arrangement was no longer effective. The same former police officer who claimed that, in previous years, "the police controlled the streets," stated that:

Today, there are areas where the police cannot enter. The police are irrelevant. You put a vase and it's the same. Now, that's not to say, "Oh, poor us." There were people inside the force who worked for this to happen.[66]

In other words, the police's extensive and disorganized corruption, combined with an absence of political control, diminished its capacity to manage crime and violence.

Escalating Criminal Violence

Particularistic negotiations in Santa Fe generated a substantial increase in homicides, driven primarily by its two main metropolitan areas: Rosario and the Capital City of Santa Fe. In the Rosario department, between 2002 and 2010, the homicide rate rarely reached 10 homicides per 100,000 individuals. In 2013, it had ballooned to nearly 21 homicides per 100,000 individuals – the highest in the district's history.[67] While there were 127 homicides recorded in 2010, in 2013 this number had risen to 264. Four of every five homicides occurred in the City of Rosario. The homicide rate was even higher in the neighboring city of Villa

[65] Interview by author with social movement activists, Rosario, November 7, 2013.
[66] Interview by author with police union delegate, Rosario, November 7, 2013.
[67] "Rosario tendrá hacia finales de este año la mayor tasa de homicidios de su historia," *La Capital*, November 4, 2013.

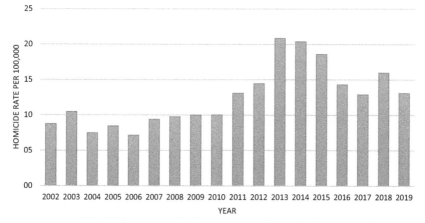

FIGURE 4.5. Homicide rates in the Department of Rosario (2002–2019)
Sources: La Capital (2002–2014) and Provincial Ministry of Security, Public Security
Observatory (2015–2019).[68]

Gobernador Gálvez – 32 per 100,000 – the highest in the entire country
that year (see Figure 4.5).

Meanwhile, in the second largest metropolitan area in the province –
the Capital City of Santa Fe and its surrounding municipalities – homicides reached record levels in 2014. While the previous highest point was
117 homicides in 2007, in 2014 there were 150 homicides in the metro
area.[69] The homicide rate for the Capital department that year was
26 homicides per 100,000 individuals, while for the city it neared 33.[70]
In contrast, between 2008 and 2011, homicide levels in the interior of the
province remained much lower – between 3 and 4 per 100,000 – and did
not increase, highlighting the fact that criminal violence in Santa Fe had
become a predominantly urban phenomenon: Rosario and the Capital,
which contain around 60 percent of the provincial population, concentrated nearly 80 percent of the province's homicides in 2011.

To put these numbers in perspective, homicide rates in Rosario and the
City of Santa Fe in 2013 were between three and four times higher,
respectively, than the national rate (7.2 per 100,000) and that of
Greater Buenos Aires (7.3). Of course, not all these homicides stem from

[68] "El primer semestre cerró con 115 homicidios, un 15 por ciento menos que 2014", *La
Capital*, Jul. 12, 2015.
[69] See "Triste récord en Santa Fe: 153 homicidios durante 2014," *La Nación*, December 31,
2014, and "Quién pone los cadáveres," *Periódico Pausa* blog, December 29, 2014.
[70] "La tasa de homicidio de la ciudad de Santa Fe fue de 32.8," *Agencia Fe*, September
9, 2015.

drug trafficking. Socialist administrations have argued that most of these crimes occurred due to "interpersonal conflicts," while only between 15 and 20 percent of homicides were drug-related.[71] Nonetheless, clearly the increase in violence in Santa Fe followed the provincial government's inability to control the police and its subsequent regulation of drug trafficking through particularistic negotiations, in which police neither confronted organized criminal actors nor reached a peacekeeping bargain with them.

Moreover, police even enticed criminals to occupy bunkers and expand their territory, regardless of the violence this generated in poor neighborhoods. Provincial prosecutor Guillermo Camporini told me of one such episode revealed by judicial wiretaps on one of the Canteros' bosses' conversations with one of his police accomplices:

El Monchi [Cantero] says: "Tell me, [street address] how is it? Talk with the guys from the police station." "Ok," says the police officer, "I'll find out and let you know." Ten minutes later, the officer calls back: "I spoke with the Number 2 and it's a go. Somebody is already paying for that bunker but if it's for you, there's no problem. Go on and we'll settle later."[72]

This episode ended with Cantero gang members raiding the bunker. They shot it up and killed a little girl who was accidentally in the crossfire. The exchange reveals how the police not only did not contain but rather stimulated competition between drug gangs, even at the expense of other units. It speaks to the rampant disorganization in the police, even for the purpose of collecting funds from crime.

Furthermore, from 2014 to 2019, between 65 and 75 percent of homicides were carried out with firearms, a typical marker of illicit markets.[73] Many of these weapons and their ammunition were stolen from police precincts and military facilities. In 2014, there were 560 reports of stolen firearms in Santa Fe, of which one in every five belonged to police officers, many of whom could not explain how the theft happened. Although there are no precise quantities, several weapons were, in fact, sold by police to criminals. Many drug traffickers then distributed these weapons to young boys recruited as "soldiers" to guard bunkers from which drugs are sold. Even when these

---

[71] The government used indicators like the perpetrator's criminal record, the prior relationship between the victims, their respective domiciles and so on.

[72] Interview by author with state prosecutor, Guillermo Camporini, Rosario, June 24, 2014. See also De los Santos and Lascano (2017) and Auyero and Sobering (2019).

[73] Public Security Observatory, Santa Fe state security ministry, 2019.

weapons showed up in homicides committed for other reasons (e.g., brawls between young men over money, women, or reputation), they can also be indirectly connected to the expansion of local drug dealing gangs.

The failure of this regulatory regime compelled the government to shift its approach. Following a spree of drug-related homicides in the first semester of 2013,[74] the governing coalition realized they needed to bring down at least one major drug gang or they risked losing the upcoming election.[75] The government subsequently backed a local judge's investigation into various homicides connected to the main drug gang in Rosario, the Canteros family, in the hopes of shutting down their operation. The prosecution of homicides by the state-level judiciary circumvented the lack of support by the federal government and prosecutor's office, who countered that the local court was infringing on federal judicial territory.[76]

As several gang leaders fell, so too did many of their police associates. This sparked a series of threats against the case judge and lead prosecutor, as well as the top political authorities in the security ministry and even the attempt against Governor Bonfatti narrated in this chapter's introduction. The ensuing judicial investigation determined that at least four police officers participated in the shooting, suggesting it was a retaliation against the provincial government's efforts to shut down their drug trafficking rings (Burzaco and Berensztein 2014, 159–62).[77] The government's investigation of the drug gangs also aimed at their police associates, further complicating the relationship between the administration and the already autonomous provincial police.

EPILOGUE: GOVERNMENTS CHANGE, THE CRISIS CONTINUES

In 2015, the Progressive Front won its third consecutive election by a tiny margin of less than 2,000 votes (0.09 percent). During the administration of Socialist Miguel Lipschitz, the state government did not implement a comprehensive police reform or make significant advances to reduce

[74] Among these, on New Year's Day 2013, a drug gang killed three social activists in Villa Moreno because they confused them for rival dealers. In late May, a succession of murders followed the assassination of the leader of the Canteros gang.

[75] Interview by author with local journalist, Hernán Lascano, Rosario, June 24, 2014.

[76] Interviews by author with state judge, Vienna and federal prosecutor, Murray.

[77] Interviewed representatives of an NGO that denounces organized criminal activities suggested an alternative version: that hitmen targeted Bonfatti in retaliation for breaking a previous compromise or pact with police and/or traffickers. Interviews by author with NGO representatives, Rosario, June 24, 2014.

police autonomy. Although scandals involving police complicity with drug traffickers were less frequent than in Binner or Bonfatti's administrations, the government hardly rooted out structural corruption within the police. Some politicians suggested that the government had reached a modus vivendi with the force, ignoring its illicit rent extraction schemes to ensure a certain peace. The reduced conflict with the police could explain the decrease in homicide rates between 2014 and 2017, although the increased presence of federal security forces in Rosario, as well as a successful violence prevention program in the provincial capital, also helped reduce violence. Nonetheless, this decrease was only temporary, as homicide rates bounced back the two following years (2018–2019). This new increase in violence surely contributed to the Socialists' loss of the 2019 election, which marked the return to power of the Peronist movement.

The situation further deteriorated as Peronist politician Omar Perotti took office as governor in December 2019. During the first few months of his administration, his security minister, Marcelo Sain, a renowned but controversial reformist politician and scholar from Buenos Aires, whom we will meet repeatedly in Chapter 5, tried to reduce police autonomy. Unsurprisingly, he encountered high police resistance. Criminal violence escalated again. The province registered more than forty homicides up to February 2020. A preliminary report counted 336 people injured due to gunshots between January and June in the city of Rosario alone.

This dynamic resembles what we saw in the first Socialist administrations. Political turnover increases policy instability and forces relationships between the government and the police to start anew. Mixed cohorts within the force drag their feet and undermine support for reform. Both external opposition and internal incoherence within the government hamper policy implementation. The police preserve their autonomy and continue to regulate illicit markets through particularistic negotiations. Criminal violence persists as gangs battle in a fractured and deregulated market. Both Socialist and Peronist administrations have fallen into this trap.

As this chapter has illustrated, informal regulatory arrangements can deteriorate over time from coordinated to uncoordinated regimes. Protection rackets are stable when the players and rules of the agreement persist but can rapidly collapse with a change in cast. The end of the Peronist unified dominance and the arrival of the Socialists resulted in unfettered, decentralized deals between police and traffickers, with alarming increases in criminal violence in the province's main cities.

The cases here and in Chapter 3 exhibited uncoordinated regulatory regimes, one that persisted for three decades (particularistic confrontation in Rio de Janeiro in Chapter 3), and one that emerged following more recent changes in political competition (particularistic negotiation in Rosario, this chapter). The following two chapters display how decreasing turnover over time allowed subnational incumbents to reduce police levels of autonomy and produce more coordinated regulatory regimes to manage the drug trafficking market. They also illustrate how fragmentation affects whether politicians reduce police autonomy through politicization or professionalization, which results in protection rackets or coordinated coexistence, respectively.

5

Coordinated Protection

The Consolidation of Centralized Corruption in Buenos Aires

OVERVIEW

On the eve of the 2015 primaries, the most popular Argentine TV show broadcast a story that the Peronist candidate for governor of the province of Buenos Aires, Aníbal Fernández, headed a drug trafficking organization responsible for the murder of three men involved in exporting ephedrine – a chemical precursor commonly used for making synthetic drugs – to México. Fernández denied the charge and accused his opponent in the Peronist primaries of feeding this slander to the TV show, a fervent critic of the national administration. Fernández eventually won the primary but lost the general election, marking the first time the Peronists relinquished control of the province since 1987. While the ensuing criminal investigation did not produce new evidence supporting these allegations, this episode exposes the brutal competition between Peronist factions in Buenos Aires, which often revolves around the issue of illegal markets.

Fernández was not the first Peronist politician in Greater Buenos Aires (GBA) accused of drug trafficking. Others, in fact, had stronger alleged – and sometimes real – connections to this illicit activity. For over twenty years, many state and local politicians and brokers had used the police to run protection rackets in the province. Protection rackets are state-sponsored exchanges with criminal actors, in which state actors demand material benefits for not enforcing the law (or enforcing it against criminals' opponents) and usually implies criminals refraining from violent behavior. This chapter illustrates this coordinated regulatory regime focusing on the often shady and sometimes tumultuous relationship between Peronist politicians and the notorious Buenos Aires police, the Bonaerense.

The Peronist party governed Buenos Aires for twenty-eight consecutive years, between 1987 and 2015. It held an ample majority in both chambers of the provincial legislature for most of this period. It controlled over 60 percent of the province's municipalities and over 70 percent in the Greater Buenos Aires region, where over 35 percent of the country resides. This partisan entrenchment and lack of opposition allowed successive Peronist administrations to politicize the police and employ it to channel proceeds from illicit activities, often using such funds to finance political machines. The subordination of police by governors did not, however, democratize or professionalize the force, which still remains plagued by inefficiency, corruption and human rights abuses. Police brokered informal agreements with criminal actors to protect their operations in return for rents and containment of violence in their turf. Thus, police regulated drug trafficking primarily through coordinated protection rackets, a regime characterized by centralized corruption and low violence.

The fact that homicide rates remained low in Buenos Aires, especially when compared to its Argentine neighbor, the province of Santa Fe (Chapter 4), is puzzling. Unlike in São Paulo (Chapter 6), there are no powerful drug gangs with whom to broker centralized pacts nor has the police become more professionalized or efficient at solving crimes. By contrast, the drug market is highly fragmented, and the police still exhibit multiple deficiencies. In this chapter I will show how the arrangement scholars and policymakers usually refer to as a "double pact" between politicians, police and criminals works in practice to capture rents and contain violence (Binder 2004; Sain 2004, 2008, 2019; Auyero and Sobering 2019).

However, the double pact was not constantly in place. When, in the late 1990s and early 2000s, political fragmentation and turnover in the province increased due to greater competition between Peronist factions, police autonomy grew as well. Not only did the police successfully resist two reform attempts, but they also started to regulate organized criminal activities via *particularistic negotiations*, or dispersed and unstable deals with criminal actors, like the ones described in Rosario in the previous chapter (Chapter 4). These changes contributed to the increase in state and criminal violence in the province during this period (see Table 5.1). This chapter shows how, despite never implementing a real reform, the Buenos Aires police became a reliable partner for governing politicians to control criminal violence and capture rents from crime.

Several scholars have focused on protection rackets as a means to regulate illicit markets and organized crime. The conventional wisdom,

TABLE 5.1. *Political turnover, fragmentation, police autonomy and drug trafficking regulatory arrangements in Buenos Aires, 1983–2015*

Period	Turnover	Fragmentation	Police autonomy	Drug trafficking regulatory arrangement
1983–1996, 2004–2015	*Low* Peronist continuity in power (PJ/FPV)	*Low* Unified cabinet and majority in legislature	*Low* No reform, Centralized capture of police illicit rents Politicization of police	*Protection rackets* High and centralized corruption Low violence by police and criminals
1997–2003	*High* Turnover between different factions	*High* Factionalized party: divided legislature and competition between leaders	*High* Reform cycles No political control of police rent extraction	*Particularistic negotiation* Inchoate police corruption Higher violence by police and criminals

Source: Author's elaboration

as Snyder and Durán-Martínez (2009) argue, associates protection rackets with centralized state *and* criminal actors, for example, hegemonic drug cartels. In this chapter, I will show how, despite the high fragmentation of the drug market in Buenos Aires, the government's centralized control of the police and police's coordinated protection scheme precluded market destabilization and deterioration into violence.

Alternative Explanations

The Buenos Aires police is one of the most notorious departments in the region. Its penchant for corruption and for contesting reformist initiatives has been extensively documented in various academic and journalistic works. Some local policymakers and specialists on the police would argue that no administration has been able to govern it successfully, much less in a democratic form (Binder 2004; Sain 2019), while others are perhaps more optimistic about the potential for reforming it (Arslanian 2008). I certainly concur that the Bonaerense's main vices, such as systemic corruption and human rights abuses, have persisted throughout different administrations. Nevertheless, as I will show, some governments have been better equipped to control this force, even if to exploit it politically. In this chapter I will show how, during the periods when protection rackets were the dominant regulatory regime, police not only had immunity to extract illicit rents from criminal activities, but they also contributed to the prevalence of relative order in the province, whereas when the ruling party faced greater turnover and fragmentation, this arrangement faltered, and police undermined the administration.

Other analyses agree with my emphasis on political competition but disagree on the locus of that competition. Studies of prominent scholars of police reform in Buenos Aires, such as Mercedes Hinton (2006) and Kent Eaton (2008), have centered on this factor. Given the province's importance in national politics – it constitutes 40 percent of the national electorate – and the fact that for most of this period, both the country and the province have been governed by Peronist politicians, the main dispute is between the governor and the president. In this intrapartisan conflict, presidents have often undermined governors' control of the police in their home state, as the rift between Duhalde and Menem in the late 1990s attests. By contrast, when governors and presidents are aligned, the former have greater political support to implement their policy agenda in the province, including police reform, as the example of Solá and Kirchner (2004–2007) shows. On the other hand, as Eaton also points out, conflict over police governance also involved mayors from Greater Buenos Aires, most of whom were also from the Peronist party, and directly enabled or even benefited from police illicit rent extraction.

These alternative explanations are not contrary but complementary to my argument. Political fragmentation, as discussed in the theory chapter (Chapter 2), refers to the challenges incumbents face when governing. Those challenges can originate from opposition parties in the state legislature but also from national or local governments. In some cases, when a party is dominant, the main conflicts will be along party factions rather than with different parties. Buenos Aires combines these two scenarios. In other words, Buenos Aires' trajectory conveys the importance of intergovernmental relations as a possible expression of political fragmentation or even turnover, as these different factions have succeeded each other in power. Moreover, these arenas are intertwined because of their occupants' respective political ambitions and the distribution of resources across government tiers. However, political pressures from other levels notwithstanding, governors and security ministers are still the main actors in charge of making security decisions and dealing with the police. This chapter revolves around this typically accommodative and sometimes fraught relationship.

POLITICIANS AND THE BONAERENSE, 1983 THROUGH THE MID-1990S

Peronist Hegemony and Factionalism

The most powerful political movement in Argentina, Peronism, governed Buenos Aires uninterruptedly between 1987 and 2015. Furthermore, the strongest contenders for the provincial executive have come from factions that split from the ruling party. Peronist governors from aligned factions (Antonio Cafiero and then Eduardo Duhalde) succeeded each other between 1987 and 1995. Duhalde reformed the state Constitution in 1994 to allow for his reelection and won in 1995. Between 1996 and 2003, however, fragmentation increased, first due to infighting between the two main leaders of the party, Duhalde and President Carlos Menem, over Duhalde's intention to succeed Menem as president; second, due to the legislative victory of an alliance that featured a former center-left faction of the Peronist party. During this interval, turnover occurred as both Carlos Ruckauf and Felipe Solá – the vice-governor who finished Ruckauf's term – hailed from different factions than their respective predecessors. However, fragmentation and turnover would decrease in subsequent years as Solá – reelected in 2003 – and Daniel Scioli (2007–2015) belonged to the same Peronist faction, headed by President Néstor Kirchner and his wife (and successor), Cristina Fernández de Kirchner. From then until 2015, the dominant Peronist faction would be under the electoral label of the Front for Victory (*Frente para la Victoria*, FPV) (Table 5.2).

Throughout this period, the Peronists governed with little legislative opposition. As Figure 5.1 shows, the PJ gained a legislative majority in eleven of the sixteen elections,[1] and held up to 90 percent of the Provincial Senate in 2011. The main challenges to the Peronists' hegemony in the province came in 1997–1999, when the party came close to losing the governorship to an alliance formed by the Radicals and the FREPASO,[2] itself made up of former left-leaning Peronists), and in 2009 and 2013,

---

[1] In Buenos Aires, legislative elections occur every two years, renewing half of each chamber.
[2] FREPASO stands for Front for a Solidary Country (*Frente para un País Solidario*).

TABLE 5.2. *Governors of Buenos Aires and their electoral performance,*
1983–2011.

Election year	Governor[a]	Governor's party	Governor's vote share (percent)	Margin of victory (percent)
1983	Alejandro Armendáriz	UCR	52	12.5
1987	Antonio Cafiero*	PJ	46.5	6.8
1991	Eduardo Duhalde	PJ	46.3	22.7
1995	Eduardo Duhalde	PJ	56.7	35.7
1999	Carlos Ruckauf*/ Felipe Solá*[b]	PJ	48.3	7
2003	Felipe Solá	PJ	43.3	30.9
2007	Daniel Scioli	FPV-PJ	48.2	31.7
2011	Daniel Scioli	FPV-PJ	55.1	39.2
2015	María Eugenia Vidal* Cambiemos Buenos Aires	PRO –	39.4	4.2

[a] (*) Indicates that the new governor is from a different party or faction than his predecessor, in other words there is high turnover.
[b] Felipe Solá finished Ruckauf's term.
Source: Author's elaboration from Andy Tow Electoral Blog.

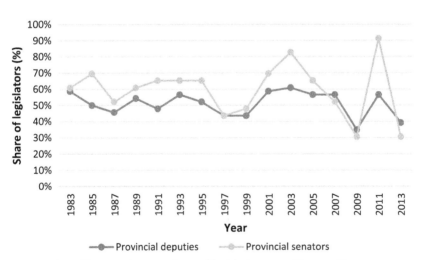

FIGURE 5.1. Governor's party share of legislative seats (Buenos Aires, 1983–2013)
Source: Andy Tow's Electoral Atlas.

when center-right Peronist factions would confront the dominant FPV. In sum, while Buenos Aires exhibits consistently low *interparty* fragmentation, it has repeatedly featured significant *intraparty* fragmentation between Peronist factions.

This intraparty conflict has often pitted the movement's two main political leaders, the president and the governor of Buenos Aires, against each other, a conflict that would permeate to the control (or lack thereof) of police forces.[3] Argentine presidents tend to have a complicated relationship with Buenos Aires governors. On the one hand, they need the province's votes, which constitute over 40 percent of the electorate and thus have an incentive to invest in the province – and sometimes the governor's – wellbeing.[4] On the other hand, they view governors as potential competitors or successors in upcoming elections. Therefore, they have an incentive to curb their ambitions, even if they share the same political affiliation and if the province suffers because of it.

"The Best Police in The World": Mutual Accommodation between Police and Politicians, 1987–1996

Between 1987 and 1996, low turnover and fragmentation enabled a mutually beneficial accommodation between state politicians and police. Politicians informally granted the police immunity to run protection rackets while also sidelining reform and allowing the police to retain their internal governance prerogatives. In return, police kicked up part of the collected funds to politicians and maintained acceptable levels of crime in the province.

During this period, provincial governments made little attempt to reform the police. The only (brief) instance occurred at the start of Governor Antonio Cafiero's administration (1987–1991). Cafiero's minister of government, Luis Brunati, a progressive Peronist, intended to cleanse the department after police officers murdered three young men in a working-class district in Southern GBA. Brunati recalled that when he took office the police brought him several gifts, including a rifle and a

---

[3] We observed a similar dynamic in Santa Fe (Chapter 4) during the period of the Ley de Lemas, which allowed rival factions to solve their dispute in the general election as opposed to having primaries.

[4] Buenos Aires is relatively poor – especially in the Greater Buenos Aires area – and receives a much lower share of fiscal revenue than what it contributes to the federal government. Given Argentina's asymmetric fiscal federalism in favor of the president, this provides additional leverage to impose their preferences on the governor.

German shepherd for "protection", as well as an envelope filled with cash. Brunati rejected the gift and, after purging several precinct bosses who participated in criminal rackets, faced multiple police protests and personal threats (Chevigny et al. 1991, 16). The reform attempt failed and, with little support from the governor or the Peronist party, Brunati resigned after one year.[5]

In 1991, Eduardo Duhalde, the former mayor of that working-class municipality (Lomas de Zamora) where police violence erupted in 1987, won the gubernatorial election, marking a partisan continuity in the state executive.[6] Duhalde had been vice-president to Carlos Menem, the charismatic caudillo from the northern province of La Rioja who defeated Cafiero in the presidential primary in 1988 and went on to win the 1989 general election. However, as the sitting vice-president, Duhalde had secured Cafiero's support in the 1991 gubernatorial elections and ran unopposed within the party.

Duhalde created the office of Secretary of Security upon taking office but did not implement any relevant initiatives to reduce police autonomy.[7] The administration lacked crime prevention plans and protocols regulating officers' use of force, as well as external accountability mechanisms to check police corruption. According to former security secretary Alberto Piotti, the province's constant security problems left no room for engaging in structural reform. As he told me, "Being in charge of security [in Buenos Aires] consists of always giving bad news. It's like having the rod of King Midas backwards."[8] During Piotti's swearing-in ceremony, in fact, Duhalde referred to the Bonaerense as "the best police force in the world" (Dutil and Ragendorfer 1997, 239), a phrase that would come back to haunt him.

Various academic and journalistic studies revealed that, during the early 1990s, the provincial police were managing multiple criminal rackets in the metropolitan area under the protection and for the benefit of local and state politicians, including the governor and his security secretary (López Echagüe 1996; Córdoba 2007; Eaton 2008). This illicit association related to a broader transformation in the Peronist party.

---

[5] "La historia de un precursor," *Página12*, April 11, 2004.

[6] Starting in 1995, state and national elections have taken place simultaneously. Governors can run for one reelection.

[7] The Secretary had the same functions as a cabinet minister. Security became a ministry in 1998.

[8] Interview by author with former Security Secretary Alberto Piotti, City of Buenos Aires, July 4, 2012.

During the 1990s, Peronism shifted from a unionist to a clientelist party, incorporating the urban poor and unemployed relegated by the national government's neoliberal reform (Levitsky 2003). These clientelistic machines, managed by brokers (*punteros*) who belonged to a local political faction (*agrupación*), delivered necessary social benefits to impoverished populations in the metropolitan area, yet often distributed them discretionally according to whether recipients showed up at campaign events or turned out to vote (Auyero 2001; Nichter 2008; Stokes 2013; Weitz-Shapiro 2014; Zarazaga 2014; Szwarcberg 2015). Police rents from criminal activities, including drug trafficking, constituted a nonnegligible source of revenue for these local machines.

Governor Duhalde declared that the Buenos Aires police would lead the fight against drug trafficking in the province and portrayed himself as a crusader against illicit drugs. By contrast, many of his political detractors alleged that he facilitated the expansion of drug trafficking in the province, although they have not backed up their claims in court.[9]

Whether Duhalde knew it or not, the Bonaerense was protecting (and profiting from) the same criminal enterprise that it was supposedly combatting. A journalistic investigation calculated that, during the 1990s, the police levied up to USD $100 million per month from illicit sources, including protection fees from drug trafficking (Dutil and Ragendorfer 1997, 113). Police not only protected but also ran drug distribution rings in Greater Buenos Aires with the aid of local Peronist machines. Journalist López Echagüe reported that local politicians allied with Duhalde protected drug dealers in key locations, such as the Central Market in La Matanza and the largest informal market in Lomas de Zamora (López Echagüe 1996).[10] Studies of urban clientelism have shown that Peronist brokers distributed drugs to mobilize activists to rallies for local mayors or state politicians (Auyero 2001; Zarazaga 2014). Although no mayor has been charged with taking money from drug trafficking, several have been accused of corruption or participation in other rackets, usually following splits in the ruling party at the local level (O'Donnell 2005).

Presumptions of complicity with traffickers also tainted the police's "successes" in the fight against drug trafficking. The two most important drug seizures by the BA police during this period were codenamed

---

[9] Among these denouncers are former Civic Coalition National Deputy Elisa Carrió, and social movement leader, Luis D'Elía (Federico 2008, 15–25).

[10] During his investigation, two active police officers who were the bodyguards of one such political patron brutally beat Echagüe.

"Operation White Coffee" and "Operation Strawberry." In the first case, while the police initially claimed to have seized 1,800 kg of Colombian cocaine, they later filed only 1,030 kg into evidence. In the second case, police seized a shipment of over two tons of cocaine in Buenos Aires but arrested only low-level handlers and intermediaries. The judiciary then acquitted all detainees due to irregular police procedures in the investigation, arousing suspicion that police had deliberately botched the case (Burzaco and Berensztein 2014, 30–34).

The linkages between governors, mayors and police would remain undisturbed for most of the analyzed period (1987–2015). Nonetheless, starting in the mid-1990s, in response to serious scandals that threatened the government's electoral prospects, the provincial administration would introduce broad reforms to reduce police autonomy (Hinton 2006; González 2020). However, increased intraparty disputes and turnover between different Peronist factions prevented these reforms from gaining traction and motivated police to resist their implementation.

FACTIONAL DISPUTES, POLICE REFORM CYCLES AND PARTICULARISTIC NEGOTIATION, 1997–2003

Between 1997 and 2003, higher fragmentation and turnover between Peronist factions increased the police's autonomy. After winning reelection in 1995, Governor Duhalde – who could not run for another term in the province – declared his intention to succeed Menem as president in 1999. Menem, however, had different ideas. He tried to reform the Constitution (once again) to run for a third consecutive term and, when this proved impossible, sabotaged the governor's campaign. This conflict between the two Peronist leaders illustrates the increasing intraparty fragmentation in the PJ (Ollier 2010, 99–100). Furthermore, the center-left FREPASO, a faction that had splintered from the national PJ in the early 1990s in opposition to the neoliberal reforms and widespread corruption of Menem's administration, allied with the UCR to defeat the incumbent Peronists in Buenos Aires in the mid-term election in 1997.[11] Finally, factional turnover occurred as Ruckauf – Duhalde's successor – distanced himself from the exiting provincial boss in the 1999 election, while his vice-governor, Felipe Solá, who came from a

---

[11] The FREPASO presented a broad security plan, with police reform as one of its main proposals. It formed the Alliance for Work, Justice and Education *(Alianza para el Trabajo, la Justicia y la Educación, ALIANZA)* with the UCR.

different faction, replaced Ruckauf midway through the term. This greater political competition would rattle security politics and the regulation of drug trafficking over the following years.

A corollary of this internecine war between the Peronist factions was a succession of police reform cycles that disrupted the provincial government's control of police rent extraction. Unlike in previous years, when police wrongdoings had remained under the radar, scandals involving extortion, kidnapping, drug trafficking and even murder by the police erupted repeatedly between 1996 and 2003. The tipping point was the arrest, on July 13, 1996, of fourteen police officers charged with participating in the bombing of the Jewish Center AMIA (*Asociación Mutual Israelita Argentina*) in 1994, the largest terrorist attack ever carried out in Argentina.[12] The scandal forced the resignations of Duhalde's security secretary, Alberto Piotti, and the provincial police chief in August 1996. As it turned out, the judge in charge of the investigation had paid a car thief protected by the BA police to denounce these officers at the behest of Menem and other members of his cabinet, evidencing the extent of internal fragmentation in the PJ.[13]

Eyeing his upcoming presidential prospects, in October 1996, Duhalde introduced an encompassing police reform (Ragendorfer 2002). This would be the first of several reform attempts followed by erosion or downright reversal between the late 1990s and early 2000s (Ungar 2009; Macaulay 2012; Flom and Post 2016). Duhalde appointed as security secretary the provincial prosecutor Eduardo de Lázzari, who immediately expelled 300 high-ranking police officers. The government also passed a judicial reform that took criminal investigation powers away from provincial judges – who relied on the police – and handed them to state-level prosecutors.[14]

However, intraparty fragmentation doomed Duhalde's reform from the start. Peronist mayors, concerned about how the reform would upset the protection rackets that fed their local machines, challenged the initiatives. As de Lázzari told me, "The municipal mayor would call and say, 'I want such and such [as street boss in their district]'; I had a lot of problems with mayors."[15] De Lázzari also stated that he cut off the

---

[12] A popular magazine story titled "Maldita Policía [The Damned Police]," exposing the police's illicit businesses, also accelerated the reform.

[13] Menem and some of his former ministers were indicted for this scheme.

[14] Law No. 11.922 (approved on December 18, 1996).

[15] Interview by author with former Security Secretary Eduardo de Lázzari, La Plata, Buenos Aires, July 7, 2012. See also Eaton (2008).

government's previous use of funds from police corruption to buy off journalists, by which former secretaries got praised in the press. As he said, "It was easier to get criticized once the payments stopped."[16]

The reform also triggered police resistance, often through violent means. The gravest example occurred on January 25, 1997, when a police unit murdered news photographer, José Luis Cabezas, at the behest of Alfredo Yabrán, an infamous businessman with links to President Menem. Duhalde claimed that "[the police] threw a corpse at my feet," and implicitly accused Menem of exploiting the case to hurt his presidential candidacy.[17] In another example of police backlash, Secretary De Lázzari had shots fired at his house and photographs taken of his children.[18] De Lázzari resigned in March 1997, after which Duhalde appointed municipal mayor Carlos Brown as secretary to repair his relationships with local politicians and police commanders (Dutil and Ragendorfer 1997, 301) and temporarily halted the reform's implementation.

The reform restarted after Duhalde's electoral defeat in the October 1997 midterm. The governor temporarily appointed a provincial legislator to restructure the police,[19] and upgraded the security secretary office into a ministry. Duhalde brought on former federal judge, León Arslanian, who redesigned the provincial security system,[20] dissolved the position of chief of police, placed civilians as heads of each division, established an external auditing agency and set up neighborhood security forums as external accountability mechanisms, among other measures.

However, political fragmentation within the PJ would again derail the reform. Arslanian complained that "[Peronist mayors were] not buying my ideas; some believed that we had to negotiate with the police. This was a generalized notion among Peronists".[21] Arslanian resigned in April 1999 when Duhalde's prospective successor, Carlos Ruckauf, notified him that he would not continue the reform,[22] a

---

[16] Interview by author with former Security Secretary Eduardo de Lázzari, La Plata, Buenos Aires, July 7, 2012.

[17] On the murder of news photographer José Luis Cabezas, see Bonasso (1999).

[18] Interview by author with former Security Secretary Eduardo de Lázzari, La Plata, Buenos Aires, July 7, 2012.

[19] Decree 4508/97, published in the Official Bulletin on December 31, 1997.

[20] Law 12.154, passed on August 5, 1998.

[21] Interview by author with former Security Minister León Arslanian, City of Buenos Aires, July 3, 2012. See also López Echagüe (2000, 159).

[22] Interview by author with former Governor Eduardo Duhalde, City of Buenos Aires, July 3, 2014.

revelation that disincentivized police compliance with the administration's proposals.[23]

Motivated by the risk of losing the 1999 elections against the ALIANZA, Ruckauf promoted an explicitly punitive approach to security to distinguish himself from his more progressive contenders (Ragendorfer 2002). Inviting police to "shoot criminals" [*meter bala a los delincuentes*], he obtained a slim victory and retained Peronism's control of the province – even as the PJ lost the presidency.

Ruckauf distanced himself from Duhalde's security proposals during the campaign and, once in office, reversed several democratizing reforms. He reinstituted the chief of police, sponsored a law reducing restrictions on police apprehension and interrogation of subjects,[24] dismantled the citizen security forums and offered a six-month bonus to police that killed criminals caught in the act. However, just like what happened with governors Moreira Franco and Alencar in Rio de Janeiro (Chapter 3), the Bonaerense's increased autonomy would soon backfire against Ruckauf's administration, as the force ousted his first security minister, former military commander Aldo Rico, after only three months (Ragendorfer 2002). Ruckauf's next minister was the former police chief, Ramón Verón, a high-ranking member of the Damned Police (*Maldita Policía*). His appointment meant that the old police bosses – including those removed during the reform period – maintained control over the force's illegal activities. Ruckauf resigned in January 2002 to take office in the national administration, and left his vice-governor, Felipe Solá, in charge.

Once more, intraparty turnover and fragmentation both prompted and hindered the administration's intention to reduce police autonomy. Solá belonged to a different faction and professed a different orientation from Ruckauf in terms of security. When I interviewed him, he described Ruckauf's punitive discourse as "populist [and] cheap."[25] Soon after Solá took office, the province experienced a new reform cycle, sparked by another episode of police violence.

During Solá's term, Argentina was experiencing a massive socioeconomic and political crisis with regular street protests. On June 26, 2002,

---

[23] After Arslanian's resignation, there were multiple police scandals involving corruption and even murder.

[24] Law 12.405.

[25] Interview by author with the former governor, Felipe Solá, City of Buenos Aires, July 3, 2012.

the provincial police violently repressed one of these protests and murdered two social movement activists. Solá claimed that sectors behind President Duhalde[26] had choreographed the repression along with the National Intelligence Agency and the provincial police. Security expert and Solá's future vice-minister of security, Marcelo Sain, called it an "open confrontation between the police and [social] organizations [to] wear down and discipline governor Solá," who had declared his intention of running for reelection in 2003 without consulting the Peronist leadership (Sain 2004, 24–26).[27]

The governor called upon two leading figures of the Peronist center-left, Juan Pablo Cafiero – son of the former governor – and Sain, to bring the police under control. They restructured the security ministry and shut down the police's rent extraction from the province's car chop shops, where most stolen cars ended (Sain 2008, 182–91). However, Solá then shifted course and instructed them to not "rock the boat" by interfering with the police in an election year (Sain 2008, 211). Before resigning in December 2002, Sain publicly alleged that police corruption funded the provincial Peronist political machine and that the administration's ongoing problems with the police stemmed from the Peronist intraparty dispute (Sain 2008, 208).

The reform provoked another brutal response by the police, who stirred up a kidnapping spree through their criminal associates in Greater Buenos Aires. Some of the victims included family members of famous actors and soccer players, which augmented the visibility and political damage of this crime wave (Sain 2008, 209–10). Police also repeatedly threatened Security Minister Cafiero, ultimately forcing his resignation in September 2003 (Klipphan 2004). Solá then appointed a former mayor and national official, conservative Juan José Álvarez, who intended to continue the reform, but resigned after only three months after changing bodyguards twice during his first month in office due to ongoing threats.[28]

Solá, unlike other politicians, survived this political turmoil. He won reelection by a landslide in October 2003, after which he reshuffled his security cabinet, placing his former minister of agrarian affairs, a man of

---

[26] In December 2001, Argentine President De la Rúa resigned, and after a week of political turmoil, Congress appointed National Senator Duhalde to head a transition government until the 2003 election.

[27] "Felipe Solá: Mi relación con Néstor Kirchner fue mala," *BA Noticias*, December 12, 2012.

[28] "Juan José Álvarez ya cambió dos veces su custodia," *La Nación*, October 16, 2003.

his inner circle but without any relevant experience, as security minister. In April 2004, a new security crisis emerged after the kidnapping and murder of Axel Blumberg, an upper-middle class student. Blumberg's father organized a massive rally in front of the national Congress demanding active government responses against insecurity. Solá called on Arslanian once again to implement an encompassing police reform. While the components resembled those of his previous reform, this time the outcome would be different.

Particularistic Negotiation: From the "Best Police in the World" to the "Damned Police"

As the Peronist's control of the police dwindled amid increasing intra-party disputes and factional turnover during the late 1990s and early 2000s, the party's coordinated protection regime broke down. Police chiefs increasingly appropriated rents from criminal activities for their personal benefit. Many bought luxurious houses, cars and boats whose costs clearly exceeded their stated income. Ultimately, this conspicuous consumption proved their undoing, as different units battled each other to capture more territories, businesses and rents. A former high-ranking official described street conflicts between police units as a "free-for-all, led by the bosses."[29] By way of illustration, in a case the press referred to as the "Narcopolice scandal," a police commander tried to expose another division's protection of traffickers, only to have his own division's racket revealed in the process. These turf wars even resulted in police murdered by fellow officers (Dutil and Ragendorfer 1997).

Police violence against criminal actors and civilians also increased during this period. According to the Center for Legal and Social Studies (*Centro de Estudios Legales y Sociales*, CELS), while between 1987 and 1990, the average number of civilian victims of police lethal violence was 138, between 1996 and 2004 it was 210 – a 35 percent increase. Many of these cases were summary executions. In line with Ruckauf's six-month bonus, the number of victims from police lethal interventions jumped by 80 percent between 1999 and 2001.

Police officers' use of deadly force also demonstrated their incapacity to regulate crime. In various situations, police killed their criminal associates to wipe out traces of their illicit activities. Two patent examples were

---

[29] "No cesa la crisis en la policía bonaerense," *La Nación*, November 23, 1997.

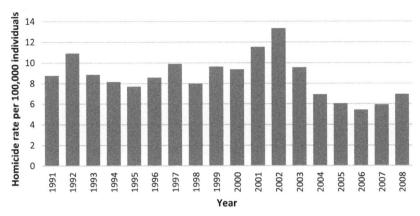

FIGURE 5.2. Homicide rates in the province of Buenos Aires, 1991–2008
Source: Sistema Nacional de Información Criminal (SNIC, National System of Crime Information).

the assassination by police of the criminals who perpetrated the hijackings of the post office in 1996 and a local bank in 1998, jobs which police themselves had authorized (Ragendorfer 2002; Córdoba 2007). This interim period reinforces the idea developed in this book that high autonomy increases police lethality.

The police also proved incapable of regulating criminal violence in the province. As shown in Figure 5.2, homicides, which had decreased steadily between 1992 and 1995, increased by 56 percent – from 8.5 to 13.3 per 100,000 individuals – between 1996 and 2002. They would decrease once more, with politicians regaining their control of police, between 2003 and 2008 (and remain low for the succeeding years).

Police themselves often fueled criminality to intimidate reformist politicians. Kidnappings, authorized by certain police sectors, spiked after Cafiero and Sain took office in late June 2002 and remained high until mid-2003, with another spike between April and May (see figure 5.3). By contrast, extortive kidnappings decreased in 2004, when the government curtailed police engagement in this illicit activity, and remained low since then. This monthly variation also casts doubt on the alternative explanation that the socioeconomic crisis was the sole determinant of increases in violent crimes, at least in the province of Buenos Aires (Figure 5.3).

In short, intraparty disputes and growing turnover during the second half of the 1990s jeopardized the mutual accommodation between the provincial government and the police. Thus, while coordinated protection rackets were the predominant regulatory arrangement until 1996, particularistic negotiations prevailed between 1997 and 2003. As conflicts

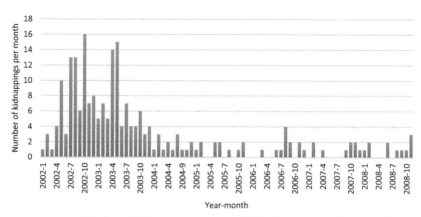

FIGURE 5.3. Number of kidnappings per month in the province of Buenos Aires, 2002–2008
Source: Sistema de Alerta Temprana (SAT, Early Warning System).

between the state-level government and the police intensified, police autonomy grew and the Bonaerense thus proved incapable or unwilling to regulate the province's drug market and criminal violence. However, as turnover and fragmentation declined in the ensuing decade (2004–2015), Buenos Aires governors managed to reduce police autonomy to restore protection rackets as the main regulatory regime in the province.

PERONIST CONSOLIDATION, THE RESTORATION OF THE PACT WITH THE BONAERENSE AND THE RETURN OF PROTECTION RACKETS, 2004–2015

From 2004 until their exit from the provincial government in 2015, Peronist governors in Buenos Aires consolidated their control over the police and effectively reduced the force's autonomy. Two factors contributed to this development. First, the party's entrenchment in power gave police commanders and their subordinates greater incentives to cooperate with the government, even in detriment of its organizational autonomy, because it enhanced their career perspectives. Second, although factional tensions in the ruling party persisted, during this period there was greater unity within the Peronist party, in other words, lower intraparty fragmentation. Interparty fragmentation also remained low, as no other party could challenge the PJ for the governorship. This political dynamic enabled state-level governments to reduce police autonomy, albeit for different purposes. While Solá's government (2004–2007) intended to reform and professionalize the police, Daniel Scioli's administrations

(2007–2015) politicized the force and tolerated – and, according to multiple sources, even profited from – the force's illicit rent extraction. During this period, low political competition and police politicization reestablished protection rackets as the primary regulatory regime of drug trafficking in Buenos Aires, with low violence by both police and criminals.

Reduced Turnover and Fragmentation in the Frente Para La Victoria (FPV-PJ)

In October 2003, Felipe Solá won reelection in the province of Buenos Aires by more than thirty points. A few months earlier, Santa Cruz governor, Néstor Kirchner had won the presidency, with the support of Duhalde's political machine in the province of Buenos Aires. The national PJ split soon after, however, as Kirchner distanced himself from Duhalde. Solá supported Kirchner in this dispute. In the mid-term election of 2005, First Lady (and future president) Cristina Kirchner defeated Duhalde's wife in the Buenos Aires national senate race, consolidating the Kirchners' control over the national PJ and decreasing intraparty fragmentation, with governors and municipal mayors falling in line.

There was no partisan or factional turnover during the next electoral cycle. As Solá could not run again in 2007, Kirchner anointed his vice-president, Daniel Scioli, as the Peronist candidate under the banner of the recently established Frente Para la Victoria (FPV). Scioli swept both of his gubernatorial elections: In 2007 he gained 48 percent of the vote with a 32 percent margin over his closest competitor and in 2011 he obtained 55 percent of the vote with a 40 percent margin. Meanwhile, political fragmentation in the province remained low until 2013, when Sergio Massa, then mayor of Tigre, a wealthy municipality in the North of Greater Buenos Aires, split from the FPV. His new electoral alliance, the Renovation Front (*Frente Renovador*, FR), which included several Peronist mayors from Greater Buenos Aires, defeated Cristina Kirchner – and Scioli – in the midterms.[30]

Of course, this period was not devoid of frictions between the provincial and national government. Scioli's relationship with President Cristina Kirchner (2007–2015) was tense, particularly after Néstor Kirchner's

---

[30] While the incumbent Peronist faction also lost in the 2009 midterm election, municipal mayors did not abandon the FPV, which soon regained its strength and won the 2011 election by a landslide.

death in October 2010 (Schmidt and Ibañez 2015). However, there were no factional splits. The national government did not support another candidate to run against Scioli in the province in 2011, although Cristina appointed Scioli's vice-governor and stacked the legislative ballot with her loyalists. Scioli, meanwhile, received offers to join the dissident Peronist faction in the congressional elections of 2009 and 2013, but passed on both opportunities. In 2015, Cristina Kirchner unilaterally resolved the issue of national succession by anointing Scioli as the presidential candidate for the FPV – unlike Menem, who refused to recognize Duhalde as his successor and undermined his bid for the presidency in 1999.[31] However, FPV politicians waged a fierce primary in the province of Buenos Aires, which, as narrated in the introduction of this chapter, included accusing one of the contenders – Aníbal Fernández, the national chief of staff – of heading a drug trafficking ring and orchestrating a triple homicide. This internal struggle took its toll. The Peronists lost the province of Buenos Aires after thirty-two years in 2015 to the electoral alliance *Cambiemos* (Let's Change),[32] which also won the presidency.

Police Autonomy During the Solá and Scioli Administrations: From Professionalizing Reform to Political Appropriation of Police Rents

As the Peronists consolidated their control over the province, the provincial police force was no longer the political liability it had been in the past. A clear indicator is the greater stability of political appointees in charge of security. While there were sixteen security ministers between 1994 and 2003, there were only four between 2004 and 2015, a significant change in a province where, as former Secretary Piotti told me, "The security minister is always the first fuse, even before the chief of police."[33]

During this period, both Solá and Scioli were able to reduce the police's autonomy. After the security crisis posed by the murder of Axel Blumberg in April 2004, at the behest of Néstor Kirchner, Solá appointed Arslanian, who once again, placed civilians as heads of police divisions, introduced

---

[31] This occurred much to the displeasure of Cristina's left-leaning supporters, who identified Scioli as a center-right candidate, and of other FPV politicians who wanted their shot at the presidency.

[32] The major members of this alliance are the center-right party PRO, which had governed the city of Buenos Aires since 2007, and the UCR.

[33] Interview by author with former Security Secretary Piotti, City of Buenos Aires, July 4, 2012. These numbers include those officials designed as secretaries of security, before it became a ministry in 1998.

statistics to measure police performance, created an Internal Affairs Division directly under his supervision, revitalized citizen security forums and even set up a new force, the Buenos Aires Police 2, unshackled by the corrupt practices of its predecessor (Arslanian 2008). The new Internal Affairs office was more active than ever. The administration expelled over 2000 police officers between September 2004 and November 2007, compared with just 172 between February 1999 and June 2004 (Arslanian 2008, 252).

As always, the police resisted. However, unlike in the late 1990s and early 2000s, greater coordination between the national and provincial Peronist governments was fundamental to sustain the reform.[34] Kirchner's support was especially crucial. When Arslanian's plan prompted a new wave of four high-profile kidnappings with police participation in two days, Kirchner instructed the federal police and the National Intelligence Agency to investigate the abductions and diffused tensions between Arslanian and Solá.[35]

Peronist municipal mayors also became more amenable to Arslanian's proposals, even though it jeopardized their gains from police rent extraction. As Solá told me, "I would ask the mayors [when they objected to Arslanian]: What do you have to offer [as minister]? A thug, a friend of the precinct boss? We've already seen that."[36] This time Arslanian remained as minister for over three years, until the end of Solá's administration in December 2007. Although several of its entrenched vices persisted, the police were no longer the politically destabilizing force of previous administrations. This reform was the most stable and effective since the return of democracy.

During his eight years as governor (2008–2015), Daniel Scioli also maintained control over the police, albeit through different means. He overturned some formal curbs on police autonomy and relied more heavily on informal mechanisms applied by his security ministers. While the police regained autonomy to manage their internal governance, the administration would control its external operations to centralize illicit rents, reestablishing protection rackets as the main drug trafficking regulatory regime.

---

[34] Interview by author with former Security Minister León Arslanian, City of Buenos Aires, July 3, 2012.

[35] "Paños fríos entre Arslanian y Felipe Solá," *Página12*, October 2, 2004.

[36] Interview by author with the former governor, Felipe Solá, City of Buenos Aires, July 3, 2012.

When Scioli took office, he quickly reversed several aspects of Arslanian's reforms. He reinstated the chief of police and dissolved the parallel Buenos Aires Police 2. However, the administration lacked concrete and stable formal security policies of its own. For example, Scioli first fused the ministries of security and justice in November 2010 and then split them again in September 2013, to keep the exiting security minister – according to critics, the key enforcer of his arrangement with the police – in his cabinet.

Additionally, Scioli did not propose laws or sanction decrees to professionalize the police, despite having an overwhelming majority in the provincial legislature. He also ignored measures demanded by the opposition, such as the creation of a Judicial Police to conduct criminal investigations. Boards of police commanders decided over promotions. The administration incorporated massively and put police on the street with little and precarious training; in 2013, it nearly doubled the size of the force to 90,000 members. Finally, although the government formally maintained the neighborhood security forums, it deactivated them in practice.

Nonetheless, members of the administration highlighted the importance of *informal* mechanisms, particularly personal leadership and attention to everyday matters, to control the police. When I interviewed him, former minister Ricardo Casal told me, "Police need political control. It's impossible to think otherwise. Not just because of its functioning, corruption and other stuff, but because security is not a reflex action; it's a policy that you apply." He then highlighted some the main control mechanisms the administration employed:

I constantly rotated police officers [especially high commanders] between local precincts: I didn't like it when police remained in the same place for a long time, so we annually rotated all personnel in strategic places. [Also] all police cars have an ABL chip that monitors where they are. It's not good to follow them because they are 20,000 [cars], but it helps to know if something bad happened, e.g., they committed a robbery here and the car was twenty blocks away and took forty minutes to get there. That's suspicious: Either there was a 'freed zone', or they were sleeping or eating somewhere.[37]

Casal's second-in-command also underscored the government's informal control of the police:

---

[37] Interview by author with former Security Minister Ricardo Casal, La Plata, January 16, 2014.

You can't demand the police to do a serious job if the political leadership is not on top of things and does not know what they are talking about. As a middle-ranking official, I lived through an enormous demand by the governor and the minister that made us aware of all the important questions. The governor might call you at seven in the morning and ask [about] something that happened at 3 a.m. ..... I would leave here at 10 p.m. and go around Greater Buenos Aires at midnight because if you fall asleep and answer the phone, it's not the same. Casal might ask you for such details that if you were not up to speed, you were screwed.[38]

Politicians' depiction of police subordination during this period is accurate. Indeed, there was little overt political conflict between the political leadership and police commanders, especially when compared to the previous period, when commanders staged crimes and intimidated government officials to destabilize reforms. In fact, Casal and his second-in-command acknowledged that they encountered little, if any, resistance from the police.

Police interviewees shared this perception of police subordination to the government. For example, the former deputy police chief said that "Casal placed chiefs because of political requests, not because of their skills," thus ensuring the commanders' personal allegiance. He recalled, for example, that "Casal told [the chiefs] he wanted one police officer per vehicle because they didn't have enough [money] for two and the bosses said 'Yes.' Why? Because they don't know, they were never in the line of fire. They don't confront [the minister]."[39]

The commanders' support of, or at least lack of open opposition to, the government also manifested during the police protests of December 2013. Lower-level officers, supported by police union leaders, left their stations and took to the streets to demand wage increases. However, police commanders did not support the protest and the unions soon reached an agreement with the government.[40] In contrast, police rebellions in other Argentine provinces, like Santa Fe (Chapter 4), generated wide-spread chaos and even forced the national government to send the national military police to contain the situation.[41]

---

[38] Interview by author with former Secretary of Security Policy and Penitentiary Affairs César Albarracín, La Plata, June 17, 2014.

[39] Interview by author with former provincial deputy police chief, Salvador Baratta, Lanús, Buenos Aires, June 16, 2014.

[40] "Scioli decretó un aumento para la policía y logró reducir la protesta en Buenos Aires," *La Nación*, December 10, 2013.

[41] "La protesta policial con más alcance de la historia argentina," *La Nación*, December 9, 2013.

The provincial government also centralized control of the police at the expense of municipal mayors, who had previously wielded greater informal influence on police politics. According to some interpretations, the state government was able to centralize police rent extraction from drug trafficking and other criminal rackets, sidelining the mayors. Marcelo Sain, Solá's former vice-minister of security, commented, "The precinct boss has to pay up to the department chief, not the mayor. What you hear from mayors is 'while this son of a bitch [i.e., the governor] makes money from this, I get the mess down here.'"[42] Mayors' dissatisfaction with the provincial government's security policies contributed to the mass defection from the FPV to Massa's dissident Peronist faction, the Renovation Front (FR), before the 2013 midterm election. After the electoral defeat, Scioli appointed the Mayor of Ezeiza, a city in GBA, Alejandro Granados, as security minister to smooth his relationship with the local bosses.[43]

In short, the Scioli administration reversed Arslanian's reforms and abandoned attempts to professionalize the police. However, it was nonetheless able to reduce police autonomy, thwart police resistance and wrestle informal control from mayors. This centralized control enabled the administration to politicize the police. The result was the reinstatement of coordinated protection rackets as the main regulatory regime in the province.

Protection Rackets: Effective Regulation of Drug Trafficking and Criminal Violence

Given the clandestine nature of protection rackets, it is extremely difficult to obtain concrete evidence of the involvement of high-level politicians in this activity. Despite several suspicions of corruption in multiple areas, no member of Scioli's administration has been charged, much less convicted, of any crime.[44] However, as I will show through my interviews and analysis of secondary evidence, there are at least three strong, interconnected indications of this arrangement.

---

[42] Interview by author with former Vice-Minister of Security Marcelo Sain, San Isidro, Buenos Aires, June 25, 2013.

[43] A high-ranking public official in Florencio Varela, for example, praised this decision because Granados was much more attentive than Casal to the needs of local governments. Interview by author, Florencio Varela, December 13, 2013.

[44] There are, by contrast, several cases investigating police officers involved in protection of drug traffickers.

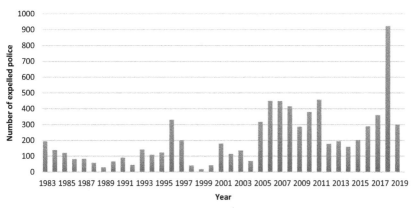

FIGURE 5.4. Number of expelled officers from the Buenos Aires police, 1983–2019
Source: Author's elaboration, based on the Provincial Registry of Expelled Police.[45]

First, numerous, unconnected sources have reported extensive police corruption in relation to drug trafficking – as well as other criminal activities – ranging from tolerance to overt participation, in various neighborhoods of Greater Buenos Aires. These cases often involve high-level officers from various districts across the metropolitan area. In other words, although the protection of traffickers does not involve the entire police force, it is an institutional rather than an individual phenomenon.

Second, internal and external monitoring agencies rarely prosecuted or even administratively punished this type of misconduct. Nor has the government improved police selection or promotion processes to root out malfeasance. In other words, there is little, if any, control of police corruption and, where it exists, it is reactive rather than preemptive. While massive purges of the police were common during the late 1990s and early 2000s, during this period there were no widespread dismissals by the provincial administration, as former security minister Ricardo Casal admitted during our encounter.[46] As we can see in Figure 5.4, the number of expelled police decreased during the Scioli administration, especially during his second term. During the four years of Solá and Arslanian's tenure (2004–2007), the administration sacked an average of 320 police per year. In Scioli's first term, this average increased to 384; however, it shrunk by more than 50 percent during his second term (183),

[45] Provincial Security Ministry. Retrieved from https://catalogo.datos.gba.gob.ar/ca/dataset/registro-expulsados.
[46] Interview by author with former minister, Casal, La Plata, January 16, 2014.

even though, as mentioned earlier, the ranks of the police nearly doubled since 2013. Furthermore, the average number of police dismissed due to corruption decreased from 148 to 59 from one term to the next, while allegations of police corruption mounted. Both indicators increased during the administration of Scioli's successor, Let's Change governor, María Eugenia Vidal (2016–2019), especially during 2018. In other words, as the government's political strength increased, its formal control of the police loosened.

Third, police corruption of this magnitude is unlikely to persist without political knowledge or protection. Furthermore, given that there are no concrete measures against police corruption and police do not confront the administration, suspecting high-level political involvement in these arrangements seems in order. Below, I use interview data and secondary evidence to illustrate the coordinated nature of corruption in relation to drug trafficking in the province of Buenos Aires.

"They Look Out For Each Other": Police and Politicians' Protection of Drug Trafficking

Like most politicians, Buenos Aires' governors adopted a confrontational stance toward drug trafficking. Solá, for instance, promoted changes in the province's legislation to allow the state police to persecute retail drug trafficking, a task previously exclusive to federal forces.[47] Scioli declared drug trafficking "public enemy number one."[48] Both governors accompanied this harsh rhetoric with increased drug policing. Between 2006 and 2013, the number of judicial investigations involving drug trafficking in the province increased by 85 percent, from 14,000 to 26,000. The volume of cocaine seizures grew by 200 percent in this period, according to the state Attorney General's Report.[49] While in 2002 there were only 52 persons detained for drug-related offenses in provincial prisons, in 2010 there were 2,161.[50] However, these actions affected mainly the lowest levels of criminal groups involved in drug

---

[47] The province adhered to the decentralization of drug trafficking investigations approved in national law 26.052 (approved on July 27, 2005) through provincial law 13.392 (approved on October 31, 2005). For an evaluation of the impact of the decentralization law, see the National Public Prosecutors' report in 2014.

[48] "Narcotráfico: el enemigo público número uno," *La Nación*, April 20, 2014.

[49] Several interviewees suggested that the police often prearranged drug seizures with traffickers or reused drugs from previous heists to bolster their statistics. See also Auyero and Sobering (2019).

[50] Source: Provincial Penitentiary System reports (2002–2010).

dealing. A different informal regulatory strategy, based on protection rackets with centralized corruption and low violence, complemented this prohibitionist approach.

Most interviewees from outside the administration hinted that the police and politicians protected (and sometimes profited from) retail drug dealing in the province. Even Scioli's former security minister Ricardo Casal admitted the police's involvement in this racket but doubted that it was extensive, "It's not rare that every now and then there is a cop arrested. Evidently [drug trafficking] needs certain collaboration. I don't think it's an institutional decision of the police to participate, but some sectors do get involved. We've arrested precinct bosses, handcuffed and everything. Local politics also matters . . .. Maybe a council member has a connection, and they finance his campaign."[51] In other words, the state security minister denied the provincial government's involvement with police in the protection of drug trafficking but shifted suspicion to local-level politicians.

The local government officials I interviewed also downplayed the magnitude of police involvement with trafficking in their districts. Two officials from the Community Prevention Office in the municipality of San Martín (Northern GBA) called the allegations "urban stories that sometimes are true and sometimes not" and could not recall concrete accusations in their two years in office.[52] Municipal officials from Florencio Varela (Southern GBA) acknowledged that police protected other criminal rackets such as car robberies and contraband but not drug trafficking.[53]

Interviewees from the political opposition at the provincial and local-level described a different picture.[54] Former Vice-Minister of Security Marcelo Sain – a state deputy at the time of the interview –was explicit and harsh in describing the government's involvement in drug trafficking:

[51] Interview by author with former minister, Casal, La Plata, January 16, 2014. Casal's predecessor, Carlos Stornelli, expressed a similar view with respect to police corruption, calling it an individual rather than institutional problem. "Stornelli: hay policías corruptos pero la institución no lo es," *La Nación*, March 12, 2009.

[52] Interview by author with local officials from San Martín, Mirta Juárez and Roberto Santillán, San Martín, Buenos Aires, October 11, 2013.

[53] Interview by author with Florencio Varela councilmembers, Héctor D'Aquino and Andrés Watson, Florencio Varela, December 12 and 13, 2013, respectively.

[54] Comparatively, these accusations across party lines were much more prominent in Buenos Aires, and to a lesser extent in Rio de Janeiro, than in Santa Fe or São Paulo.

The *sciolismo* [Scioli's faction] started to finance itself with [police corruption money]. The great leap in the magnitude of fundraising by the police occurs when the *sciolismo* orders greater levels of retribution by the police. This coincides with its calculus, at that time [2011], which leaned towards breaking with Cristina [Kirchner]. The large drug market [in the municipality of San Martín] is handled by [the largest dealer] directly with the DDI (Police Department of Investigations) and the departmental boss: what's where the big money is. Where there are better business opportunities, they [i.e., the provincial government] send better business managers. The police are a source of financing.[55]

Sain is not by any reach the only politician to make these allegations. Another provincial deputy from the opposition, said, "There's a slight suspicion that, more than discussing the chain of command or worrying about people's security, [the governor and the mayors] are discussing who handles police rackets. That's my personal opinion. They are discussing if the paycheck goes to the security minister or the mayor. If you ask me, now it goes to both."[56] A third provincial deputy not only ratified this view but also involved the provincial judiciary in the collusive scheme, "I am absolutely convinced that there is a generalized illegal activity as far as allowing the installation and functioning of drug trafficking production and distribution, human trafficking, arms trafficking, with protection from the judicial power."[57] Finally, three police union representatives pointed to the links between politicians and the organization's high command:

A: Is there complicity between politicians and the police? Yes, because they look out for each other.
Q: At what level?
A: At the level of the high command, always.[58]

Some interviewees also narrated specific episodes to explain how these arrangements worked. Former police deputy chief Salvador Baratta connected police protection of drug trafficking with political interference in the selection of precinct bosses in San Martín, one of my chosen fieldwork sites:

[55] Sain was a state deputy for the party, New Encounter, an electoral ally of the national FPV (Cristina Kirchner) while simultaneously a critic of the Scioli administration.

[56] Interview by author with Civic Coalition state deputy, Marcelo Díaz, La Plata, October 8, 2013.

[57] Interview by author with state deputy for the Renovation Front (FR), Jorge D'Onofrio, La Plata, August 13, 2014.

[58] Interview by author with three police union representatives, La Plata, December 17, 2013.

When I [got back from my vacation] they had switched three precinct bosses from the biggest precincts in San Martín because of a political request. Those are just the ones through which all the drug comes into the Northern Area [of Greater Buenos Aires]: It comes through routes eight and nine, is fragmented in San Martín and from there it is distributed to the province. *You can't put a fox to take care of the chicken coop.* When I returned from my break, they wanted me to sign the transfers and I refused because there were police bosses [whom] I was convinced would not pass a rhinoscopy.[59]

Other cases in this municipality during this period point to police complicity with drug trafficking with the provincial government's complaisance, if not involvement. The most resounding case was the kidnapping and murder of Candela Rodríguez, a nine-year-old girl, in August 2011. A legislative commission concluded that the police had deliberately manipulated the investigation to conceal its own links with the drug traffickers who had abducted the girl and recommended the dismissal of the security minister, the police chief and deputy chief, and the district boss.[60] While the government dismissed the district boss in December 2012 (almost a year and-a-half later), the top commanders and political authorities remained in their place, which showed how little leverage the opposition had to investigate the government's links with drug trafficking.

A provincial legislator from the opposition told me of a similar incident in which the provincial chief of police protected one of the main drug traffickers from this municipality:

I had the testimony of a police officer who told me about a drug deal in a car shop. They get in; they arrest two armed guards and see [the dealer] speaking on the phone in the back, unfazed. [The officer] starts walking and his phone rings. The voice on the other side says, "Pick up." He says, "I'll call you back boss, I'm on a job." "Pick up NOW." He had to leave the scene. The voice on the other end was the current chief of police and he was the one speaking with [the dealer]. This is entirely corrupted from top to bottom, and it's not so generalized at the bottom, but they follow orders.[61]

A judicial investigation into another of the district's top traffickers revealed that he paid protection money to local precinct officers. This dealer also claimed that politicians "cannot play dumb with respect to

[59] Interview by author with former Deputy Chief Baratta (emphasis added), Lanús, June 16, 2014.
[60] See the commission's report in www.senado-ba.gob.ar/informe_candela.aspx. See also "Separaron de la policía bonaerense al comisario que investigó el caso Candela," *Clarín*, December 13, 2012.
[61] Interview by author with state deputy, D'Onofrio, La Plata, August 13, 2014.

cocaine because they are knee-deep in it. How do you think they finance their campaigns?" (cited in Federico 2008, 130, my translation). However, no high-ranking officer or politician was investigated, much less convicted, regarding these accusations.

Finally, in 2015 a Federal Police investigation discovered that two San Martín drug traffickers gave ARS $5,000 (around USD $500) per week to a local precinct boss, as well as ARS $30,000 (around USD $3,000) to his superiors in the Departmental office and the Drug Trafficking Division. The police, in turn, provided the dealers with drugs seized from other raids and alerted them of the moves of their rivals, thus regulating gangs' territorial expansion in the metropolitan area.[62] The dealer had thirteen officers listed as contacts on his phone, a clear indication that groups of police protected him. Furthermore, it took a Federal Police investigation to shut down this racket. Again, no politician was held accountable.

Federal authorities and municipal public officials in San Martín also questioned the provincial government's commitment to confront drug trafficking. The lead federal prosecutor in the district hinted that the state government complicated judicial investigations into drug trafficking gangs because it continuously changed police commanders, whereas such inquiries required establishing long-term relationships and trust between prosecutors, judges and the police.[63] The municipal security secretary also complained about this issue, "We established a trusting relationship between the police and the prosecutor's office and carried out several seizures in 2012, but at the end of that year the head of drug trafficking was changed and now there is much less work."[64] He was also suspicious about leaks to drug dealers in impending raids, "I ask to be informed of drug seizures only ten minutes before [they take place] so that everybody knows that we didn't leak anything. I often got angry calls from prosecutors saying that they had surveilled a place and recorded drug sales for 15 days, then they ordered the seizure and there's nobody there. Somebody talked."[65]

---

[62] See "Creen que policías daban a traficantes drogas para su venta," *La Nación*, June 26, 2015, and "Descubren que un narco tenía a trece policías en su agenda telefónica," *Perfil*, June 27, 2015. See also Auyero and Sobering (2019).

[63] Interview by author with federal prosecutor in San Martín, Jorge Sica, San Martín, December 18, 2013.

[64] Interview by author with San Martín municipal security secretary, José María Fernández, San Martín, October 11, 2013.

[65] Interview by author with municipal Security Secretary Fernández, San Martín, October 11, 2013.

Police and political protection of drug dealers is not exclusive to San Martín. Several secondary sources have noted similar patterns in various other municipalities across GBA. For example, the Provincial Memory Commission's (CPM) reports of 2012 and 2013 alleged that, in Florencio Varela, a local trafficker involved in two murders was a Peronist broker who sold drugs right next to the headquarters of a powerful local politician, naturally with police protection as well (CPM 2012, 248; CPM 2013, 403–405).[66] In their ethnographic work in Lomas de Zamora, Auyero and Berti recorded testimonies of dealers who claimed, "Police came every weekend to collect ... they knew we sold drugs but they did not bother us, they freed the area ... they come by themselves to get their commission .... If you give them ARS $500–600 [about USD $50–60] a night they leave you alone" (2013, 120–27). Zarazaga's extensive fieldwork in the metropolitan area registered 85 out of 100 brokers who stated that paying party activists with drugs was a common practice, and twelve who actually admitted to having paid people with drugs to go to rallies (2014, 32). As in the 1990s, most of these brokers received protection from both the police and the political bosses in their districts.

State connections to drug trafficking in Buenos Aires extend beyond poor neighborhoods – or the police. A federal prosecutor from San Isidro, one of the wealthiest municipalities in the province, faced impeachment and is awaiting trial for covering up the murder of two Colombian traffickers in 2008.[67] Another federal judge faced a similar fate due to his "mishandling" of the investigation of an ephedrine ring in Campana, a municipality located in the outskirts of the province.[68] Before, during and after the 2013 midterms, political rivals cast suspicion upon Tigre mayor and dissident Peronist leader Sergio Massa, since several renowned Colombian traffickers lived in private neighborhoods in his district.[69]

The expansion of drug trafficking in the province, the persistent links between police, drug trafficking and political brokers, and the spotty political response to prevent or punish these linkages, belies the government's claim that it is attempting to confront drug trafficking head-on. On

---

[66] See also "Un modelo agotado", *Página12*, February 5, 2012.

[67] "Julio Novo, fiscal general de San Isidro a juicio político por presunto encubrimiento," *Perfil*, September 28, 2015; "Revés para el ex fiscal Julio Novo: quedó a un paso de ir a juicio por encubrir narcos," *Clarín*, December 28, 2018.

[68] "La Corte ratificó la destitución de Faggionato Márquez," *La Nación*, June 7, 2012.

[69] See "Autos, viajes y negocios: cómo vivían los narcos colombianos," *Perfil*, Nov. 2, 2013, and "Rossi: Los narcos están en Nordelta," *Página12*, October 5, 2015.

the contrary, it suggests that the government and the police coordinated their rent extraction from this illicit activity.

Successful Violence Containment

In protection rackets, police seek to establish long-term relationships with criminals. Such linkage requires lower levels of violence by both parties. Police employ less violence because, since their protection is credible, they rarely need to extort criminals to obtain rents or discipline them for deviating from the arrangement. Meanwhile, criminals resort less to violence to keep their protection, avoid excessive attention by the state and preserve their business.

Available statistics support this argument.[70] While retail drug trafficking exploded in Buenos Aires, criminal violence remained stable. Between 2008 and 2015, homicide rates in Buenos Aires increased by only 7 percent, from 6.8 to 7.3 per 100,000 individuals, compared to a 40 percent increase in Santa Fe province (Chapter 4) during the same period. Recall that in Rosario, Santa Fe, the homicide rate in 2013 nearly tripled that of Buenos Aires.

This low criminal violence in Buenos Aires is puzzling given its highly fragmented drug market. Unlike in São Paulo (Chapter 6), there are no powerful drug gangs with whom to broker centralized pacts nor has the police become more professionalized or efficient at solving crimes. Additionally, criminal violence in Buenos Aires decreased or remained stable after the best years of economic growth, between 2002 and 2008, had passed.

This pattern is not exclusive to homicides. Between 2009 and 2012 nine out of thirteen indicators of crimes against individuals decreased. This trend contrasts with the late 1990s and early 2000s, when the police frequently stirred up violent crime waves or unshackled their criminal acquaintances to destabilize political authorities. Homicides and other violent crimes increased, however, between 2013 and 2014, coinciding with the greater fragmentation within the Peronist party and the anticipation of turnover given the term limits facing Scioli's administration.

While there are no reliable statistics on confrontations between drug gangs, in the early 2000s there were several clashes and even kidnappings between local groups, especially in the municipality of San Martín. In contrast, after 2007, violent confrontations between gangs in this district were rare, with only two feuds, in 2009 and 2011, which resulted in four

---

[70] Homicide statistics come from the National Crime Statistics Office. The province did not publish official statistics between 2009 and 2013.

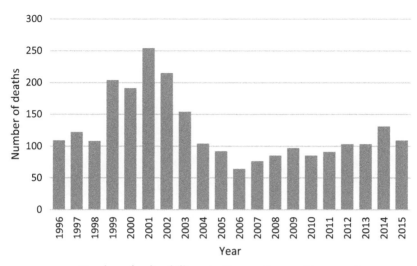

FIGURE 5.5. Number of police killings in Greater Buenos Aires, 1996–2015
Source: Author's elaboration from Centro de Estudios Legales y Sociales (CELS, Center for Legal and Social Studies).[71]

casualties (for a description of these conflicts, see Sain 2019). The fact that drug trafficking gangs in Buenos Aires rarely grow beyond their local territory (and do not typically confront each other) highlights the police's efficient regulation.

The politicized BA police rarely applied lethal violence to regulate this illicit market. As Figure 5.5 shows, the number of victims killed by police in the Greater Buenos Aires increased dramatically between 1996 and 2001,[72] peaking at 254 that year, during the stint of greatest police autonomy and regulation through particularistic negotiations. Afterwards, however, lethal interventions decreased and remained stable between 2004 (104) and 2015 (109), through the periods of attempted professionalization by Solá and Arslanian (2004–2007) and the politicization led by Scioli (2008–2015).

Finally, violence against police by criminals also remained low when protection rackets prevailed. As we can see in Figure 5.6, the number of police killed in Greater Buenos Aires jumped between 1997 (38) and 2002

---

[71] Data retrieved from Centro de Estudios Legales y Sociales (CELS): www.cels.org.ar/web/letalidad-policial-estadisticas/

[72] While this figure refers to police killings in GBA (and not the whole province) and does not distinguish officers' institutional affiliation, it is safe to assume that it represents a vast majority of police lethal interventions in the whole province and that most individuals belong to the provincial police.

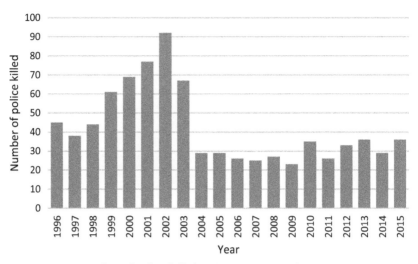

FIGURE 5.6. Number of police killed in Greater Buenos Aires, 1996–2015
Source: Author's elaboration from CELS.

(92). During this period police killed more frequently, giving criminals greater motivation to shoot first – which fueled further police violence. However, the number of fallen police officers declined and hovered around thirty per year between 2004 and 2015, even though police are only marginally better trained or equipped than they were two decades ago. Since the ranks of police have increased substantially in the last decade, a further implication is that the likelihood of officers getting killed is much lower than before. Drug dealers' carefulness to not draw excessive police attention, their willingness to broker stable deals with police and their relative disadvantage vis-à-vis the state, surely contributed to these low levels of violence.

In short, low political competition and politicized police enabled protection rackets, a drug trafficking regulatory regime built on centralized protection and low violence, in Buenos Aires.

EPILOGUE: DID WE CHANGE?

In October 2015, the people of Buenos Aires elected a non-Peronist governor for the first time in thirty-two years. The media report portraying the Peronist candidate as a drug trafficker narrated in this chapter's introduction (see Section, "Overview") certainly influenced this outcome. The new governor, PRO (*Propuesta Republicana*) politician María Eugenia Vidal, promised to fight drug trafficking and cleanse the provincial police, in line with her coalition's name, Let's Change. She instituted mandatory filing of income tax returns and doping tests. Police responded by ransacking the offices and homes of the governor and her ministers, and (once again) kidnappings increased. The governor relocated herself and her children to a military base, where she spent her entire term. Following this initial resistance, however, conflict between the administration and police abated. The government did not pass any further meaningful reforms.

Nonetheless, the security situation in the province did not deteriorate, even despite worsening economic indicators. Criminal violence actually decreased during Vidal's tenure: Homicide rates fell from 7.3 per 100,000 individuals in 2015 to 5.2 per 100,000 individuals in 2019.[73] Police lethal violence decreased as well. The human rights NGO CELS registered 368 police fatal shootings in Greater Buenos Aires between 2016 and 2019, an average of 92 a year, whereas there were 446 (111.5 average) during the previous four years (2012–2015). Finally, the number of murdered police dropped as well: There were 110 police killed during Vidal's administration in contrast with 134 during Scioli's second term.

These numbers indicate that, contrary to expectations of what happens when a new government takes power – especially after a prolonged period of party rule – the regulation of crime did not deteriorate into greater violence. It is possible that the administration, a newcomer in a broad coalition with divided government, managed to achieve police loyalty, efficiency and integrity. However, the government did not make significant reforms to professionalize the police, who seem to retain most of their historical rackets. In short, the administration could have agreed to tolerate high-level police corruption, while cracking down on lower-ranking officers, to maintain lower levels of crime, as their Peronist predecessors did, to prevent backlash from the institution.

During the twenty-eight consecutive years of Peronist rule in the province of Buenos Aires, protection rackets prevailed but for brief, albeit furious, periods of internecine disputes. For most of this period, governments sidelined reform, politicized the police and used it to run protection rackets from which they benefited politically if not materially. The following chapter illustrates how governments can professionalize police to establish a regime of coordinated coexistence, based on tolerance of crime rather than its protection for material gain.

---

[73] National Ministry of Security Crime Statistics Report, 2019. Available upon request. Data from the Provincial Prosecutor's Office also confirms a substantial drop in homicides in the province.

6

Coordinated Coexistence

The Consolidation of a Police–Gang Truce in São Paulo

OVERVIEW: "O ACORDO DE CAVALHEIROS
[A GENTLEMEN'S AGREEMENT]"

"*Você nunca tem visto uma biqueira?* [You've never seen a drug den before?]" Corporal X asked after he picked me up at the train station in one of the southern neighborhoods of São Paulo's sprawling metropolis. We started driving to his house and I noticed he didn't put on his seatbelt. I asked him why and he said he wanted to have more mobility to reach for his gun in case he was attacked by members of the state's most important gang, the Primeiro Comando da Capital (First Command of the Capital, PCC). On the way, he identified at least ten locations he knew to be drug selling points: a store with a hair salon on the bottom floor; a narrow passageway; a run-down public park; and several vacant lots. When I asked him about the government's response to the PCC, he told me that there was an "*acordo de cavalheiros*" (gentleman's agreement) between the state and the gang "not to mess with each other." This phrase synthesizes São Paulo's distinctive regulatory arrangement: *coordinated coexistence*, which contained violence even though, as the Corporal's behavior indicates, police officers still feel threatened and, one might presume, criminals as well. This chapter explains how this regime emerged and persisted for more than two decades.

This arrangement, however, did not always exist. São Paulo's regulation of drug trafficking initially resembled that of Rio de Janeiro (Chapter 3). Following the democratic opening in 1982, high partisan turnover and fragmentation increased the autonomy enjoyed by the state police, which maintained corrupt and violent practices deployed during the dictatorship. In turn, high police autonomy led to the emergence of *particularistic confrontation* as the main regulatory arrangement of drug trafficking and crime, consisting of dispersed violence and corruption by both Military and Civil Police forces.

However, in the mid-1990s politicians began to restrict police autonomy. Partisan turnover ceased: Between 1994 and 2018, the Brazilian Social Democratic party (Partido da Social Democracia Brasileira, PSDB) won all state executive elections in São Paulo. At the same time, political fragmentation remained high. Despite its executive dominance, the PSDB could never achieve a majority in the state legislature. Furthermore, it often faced highly competitive elections, mostly against conservative, pro-law-and-order parties, which it defeated in runoff contests, and had to form broad coalitions to govern. This political fragmentation explains why successive administrations opted to professionalize the state police and ultimately favored a regime of coordinated coexistence, unlike what we observed in Buenos Aires in the previous chapter, where the ruling party took advantage of far fewer checks from the opposition to politicize the police and deploy protection rackets as a regulatory strategy.

The professionalization of the São Paulo police reduced deaths from police interventions and contributed to a massive drop in criminal violence in São Paulo since 2000. Furthermore, it enabled a *coordinated coexistence* regulatory arrangement of drug trafficking, which appeared most clearly since 2006, when the state sanctioned an implicit truce with the Primeiro Comando da Capital (PCC, First Command of the Capital), the strongest drug gang in São Paulo, if not in Brazil.

This pact stabilized low levels of violence by both police and criminals, yet the initial decrease in these indicators preceded its sanction. Therefore, one cannot solely attribute the relative peace in São Paulo to the PCC's dominance of the drug market. In this chapter, I will show how the state's policies contributed to the growth and hegemony of the PCC. Table 6.1 summarizes this intertemporal evolution.

Alternative Explanations

Few would dispute my argument that São Paulo represents a case of a relatively ordered drug market with a tacit coexistence between police and the main drug gang, the PCC. A greater dissonance, however, springs with respect to the reasons for the emergence of this regime, especially the role of the police – and the politicians behind them. The first disagreement

TABLE 6.1. *Political turnover, fragmentation, police autonomy and drug trafficking regulatory arrangements in São Paulo, 1983–2014*

Period	Turnover	Fragmentation	Police autonomy	Drug trafficking regulatory arrangement
1983–1994	*High* Turnover between PMDB factions	*High* No legislative majority Divided cabinets	*High* No reform No political control of police rent extraction	*Particularistic confrontation* High violence by police and criminals High and anarchic corruption
1995–2014	*Low* Continuity in power of PSDB	*High* No legislative majority Unified cabinets	*Low* Reform Political restriction of police rent extraction	*Coordinated coexistence* Low police and criminal violence Frequent but nonpredatory corruption

Source: Author's elaboration

is that the relative peace in São Paulo is predominantly a function of the PCC's temperance of crime in the periphery (Feltran 2011; Dias 2013), regardless of the state's intervention. Other accounts do include the police as key interlocutors with criminal actors. For example, Graham Denyer Willis' fantastic ethnography refers to an "unspoken consensus" on legitimate killings between the police and the PCC as the logic behind the violence – or lack thereof – in São Paulo (Denyer Willis 2015). However, it does not, probably for reasons of disciplinary focus, venture into the political determinants of such interactions.

There are at least two problems with these explanations. On the one hand, this perspective overlooks the fact that homicide rates in the state began to decrease in the early 2000s before the truce brokered with the PCC in 2006. In part, this drop traces to different political initiatives to prevent crime implemented by the police (see Freire 2018). On the other hand, and more importantly, these narratives overlook the political conditions that have led police to contain their penchant for violence in order for the truce to be effective. In other words, police professionalization, as opposed to rampant killings (and corruption) of the type predominant in Rio de Janeiro (Chapter 4), has a political explanation behind it.

That brings us to the second disagreement, which is that it is remiss to speak of police professionalization, much less reform, in the case of São Paulo. Yanilda González's book, for instance, makes a convincing case that *paulista* governors enacted superficial changes to deflect popular discontent with police brutality without modifying its organization, structure or functions. She proposes that the lack of electoral threats to the PSDB's claim to the governorship impeded more profound police transformations (González 2020). This argument certainly has merit. Police-related deaths and nonlethal violence continues, especially directed at poor, young men of color (Alves 2018). While horrendous practices like use of torture devices in police stations have perhaps faded, police violence and its associated corruption undoubtedly persists.

I do not deny that São Paulo's police are far from being a democratic security force. At the same time, it is necessary to place São Paulo in a comparative perspective, both with other cases and with its own past. First, while still undoubtedly high, levels of police lethality in São Paulo are substantially lower than those in Rio de Janeiro, except for the brief interval of Pacification's success (2008–2013, see Chapter 3). In the absence of broad reform, incremental policies governing the use of lethal force have certainly not eliminated violence but have at least reduced the frequency with which police applied it. Second, it is also important to follow the evolution of police's relationship with the government over time to understand why police violence declined (if slightly) and remained relatively stable since the mid-1990s. While the police openly confronted Governor Franco Montoro's reformist initiatives in the 1980s, they acquiesced to similar proposals in subsequent administrations. While González argues that the lack of political competition reduces incentives for more aggressive reforms, I argue that it enabled the solidification of incremental changes, whereas in previous situations, it had served to undermine those initiatives. Just as the state's rampant response to crime, especially drug trafficking, fueled the growth of the PCC in its prison system, the state's more moderate – albeit still violent – response in the ensuing decades enabled the gang to maintain its hegemony. In short, accounts of the relative peace in São Paulo not only need to address the role of both the police and the PCC, but also to recognize the changes in police behavior that make this agreement possible.

THE POLICE THAT KILL: São PAULO AFTER
REDEMOCRATIZATION, 1983–1994

Failed Reforms and Punitive Shifts

Both the Military (PM) and Civil Police (PC) in São Paulo have a long record of inefficiency, corruption and human rights abuses. Several studies point to the Civil Police force's historical use of torture to extract confessions or bribes from detainees (Mingardi 1992; Chevigny 1995, 149). During the dictatorship, the Civil Police formed death squads (*esquadrões da morte*) to take out suspected criminals in a perverse attempt to keep up with the fiercer Military Police (Huggins 1991; Bicudo 2002). The São Paulo PM has a well-earned reputation as one of the most violent police forces in the country. Between 1980 and 2000, it killed over 10,000 people, far more than during twenty years of dictatorship in all Brazil. In particular, the ROTA,[1] the PM's elite squad – akin to Rio de Janeiro's BOPE – registered over 3,500 murders between the 1970s and the early 1990s (Barcellos 2005, 318, 328). The ROTA killed indiscriminately and arbitrarily: Most of its victims had no prior criminal records, did not carry firearms at the time of death – sometimes these were planted by the officers involved – and often exhibited execution-style gunshot wounds in the back (Barcellos 2005). Its brutality earned it the moniker "*a polícia que mata*" (the police that kill), which could also have applied to the entire São Paulo police.

During the first decade of the democratic period, high political turnover and high fragmentation in São Paulo hindered the state government's efforts to reduce police autonomy. In 1983, elected Governor Franco Montoro, from the PMDB, promised to conduct a major reform of the police, like that attempted by Leonel Brizola in Rio de Janeiro (Caldeira 2000, 165), although he focused primarily on the Civil Police, over which the state government had greater formal control. He initially appointed pro-human rights secretaries of Security and Justice, strengthened the Civil Police's internal Auditing Agency (*Corregedoria*), created the Community Security Councils (*Consegs*),[2] and even though he could

---

[1] "ROTA" stands for *Rondas Ostensivas Tobias de Aguiar* (Tobias de Aguiar Ostensive Rounds), in recognition of the PM's historical patron.
[2] The CONSEGs were created by State Decree 23.455 (1985) and regulated by resolution SSP-37 (1985).

not dissolve the ROTA, took several of its most notorious killers off the street.

However, Montoro faced heavy political opposition, even from within his own party, which weakened his capacity to control the police. His own vice-governor, Orestes Quércia, from the PMDB's conservative faction, campaigned against Montoro's chosen candidates for key elections, including the mayoralty of São Paulo. In addition, Montoro lacked a legislative majority, and his proposals drew criticism from across the political spectrum, which decried his plan to withdraw the ROTA from the streets (Mingardi 1992; Caldeira 2000, 170).

Montoro also encountered heavy police resistance. Police officers dragged their feet to delay the implementation of the reform, sabotaged it through deliberate acts of violence and openly rebelled against it in the streets (Mingardi 1992; González 2020). Political opposition emboldened police to protest against the administration. For example, during the 1986 municipal campaign, several Civil Police delegates signed a manifesto criticizing the reform (Caldeira 2000, 166). Montoro ended up partially reversing these initiatives at the end of his term, and police autonomy remained largely undisturbed (Pinheiro et al. 1991).

In the next two election cycles, politicians from different factions in the governing PMDB turned against each other. This high partisan turnover generated frequent, drastic switches in the government's stance toward security and policing. Montoro's vice-governor, Quércia, won the state election in 1986. Along with his security secretary – former ROTA officer and subsequent governor, Luiz Antônio Fleury Filho – Quércia reversed Montoro's reforms and adopted a punitive approach to control crime. Both Quércia and Fleury explicitly supported "tougher police" that "acted boldly" (Caldeira 2000, 170–72) and upheld the creed "*bandido bom é bandido morto*" (a good criminal is a dead criminal). Although winning the 1990 election with Quércia's support, Fleury then accused his predecessor of corruption and leisurely spending, raising the tension between the two leaders.[3] Fleury's administration particularly favored punitive policies. Reversing Montoro's mandate, he remobilized the ROTA and provided it with new cars and equipment. Already beset by internal differences, the PMDB split in 1988, as its more progressive leaders left to form the PSDB, including former governor, Montoro,

---

[3] Fleury left the PMDB at the end of his administration and returned to the party after Quércia's death. "Com morte de Quércia, Fleury Filho volta ao PMDB," *Valor Econômico*, August 10, 2011.

future president, Fernando Henrique Cardoso and future governors, Mário Covas Jr., Geraldo Alckmin and José Serra.[4]

Particularistic Confrontation: Creating an Enemy

The high police autonomy during the 1983–1994 period resulted in particularistic confrontation as the predominant regulatory arrangement against drug trafficking and crime in general. Drug consumption, incipient in the 1980s, expanded in the 1990s, especially that of white powder and crack cocaine. While the Narcotics division detained only 284 individuals for drug-related offenses in 1991, it arrested 689 people in 1996 (Mingardi 1999, 14). The drug business was also highly fragmented: Around 80 percent of those arrested for trafficking sold crack stones – single doses, worth between USD $3 and $8 – and small amounts of marijuana (Mingardi 1999, 21; 2001, 380). São Paulo's drug market lacked a centralized territorial control by organized criminal actors.

Meanwhile, police lethal violence escalated during Montoro's tenure, probably to destabilize the government's reforms (Mingardi 1992; Caldeira 2000) and worsened during the enabling administrations of Quércia and Fleury. Fleury's first two years in office were the bloodiest in São Paulo to date, with 1,140 casualties from police intervention in 1991 and 1,470 in 1992. The paradigmatic example of institutional violence promoted by the Fleury administration was the execution of 111 prisoners, who had already surrendered, in the Carandiru prison on October 2, 1992.[5] This episode would play a central role in the history of drug trafficking in São Paulo. After this incident sparked massive local and international outrage, the government was forced to rein in the police. Hence, the number of police fatalities dropped to 409 the following year.[6]

It is more difficult to provide a systematic account of police corruption since there was no external controlling mechanism at the time, indicative

---

[4] "Conheça trajetória política do ex-governador Orestes Quércia, que morreu hoje aos 72 anos," *O Globo*, December 24, 2010.

[5] In a display of the impunity and inefficiency of the São Paulo judicial system, twenty-three police were convicted of these murders only in 2013, more than twenty years after the event. The commander, in turn, was acquitted in 2006. See "Police sentenced over Brazil Carandiru jail massacre," *BBC*, April 3, 2014.

[6] Nonetheless, several politicians and social sectors supported the police's violent intervention. Some former police officers even ran for office with '111' as their electoral identification number, celebrating the number of deaths that took place in the prison.

of the force's high autonomy. In 1999, the *Ouvidoria* (Police Ombudsman) reported that the organ in charge of monitoring corruption complaints – the *Conselho Justificativo* (Justification Council) – was extremely bureaucratic, slow and inefficient. An in-depth study on Montoro's reform in the Civil Police suggested that traditional corrupt practices, frequently associated with torture and other violations of detainees' rights, continued during this period (Mingardi 1992). Furthermore, the heads of the Civil Police under Quércia and Fleury were sentenced to prison after their mandates, convicted of organizing corrupt procurement processes during these governors' administrations.[7] Police corruption in São Paulo, as in Rio and most Brazilian police forces, was high and mostly uncoordinated, unlike the coordinated corruption exhibited in Buenos Aires (Chapter 5) or initially in Santa Fe (Chapter 4).

The state's uncoordinated violent and corrupt regulatory approach enticed criminals to organize against it. The criminal gang PCC emerged in the prison of Tabuaté in 1993, to defend the rights of prisoners who were housed in abhorrent conditions and subject to constant abuse by prison personnel, as the Carandiru massacre exemplified. For most of the 1990s, the PCC remained primarily a prison gang, although its members also engaged in different organized criminal activities outside the prisons, such as kidnapping, bank robberies, murders and extortion, and executed several impressive prison breakouts. For a long time, government officials refused to acknowledge the PCC's importance and claimed it was little more than a media fabrication (Souza 2007). The government's initial passivity enabled the PCC to expand its control of the prison system and eventually become the most powerful criminal gang in São Paulo. Its relationship with the state would considerably change during the following decade.

PSDB CONSOLIDATION AND POLICE PROFESSIONALIZATION, 1995–2014

After the conservative governments of Quércia and Fleury, the second attempt at police reform came during the first administration of Mário Covas, Jr., starting in 1995. Covas, one of the founding members of PSDB, led his party to narrow victories in the 1994 and 1998 gubernatorial elections, both times defeating populist-right wing candidates in the

---

[7] See "Ex-chefes da Polícia são condenados à prisão em São Paulo," *Folha de São Paulo*, December 6, 2005.

second round.[8] Following Covas' death in 2001, the PSDB would win the following five gubernatorial elections – 2002–2018 – consolidating itself as the dominant party in São Paulo (see Table 6.2).

Their political stability enabled PSDB governors to implement and sustain several initiatives to reduce police autonomy. On the one hand, PSDB administrations faced high political fragmentation. In their twenty years in power, the PSDB never gained more than 25 percent of the seats in the State Assembly (see Figure 6.1). As shown in Table 6.2, all PSDB governors secured power through electoral coalitions – and the first three after runoffs.[9] This fragmented scenario inhibited the administration from centrally capturing illicit rents and motivated it to control the police to avoid other politicians profiting from it. On the other hand, these governments displayed less internal fragmentation – in other words, cabinet splits – than in the other cases analyzed in this book, which afforded greater coherence to their policies. In short, while the lack of turnover made reducing police autonomy possible, fragmentation made police professionalization necessary.

The Tucanos in Charge of the Police

Despite having a legislative minority, the Covas administrations (1995–2001) managed to sanction several initiatives that reduced the police's autonomy.[10] On his first day in office, Covas created the figure of police ombudsman "to monitor irregular acts committed by police," and appointed the head of a well-known human rights group to preside over it.[11] He also instated the Recycling Program for Officers Involved in High Risk Situations (*Programa de Reciclagem de Policiais Envolvidos em Situações de Alto Risco*, PROAR) by which all police officers involved in fatal shootings were temporally taken off the streets (Caldeira 2000, 179; author's interview with Guaracy Mingardi). Through these initiatives, the government sought to restrain police rent extraction and abuse of lethal force, two key features of the force's autonomy.

The governor accelerated reforms after the infamous massacre at Favela Naval on March 3, 1997, in which Military Police officers were

---

[8] Governors – and other executives in Brazil – can run for reelection since the 16th constitutional amendment of 1997.

[9] This trend would shift after 2006, as Serra and Alckmin earned resounding first-round electoral victories in 2006, 2010 and 2014.

[10] Tucanos (toucans) is the popular name by which members of the PSDB are known.

[11] Decree n. 39.900, January 1, 1995. www.dhnet.org.br/dados/livros/dh/br/livro_santo dias/06_nasceouvidoria.htm.

TABLE 6.2. *Governors' electoral performance in São Paulo, 1983–2014*

Election year	Governor[a]	Party[b]	Coalition	Winner's vote share (margin of victory)
1982	Franco Montoro	PMDB	None	44.92 (21.4)
1986	Orestes Quércia	PMDB**	(PMDB, PSB, PC do B, PCB)	40.78 (13.9)
1990	Luiz Antônio Fleury	PMDB**	(PMDB, PL, PFL, PSD, PTdoB, PTR)	28.17 (3.5) **
1994	Mário Covas	PSDB	PSDB/PFL	46.84 (12.2) **
1998	Mário Covas – Geraldo Alckmin*	PSDB	PTB / PSD / PSDB	22.95 (10.7) **
2002	Geraldo Alckmin – Cláudio Lembo*	PSDB	PSDB / PFL / PSD	38.28 (17.2) **
2006	José Serra	PSDB	PSDB/PFL/PTB/ PPS	57 (26)
2010	Geraldo Alckmin	PSDB	N/A	50.59 (15.3)
2014	Geraldo Alckmin	PSDB	PSDB / DEM / PEN / PMN / PT do B / PTC / PTN / SD / PPS / PRB / PSB / PSC / PSDC / PSL	57 (36)
2018	João Doria	PSDB	PSDB / DEM / PSD / PRB / PP / PTC	31.77 (10)

[a] (*) Indicates that the vice-governor finished the term after governor resigned
[b] (**) Indicates that the new governor belongs to the same party but a different faction than his predecessor, in other words, there is partisan turnover.
Source: Author's elaboration from *Tribunal Superior Eleitoral* (TSE)

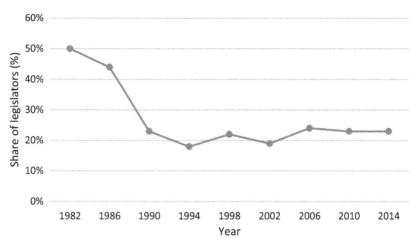

FIGURE 6.1. Governor's party share of legislative seats, São Paulo (1982–2014)
Source: Author's elaboration from Tribunal Superior Eleitoral (TSE, High Electoral Court).

filmed humiliating, torturing and executing residents. Covas publicly apologized for the event and described the scenes as "deplorable." He sent a large reform package to the legislature.[12] He also sponsored a law formalizing the Ombudsperson's Office by law, which was approved unanimously. After initial resistance from the police leadership, in December 1997, the new commander of the Military Police presented a community policing proposal "to protect the life, liberty, equality and integrity of all persons" (Neme 1999, 87), the first time that the PM explicitly recognized the importance of protecting human rights, following the recommendations of the ombudsperson. The PM also began training its soldiers with a new method, developed by one its own colonels, which focused on deescalation techniques and using firearms to minimize third party casualties. These programs remain in place today.

Covas' administration also reduced police autonomy through clear and consistent policy objectives and alternative crime control initiatives. By the late 1990s, São Paulo's homicide rates were increasing rapidly, peaking at 35 per 100,000 individuals in the State with over 50 in the Capital and Greater Metropolitan Region. Covas' administration made reducing homicides a top priority. Instead of promoting punitive policing, as Quércia and Fleury did, the government invested heavily in alternative

---

[12] "Dez anos depois, tragédia vira lição," *Secretaria de Segurança Pública*, March 5, 2007. www.ssp.sp.gov.br/noticia/lenoticia.aspx?id=8045.

crime control policies with concrete goals to guide police behavior, such as an ambitious disarmament plan. As former Security Secretary Petrelluzzi told me, "We forced the police to apprehend weapons. We apprehended around ten, twelve thousand weapons each month and it was mandatory for patrols to do this in four or five neighborhoods each night."[13] The administration also imposed curfews on bars and night-clubs to reduce violence provoked by excessive alcohol consumption and installed a CompStat system to monitor police officers using real-time data (Veloso and Ferreira 2008; Goertzel and Kahn 2009).[14] The government tested these initiatives first in the city's most violent neighborhoods – "the corpse suppliers," as a former Civil Police chief referred to them in our interview – so that "the police regained the trust of the community."[15]

The Covas administration also created specialized divisions within the Civil Police to investigate homicides and kidnappings. According to the former head of the State Division of Homicides and Personal Protection (*Delegacia Estadual de Homicídios e Proteção a Pessoas*, DHPP), the government "territorialized the specialized police and specialized the territorial police."[16] In other words, the administration placed the specialized DHPP alongside territorial Civil Police precincts to increase the homicide clearance rate and reduce perceptions of impunity. The government also strengthened specialized divisions to investigate organized crime – the State Department of Criminal Investigations (*Departamento Estadual de Investigações Criminais*, DEIC) – and drug trafficking – the State Department of Prevention and Repression of Narcotics (*Departamento Estadual de Prevenção e Repressão ao Narcotráfico*, DENARC) – a policy most subsequent administrations maintained.

Covas consolidated his reformist proposals during his second term. His two security secretaries – José de Afonso (1995–1999) and Marco Petrelluzzi (1999–2002) – former members of Montoro's administration, combined compromises with the police with firm decisions that increased the government's control of the force. They instilled a culture of respect

---

[13] Interview by author with former Security Secretary Marco Petrelluzzi, São Paulo, November 12, 2014.

[14] The state government first tested this program in the high-crime neighborhood of Diadema and then expanded it to the rest of the city and metropolitan area.

[15] Interview by author with former Chief of Civil Police, Marco Desgualdo, São Paulo, November 5, 2014.

[16] Interview by author with former Division Chief, Domingos Paulo Neto, who would then become the chief of the Civil Police, São Paulo, November 12, 2014.

for human rights in the Military Police to restrain its use of lethal force, while also improving its equipment, technology and overall professionalization. When I interviewed him, former Secretary Petrelluzzi stated that, "There was a saying in São Paulo that you couldn't control the police; it's baloney. We set goals and they complied with most of them." He also stressed the importance of politicians' discourse in limiting police actions:

> With the police, it is like this: You make a speech that you think is only for the crowd, but the police are listening. So, if you say things like [raises voice], "Police will be hard! It will confront crime! It will leave no stone unturned!" [bangs on the table] the cop on the street thinks that you're freeing him up and he goes full steam ahead.[17]

Petrelluzzi also told me how he attempted to foster collaboration between the PM and PC, giving them policy targets and holding them accountable for reaching them:

> When I took office, I noticed that the jurisdictions of both police were anachronistic, noncompatible. The first decision I made was to unify these areas and make them compatible. Afterward, we tried to create integrated work routines because it was fundamental to have accountability for either success or failure. How do you do that? Every month, territorial chiefs, the PM Captain, and the head delegate, had to turn in a signed report, talking about the crime problems in the area and proposing ways to confront it. That was necessary to be promoted. It was the only way I could find.[18]

Following Covas' death in 2001, his successor, Geraldo Alckmin, invited Petrelluzzi to remain in his post and continue these initiatives. After Alckmin won the 2002 election, Petrelluzzi resigned and was replaced by fellow state prosecutor Saulo Castro Abreu. Although Saulo was, according to Petrelluzzi, against his position on human rights, the government's course did not change drastically. Saulo kept the main authorities of the Military and Civil Police, as well as those of the main specialized divisions, and maintained the crime prevention programs begun during Covas' administration, such as disarmament, community policing and witness protection programs (Sapori 2007).

After Alckmin left to run for president in 2006, José Serra – the PSDB mayor of São Paulo at the time – won the state gubernatorial election.

---

[17] Interview by author with former Security Secretary Petrelluzzi, São Paulo, November 12, 2014. Caldeira describes a similar episode involving a dialogue between Montoro's secretary Reale and Fleury in 1986 (Caldeira 2000, 168–69).

[18] Interview by author with former Security Secretary Petrelluzzi, São Paulo, November 12, 2014.

Serra's first security secretary, Ronaldo Marzagão (2007–2009), continued the reforms established during the Covas administration.[19] Two of his core principles were to "Privilege intelligence over force [and] to guarantee security while preserving basic human rights."[20] In this sense, he created the Center for Integrated Intelligence for Security (*Centro de Inteligência Integrada para Segurança*, CIISP) and frequently monitored Military Police operations personally to deter unnecessary use of violence. He particularly recalled an uprising in the favela of Paraisópolis, in which four military police officers were shot but no PM fired back, which signaled the government's effective control of police lethality. Marzagão resigned in 2009, the result of extreme stress (he recalled, "We had to deal with over 12,000 calls on a normal day, without emergencies") and a corruption scandal involving his undersecretary. Nonetheless, his resignation did not dissipate the government's efforts to restrain the police.

Although Marzagão's successor, Antônio Ferreira Pinto, favored harsher law-and-order policies, the reduction of police autonomy persisted. For instance, Ferreira Pinto preserved the Community Security Councils, or Consegs – originally conceived by the Montoro administration – a participatory institution for citizens to relay problems to the police and hold them accountable for their performance.[21] However, Ferreira Pinto eased pressure on the PM and focused primarily on the Civil Police, which had been involved in the corruption scandal that led to Marzagão's resignation. Ferreira Pinto's most significant decision was to place the PC's Internal Affairs division (*Corregedoria*) directly under his control.[22] During his first year in office, he opened more than 7,500 internal reviews of Civil Police officials, forcing 81 of them to leave the force, and admonishing another 500.[23] He also transferred leading Civil Police officers from central to peripheral police stations. Moreover,

---

[19] Marzagão had also been a member of Franco Montoro's original cabinet (1983–1986).

[20] Interview by author with former Security Secretary Ronaldo Marzagão, São Paulo, November 13, 2014.

[21] Conseg participants meet every month, with the presence of the district's Military and Civil Police commanders. There are 84 Consegs in the Capital, 55 in the metropolitan Region and 337 in the Interior. www.conseg.sp.gov.br/historia.aspx. For more, see González (2020).

[22] Former Civil Police Chief Domingos Paulo Neto, told me he objected to this initiative because the PC had been, in his mind, efficient in controlling itself internally (Interview by author, São Paulo, November 12, 2014). Ferreira Pinto did not apply the same measure to the Military Police force, which retained its Internal Affairs Division.

[23] "Conheça Antônio Ferreira Pinto, o secretário de Segurança Pública," *Veja*, April 30, 2010.

Ferreira Pinto relied increasingly on the elite squad ROTA to lead investigations against the PCC drug gang, a decision which would have dire consequences for the regulation of drug trafficking and criminal violence in the state.

After Geraldo Alckmin won the 2010 state election, Secretary Ferreira Pinto, the heads of the Military and Civil Police and the commander of the ROTA maintained their posts, an unfamiliar occurrence in the other cases in this book (and in Latin America in general).[24] The head of the Military Police, Colonel Camilo, told me he was invited to stay because "In 2010, safety was so good it was not an issue in the election."[25] Colonel Camilo not only endorsed the administration's reforms but also maintained the support of his troops to implement these changes. He switched the ammunition used by the force, ditching previous calibers that passed through the bodies of intended targets and hit innocent bystanders.[26] He also tried to convey a different response to cases of lethal violence. After the PM murdered a delivery boy in 2009, Camilo immediately reached out to the media and human rights groups to explain that the PM did not accept these actions and expelled the officers involved. These examples illustrate how an internally coherent government reduced dissent within the police and enabled police professionalization to persist.

Unlike during Montoro's tenure, the police barely resisted the PSDB's initiatives. For instance, when in September 2008 an association of Civil Police delegates went on strike to demand better wages and working conditions, the government repressed it through the Military Police without major repercussions. By contrast, police officers have shirked their crime control duties or heavily repressed social protests to undermine the former mayor of the city of São Paulo, Fernando Haddad, a member of the PT (Workers' party), who was not aligned with the governor.[27]

Leaving "the Police that Kill" Behind

As the government endowed the police with more defined security goals, better training procedures and alternative conflict resolution mechanisms,

---

[24] The only other similar instance took place in Rio de Janeiro, as Security Secretary Beltrame remained in his post following the transition from Sérgio Cabral to Luiz Pezão in 2013.

[25] Interview by author with former Military Police Commander General Colonel Camilo, São Paulo, October 30, 2014.

[26] Interview by author with Colonel Camilo, São Paulo, October 30, 2014. See also "Comandante-geral da PM: 'o pior bandido é o de farda,'" *Veja*, April 30, 2010.

[27] González 2020.

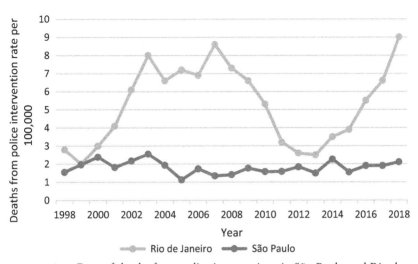

FIGURE 6.2. Rate of deaths from police interventions in São Paulo and Rio de Janeiro (1998–2019)
Source: Author's elaboration from São Paulo's and Rio de Janeiro's Secretariat of Public Security.

institutional violence decreased and then remained stable. Deaths from police intervention declined compared to the previous period (1983–1994), especially during Covas' first term (1995–1998). Police violence increased slightly between 1999 and 2003 although at a slower rate than during the 1980s; it then decreased and remained stable until 2014. Since 1998, the rate of police homicides in São Paulo has mostly hovered around 2 per 100,000 individuals. It is by no means small, but certainly lower than the rates of police violence observed in Rio de Janeiro, which fluctuated much more drastically and reached up to 9 per 100,000 people in 2019 (see Figure 6.2).

A further measure of police brutality is the ratio of dead to wounded civilians resulting from police interventions. A higher ratio suggests that police primarily shoot to kill rather than to immobilize a suspect (Pérez Correa et al. 2020). According to the Center for the Study of Violence of the University of São Paulo (*Núcleo de Estudos da Violência, Universidade de São Paulo*, NEV/USP) this ratio, which had increased up to 8:1 in 1992, decreased and remained below 1:1 afterward (see Figure 6.3). In other words, while São Paulo's police killed eight people for every one they wounded in 1992, they killed one person for every wounded person in subsequent years, when, as we have seen, police lethality rates were also lower. This trend suggests that PSDB administrations managed to restrain police lethality *before* the start of the truce

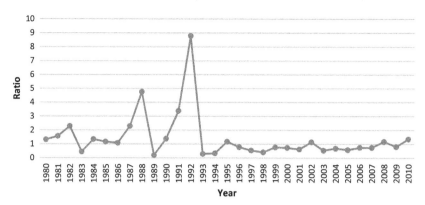

FIGURE 6.3. Ratio of dead to wounded civilians as a result of police intervention
(1980–2010)
Source: Banco de Dados da Imprensa – Núcleo de Estudos da Violência/Universidade de São
Paulo (NEV/USP, Newspaper database – Center for the Study of Violence, University of São
Paulo).

with the PCC in 2006. In other words, it was the government's initiative
and not only the gang's strength which led to this change in policing
behavior.

Since Covas' first term (1995–1999), Military Police commanders have
complied with the government's mandate to reduce the force's propensity
for lethal violence. One way to achieve this goal was through changes in
police training. As former PM Commander Colonel Camilo told me, after
the massacre in Favela Naval in 1997, "The commander at the time,
Carlos Alberto Camargo, created a human rights commission in the PM
and the police placed a human rights course in all of its curricula. Also,
[Camargo] brought these human rights concepts to all other courses, such
as approach procedures, and then created the Human Rights department
in the PM, I think in 2000."[28]

Other mid-ranking officers corroborated this aspect of the Military
Police's professionalization. A current PM captain emphasized the
importance of police training in improving relations with the community
and reducing police mistreatment, "There are courses, constant special-
ization. There is a great focus in improving the police's relation with the
community, which has improved a lot. We have not had complaints or
allegations of mistreatment lately."[29]

[28] Interview by author with Colonel Camilo, São Paulo, October 30, 2014.
[29] Interview by author with Military Police captain, Eastern Zone precinct, São Paulo,
November 6, 2014.

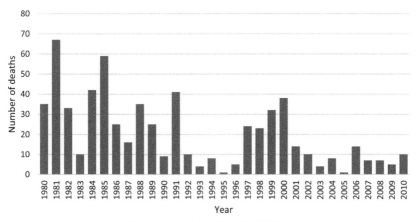

FIGURE 6.4. Number of deaths resulting from ROTA operations (1980–2010)
Source: Author's elaboration from NEV/USP.

Lower-level officers were more skeptical. A young soldier from the same precinct explained a problem generated by the renewed training, "It's contradictory, because if I go on patrol with a more experienced cop, who was educated with the logic of the 1970s – the dictatorship and fighting guerrillas – and he wants to hit a suspect, I can't say anything. Even if we are of the same rank, if he has one more year of experience than me, he is my superior. At the same time, I took over 100 hours of human rights courses."[30] Despite the restrictions to police violence, there are still issues to resolve on this matter.

Another indication of the administration's restrictions of police brutality is that the number of fatalities caused by the elite squad ROTA also declined during this period, particularly after 2000 (see Figure 6.4). Unlike in Fleury's administration, most PSDB governments contained the ROTA instead of using it as the main instrument to combat crime and drug trafficking. The Tucanos' ability to control the elite squad also contrasted with Montoro's administration (1983–1986), which endured an increase in ROTA violence, as the spike in 1984–1985 shows.

Furthermore, while previously the ROTA intervened without political authorization, presently, most operations are agreed upon with the political leadership, at least according to one of its current commanders. This commander stated that, "The force has become more technical and less

---

[30] Interview by author with Military Police soldier, Eastern Zone precinct, São Paulo, November 6, 2014.

political in choosing where and how it acts," using tools such as geo-referencing to distribute its personnel according to crime hotspots in the state, another sign of professionalization.[31]

PSDB governments have also professionalized the Civil Police, notorious for torturing detainees to extract bribes and confessions. A current PC delegate described how these practices changed, "Thirty years ago, police worked with the system from the dictatorship, which consisted in getting information through torture. That does not exist anymore. Technology has replaced torture as a way of getting information by the police. Of course, there are still [members] of the old guard who still cling to these practices. Today the investigator does not need a gun; he needs to learn how to use a laptop."[32] The PC's acceptance of these changes implied a restriction of its everyday rent extraction, something that Montoro's administration tried but failed to limit.

Notwithstanding these relevant changes, police violence in São Paulo remains high. In 2009, a Human Rights Watch report documented 397 killings by on-duty police the previous year filed as "homicides resulting from police intervention," and therefore considered legitimate, although several casualties showed evident markings of summary executions (HRW 2009, 22). Furthermore, there were over 500 killings by presumed police death squads between 2006 and 2008 (HRW 2009, 44). Finally, the report unmasked persistent police malpractice in the investigation of these homicides, including frequent cover-ups. Nonetheless, police lethal violence has decreased significantly since the first democratic administrations and is certainly more restrained than in Rio de Janeiro, the other Brazilian case analyzed in this book.

Controlling Police Corruption

While police corruption in São Paulo is still problematic, most interviewees noted that it had few (if any) links with trafficking or the PCC and was rare among the top police ranks, unlike what we saw in Santa Fe (Chapter 4) or Buenos Aires (Chapter 5). Former secretaries Petrelluzzi and Marzagão downplayed the magnitude of corruption in the force. Former PM Commander Colonel Camilo recounted that, at least during

---

[31] Interview by author with the operational commander of ROTA, São Paulo, November 21, 2014.

[32] Interview by author with current Civil Police investigator, Southern Zone of São Paulo, November 18, 2014.

his tenure, slot machine rackets were more frequent than corruption related to drug trafficking.

During the Tucanos' administrations, no PM commander or PC chief has been forced to resign under allegations of corruption. There was only one major scandal involving corrupt government officials: In 2008, the undersecretary of security took bribes for wiping the records of various Civil Police officers who had participated in racketeering. It is important to point out that other officials in the Civil Police uncovered this scheme, whereas, in the other cases, an external actor, such as the federal police, had exposed this corrupt behavior (see Chapters 4 and 5 on Rosario and Buenos Aires). While acknowledging the government's pact with the PCC since 2006, opposition politicians, police officers and other observers I interviewed did not accuse governors or security secretaries of taking money from drug trafficking, either by themselves or through the police.

Police corruption in São Paulo during the PSDB tenure is less extensive and more rigorously monitored than in the other cases analyzed in this book. PSDB administrations have not only tried to control police corruption through the Ombudsperson's office but also by enhancing internal controls within the police and improving their training. Some higher-ranking military and civil police officers, while recognizing extant corruption, also hinted at police efforts to control and punish it internally. For example, as the Military Police captain of a precinct in a poor neighborhood in the Eastern Zone told me, "[Corruption] here in the precinct used to be very high; it's always worse in areas where there are many shops, drugs and prostitutes. We switched the troops completely, rotated the entire troop in less than one year and tried to instill in them caution in how they proceed and be on the lookout."[33]

These internal monitoring practices are not without obstacles. A PM commander in the City of São Paulo told me that the extension of civil rights to the police has made its internal control of malfeasance more difficult:

[Police corruption] increased, I think, in the last twenty-five years because with democratization, police started having more rights. Before, it was very easy to conduct an internal investigation if you suspected a police officer was involved in criminal affairs. Within a month, they kicked him out, just based on suspicion. Today, this procedure takes more than a year because the police officer has a right to counsel, to see the evidence against him. These are the constitutional guarantees

---

[33] Interview by author with Military Police captain, Eastern Zone precinct, São Paulo, November 6, 2014.

we have, but it makes punishment more difficult. The alternative is to transfer them to another unit.[34]

Similarly, low-level officers acknowledged that police corruption is hard to uproot and reporting it can be dangerous. A PM soldier told me that if he saw his partner involved in crime, he would ask to be transferred instead of reporting him, since "[My partner] walks around armed in the street and can also give information to the criminals."[35] In general, although both Military and Civil Police recognized that corruption is a problem, they also acknowledged that the institution made efforts to mitigate it, which is more than what can be said for the other cases during most periods.

In short, the PSDB's entrenchment for over twenty years in power provided the necessary policy stability to reduce police autonomy. Although different security secretaries in São Paulo often had contrasting views on fundamental issues, including the importance of police respect for human rights, important initiatives like the creation of the Office of the Ombudsperson, the recycling program for officers involved in shootings, the Community Security Councils and the alternative policing strategies originally proposed by the Covas administration persisted throughout this period. These changes affected the police force's regulation of drug trafficking, diminishing its propensity for systematic and uncoordinated violence and corruption.

COORDINATED COEXISTENCE AT WORK: THE TRUCE WITH THE PCC, 2006–2015

The professionalization of São Paulo's police shifted its regulation of drug trafficking from particularistic confrontation toward coordinated coexistence. While this change was evident since the mid-1990s, it was especially palpable after 2006. By then, drug trafficking was the major organized criminal activity in São Paulo and the main criminal gang – the PCC – had a near monopoly on drug distribution in the state. After a series of PCC attacks in May 2006, the state finally recognized the PCC's power and brokered an implicit truce to prevent further outbreaks of violence between the gang and the police. This pact would preserve the gang's

[34] Interview by author with high-level Military Police commander, São Paulo, November 24, 2014.
[35] All Military Police interviewed claimed that corruption was substantially larger in the Civil Police than in their force.

hegemony and maintain relative peace, whereas uncoordinated police attacks could have fractured the organization, destabilized the drug market and ignited violent spirals. In this section, I analyze the expansion of the PCC and the mechanisms that enabled the truce between the state and the gang to persist between 2006 and 2014. I focus on the restriction of violence in the prisons and the streets in the urban periphery by both the state and the gang. Finally, I explain why the pact suffered a temporary lapse in May 2012 following a decision by then security secretary, Ferreira Pinto.

The State-Sponsored Hegemony of the PCC

While the PSDB consolidated its political hegemony in the state government, the PCC was establishing its hegemony in São Paulo's prisons and streets. The PCC was born in a single prison (Tabuaté) in 1993 but grew to control at least 80 percent of state penitentiaries twenty years later (Dias and Salla 2013, 399). The core of the gang's power resides in the prisons. According to an investigation by the newspaper *O Estado de São Paulo* in 2014, out of 7,800 PCC members in the state, 6,000 were imprisoned, including most of the gang's leaders.[36] Imprisoned leaders run the organization's criminal activities and order street-level members to either confront the state or withhold retaliation. Incarcerated PCC members even convene tribunals via conference calls to judge and sentence those who have broken the gang's rules.[37]

The PCC dominated prisons not only by eliminating its competitors but also by disciplining prisoners' conduct. The gang prohibited rapes, knives and crack consumption within the prison. Gang members also bargained for better housing conditions with prison authorities, which gained them the respect of other inmates (Biondi 2016). Simultaneously, they gradually increased their presence outside the prisons, engaging in kidnappings, extortions and bank robberies to sustain the organization and finance their breakouts. They also began to confront the state more directly, murdering three municipal mayors in 2002 and a state judge in 2003.

---

[36] "Entenda o funcionamento do PCC e a sua influência," *Estado de São Paulo*, February 26, 2014.
[37] "Brazil prison gang conducted ten-hour conference call," *InsightCrime*, December 5, 2012.

Gradually, the PCC also shifted to drug trafficking as its main criminal activity, eventually controlling the vast majority of drug selling points in the state.[38] Internally, it also experienced a key change in the early 2000s as Marcos Willians Camacho, "Marcola," expelled the gang's two most prominent figures. From then on, the PCC conceived itself as a horizontal organization, without a single leader and made decisions through collective tribunals (Dias 2013; Biondi 2016).

During both Covas' and Alckmin's administrations (1995–2006), the state government largely ignored the threat posed by the PCC. Former Security Secretary Petrelluzzi acknowledged that, during his tenure, "Our main concern was everyday crime [as opposed to organized crime and that] the PCC was mainly the responsibility of the penitentiary administration staff." The former secretary also admitted that the government involuntarily contributed to the PCC's prison expansion:

We identified six or seven gangs in prison, not just the PCC. And our government made a mistake, motivated by the respect for human rights. The secretary for penitentiary affairs, worried about rebellions, thought the best thing was to separate the organizations in different prisons. What we did not foresee is that when you have a lot of organizations in the same prison one controls the growth of the other: In a rebellion, they fought [each other] and the winner killed the others, sometimes cut off their heads and threw them outside. To prevent this, we said, "Let's separate the factions." But we allowed them to grow even bigger. [By the time] we identified this, it was too late.[39]

After they realized the PCC threat was real, PSDB administrations mostly adopted an intelligence-centered strategy, which helped avoid unnecessary confrontations with the gang. Specialized divisions within the Civil Police, such as the Department of Criminal Investigations (DEIC) and the Department of Drug Prevention and Repression (DENARC) headed operations against the PCC, unlike in previous decades when the ROTA commanded operations against organized criminals. These specialized units apprehended various notorious PCC members and affiliates, which, ironically, saturated state prisons and further strengthened the gang. In short, unlike in Rio de Janeiro – where the police indiscriminately attacked traffickers – governments in São

---

[38] Interview by author with the chief delegate of Department of Criminal Investigations (DEIC), São Paulo, November 26, 2014.
[39] Interview by author with former Security Secretary Petrelluzzi, São Paulo, November 12, 2014.

Paulo supervised the police's confrontations with the PCC, which ended rapidly and did not result in spirals of violence.

The May Attacks and Pact

May 12, 2006 is a night most politicians, police and criminals in São Paulo vividly remember. After state penitentiary authorities attempted to relocate prominent PCC figures to federal maximum-security facilities, the gang rebelled in over seventy state prisons. Violence spread to the streets, as criminals attacked police stations and other government buildings. The following days would leave almost 500 people dead, including forty-three police officers, and literally shut down the city (Adorno and Salla 2007). The Military Police was responsible for the lion's share of the casualties, as it had been authorized to respond in full force by acting Governor Cláudio Lembo.[40] This moment was a turning point in the relationship between the state and the PCC.

The attacks only subsided after a truce between the state and the PCC, signaled by a meeting between PCC spokesperson Marcola and leading Civil Police officials.[41] Thus began an implicit pact between the government and the PCC that persists. In return for avoiding further prison riots and regulating violence in the urban periphery, the PCC would maintain its drug trafficking enterprise, while the police would restrain its attacks against gang members. While the government has not officially recognized this truce, the police officers and politicians I interviewed, as well as several media and scholarly sources, attested to its existence. This *acordo* contributed to the decline of criminal and police violence throughout the state.

How the State Avoided PCC Prison Riots

The state could threaten the PCC's prison leadership through three main instruments. The first is by transferring leaders to federal maximum-security prisons, which impose a 22-hour lockdown. The second is placing them in a harsher disciplinary regime within state-level penitentiaries, known as *Regime Disciplinar Diferenciado* (Differential

---

[40] Although the government claims that all the civilian victims belonged to the PCC, family members of the deceased dispute this notion. Interview by author with representatives from human rights NGO, Eastern Zone of São Paulo, November 25, 2014. See also www .maesdemaio.com.

[41] One of the Civil Police officials who participated in the meeting confirmed this in our interview. See "Estado fez acordo com PCC para cessar ataques de 2006, mostra depoimento," *Estado de São Paulo,* July 27, 2015.

Disciplinary Regime, RDD). Finally, the government can obstruct PCC communications with its members and affiliates on the street by blocking cellular signals around prisons or by seizing the cell phones gang members' attorneys and relatives smuggle into the prisons.

After the truce, the São Paulo state government avoided confronting the PCC on all these fronts. In return for keeping leaders in state penitentiaries, these high-ranking members maintained relative order in an overpopulated prison system, preventing further riots and rebellions (Dias 2013).[42] The government also eschewed the harsher disciplinary regime (RDD).[43] Marcola, the PCC leader, for example, was only sent to RDD once during this period.[44] Finally, PSDB administrations have not disrupted cellular phone signals around the prisons and penitentiary system personnel have allowed the smuggling of phones into the prison to continue, often to illegally profit from it.[45] As the Military Police lieutenant quoted in this book's introduction told me:

The PM never again raided a prison, or entered a cell to look for weapons, drugs, or cell phones. Prisoners have more freedom to have these things, to talk on their cell or to use the Internet in the prison. It's part of the agreement (*acordo*) with the government. The state backed away and the PM lost as a result.[46]

This does not imply that the state never punished the gang in prison. A high-ranking official from the Civil Police's Criminal Investigations (DEIC) unit told me: "In 2012 [sic], Marcola was in RDD for sixty days and nothing happened. They were preparing an escape plan, so they knew that the punishment was appropriate. When they perceive that there is justice, they do not react violently."[47] One of the leading investigators of the PCC added, "Marcola owes me his 300-year jail sentence. I put his wife in jail for money laundering. They do not like me, but they respect me because I never altered evidence to put them in jail."[48] These quotes

---

[42] See also "¿Por que Marcola, suposto líder do PCC não está em um presídio federal?" *iG São Paulo*, August 20, 2014.

[43] See discussion of relevance of RDD and the decrease of PCC members in that condition in Dias (2011, 319).

[44] "Marcola foi uma vez para regime disciplinar diferenciado em 9 anos," *Estado de São Paulo*, July 28, 2015.

[45] Interview by author with former Civil Police Chief Marco Desgualdo, São Paulo, November 5, 2014.

[46] Interview by author with Military Police lieutenant, São Paulo, October 30, 2014.

[47] Interview by author with DEIC chief delegate (Civil Police), São Paulo, November 26, 2014.

[48] Interview by author with senior DEIC investigator, São Paulo, November 26, 2014.

illustrate another aspect of the implicit pact: Both police and criminals recognize when state repression or criminal violence is appropriate.[49]

Overall, the state government did not dispute the PCC's control in most of São Paulo's prisons. This not only allowed the PCC to consolidate its drug market hegemony in the São Paulo prison system but also to regulate the use of violence in the periphery, including against the police. Since 2006, there have been no major prison riots, rebellions, or attacks by the PCC against the government.

Restriction of Police Confrontations with the PCC

The government's reduction of police autonomy also enabled the truce to persist in the streets. The restriction of police violence and rent extraction against the PCC prevented the escalation of confrontation with the gang. Police did not always take such restrictions gladly. In fact, several Military Police officers complained of "political interventionism in police affairs." Furthermore, they claimed that PM commanders – following the governments' orders – were keeping the rank-and-file from lashing out against the gang, even after other police were killed. While showing me pictures of dead police officers sent by one of his WhatsApp groups, Corporal X told me that the administration reported these deaths as *"latrocínios"*(deaths following robberies) to disguise the PCC's targeting of police officers and to prevent violent retaliation by the police.[50] Two mid-ranking Military Police officers supported this interpretation. A lieutenant in Guarulhos, a northern district in Greater São Paulo, told me:

It used to be that when a police officer was the victim of robbery or homicide, those who were in his Company or Battalion increased searches so that the crime would not be left unpunished. Today, that information is not released, so that police do not act. Murders are disguised. Police find out anyway because of the images that circulate in WhatsApp groups. They don't disclose the facts in the Police intranet either. The troops feel neglected and [that criminals are acting with] a sense of impunity.[51]

Similarly, a lieutenant from a precinct in the Western Zone of the City of São Paulo added, "The state says the cop dies in a robbery or off-duty

---

[49] Denyer Willis presents a similar argument in his extraordinary ethnographic work of the state police (2015).

[50] Overall, robberies followed by homicides (*latrocínios*) decreased between 2001 and 2013, but grew during the last years of this period, particularly after 2010.

[51] Interview by author with Military Police lieutenant, São Paulo, October 30, 2014.

but that's not what happens. They are killed by order of the leaders of the criminal gang [*facção criminosa*, i.e., the PCC]. [Politicians] say the police died in an attempted robbery, to not alarm the population."[52]

Street-level police officers perceived that the government was appeasing the PCC, leaving police unprotected. The same feeling was conveyed by former ROTA captain and then city Councilmember Conte Lopes, "We had two police who were attacked by the PCC, the criminals shot at them eight times. To take care of their family, we rented a house in the periphery so that they could move there. The police took away his gun, leaving the comrade unarmed. There is no support for the police. The criminal has more support than the police."[53]

Police commanders also confirmed the intentional restrain of police violence to avoid escalated confrontation with gang members. As a high-ranking officer in the Capital City precinct explained, "Police are scared of being the next victim. That stress leads them to react inappropriately and shoot innocent people .... This generates a self-reinforcing circuit, because the police kill someone, this generates anger against the police, someone wants to kill the police, police want revenge, etc."[54] Police commanders, acting on behalf of the administration, sought to prevent violent confrontation, if not from emerging, at least from spiraling. Reduced police autonomy facilitated this goal.

Additionally, several higher-ranking Military Police officers told me that suppressing drug trafficking was not one of their main priorities. The lieutenant from Guarulhos cited above commented, "There are no operations against drug trafficking. In general, it is not a concern of PM Battalions. We focus on five main indicators: homicides, vehicle theft, vehicle robbery and other thefts and other robberies."[55] Low and mid-level officers interpreted this selectivity as a way to avoid potential conflicts with the PCC.

For coordinated coexistence to persist, the police should also restrain their rent extraction from drug trafficking as extortion of drug dealers is likely to trigger violent responses by the gang. As I argued before, corruption is still present in São Paulo's Civil and Military Police, but, according to most interviewees, it is not extensively related to drug trafficking.

[52] Interview by author with Military Police lieutenant, Western Zone Precinct, São Paulo, November 7, 2014.
[53] Interview by author with council member, Conte Lopes, São Paulo, October 23, 2014.
[54] Interview by author with a high-ranking Military Police officer in the Capital precinct, São Paulo, November 24, 2014.
[55] Interview by author with Military Police lieutenant, Guarulhos, October 30, 2014.

Corporal X told me that several officers he knew were on the take, although they were not taking money from drug trafficking but taxing businesses to let them operate without the required licenses. This diversification of sources of illicit rent extraction might be a way for police to avoid confrontation with the PCC, while still giving officers a supplementary income.

Meanwhile, governing politicians' supposed appeasement of the PCC served to justify police corruption due to apathy or lack of job motivation. In this sense, a PM soldier stated, "Many police are unmotivated because of the government's insufficiently aggressive response and, in addition to being less willing to go out and do their job, are turning to corruption."[56] Police corruption certainly persists in São Paulo; however, it is generally concentrated among lower-ranking officers and does not seem to involve police commanders or governing political authorities, at least according to interviewees and secondary sources. This limited rent extraction by police and politicians also enables coordinated coexistence to persist.

Keeping Their End of the Bargain: PCC Regulation of Criminal Violence in the Periphery

Coordinated coexistence requires restrained conflict between state and criminal actors. Like the police, the PCC have also refrained from continuous or major attacks against the state and maintained relative peace in the urban periphery. The PCC's leadership often tried to contain violence against police since they recognized that confrontation would not only incite a violent backlash but also, more importantly, decrease profits from the drug trade. Therefore, they sought to moderate conflict from within the prison system. As the current head of the Organized Crime Unit (DEIC) told me:

In São Paulo, the PCC has one person responsible for each area. From the prison, they manage things, debating on the phone. We've intercepted 6-hour conference calls. After a *dono* [local boss] was killed in a shooting with the police, they debated; some members wanted to go to war, but they resolved to hand over the dead man's franchise to a friend of theirs. In another case, the police killed four individuals, including a son of one of the leaders in prison. They were waiting for a large drug shipment. The dead man's friends – in the street – said they were going to retaliate, but [those in prison] said they cared about the money, not about revenge. They had to administer the business, not mess with the police. There is a

---

[56] Interview by author with Military Police soldier from Guarulhos, November 14, 2014.

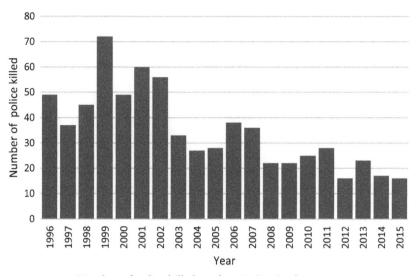

FIGURE 6.5. Number of police killed on duty in São Paulo, 1996–2015
Source: Secretaria de Segurança Pública do Estado de São Paulo (SSP-SP, Secretária of Public Security of the State of São Paulo).

difference between the voices of the street and the prison. In the street, sometimes they forgive debts for killing police [officers] and that starts a spiral of four, five deaths until the prison command stops it.[57]

Lethal violence against police has decreased markedly over this period, revealing the effectiveness of the PCC's containment policy. The number of police killed on duty decreased from forty-nine in 1996 to sixteen in 2015. The numbers are particularly low after 2006, when the pact between the state and the PCC began (see Figure 6.5). Unfortunately, this data does not include the large number of killings of off-duty police officers, which accounts for why several PM soldiers and officers feel vulnerable.

The PCC also helped contain criminal violence in the urban periphery (Manso 2009; Feltran 2011). As Figure 6.6 shows, homicide rates in the state, the city and the São Paulo metropolitan region decreased and remained low before and during the years of the pact (2006–2015). Between 2001 and 2015, homicide rates decreased by 70 percent, from 35 to less than 10 murders per 100,000 individuals. This drop was even more pronounced in the Capital and the Greater Metropolitan Region of São Paulo, which saw a decline from 50 homicides per 100,000

[57] Interview by author with current head of DEIC, São Paulo, November 26, 2014.

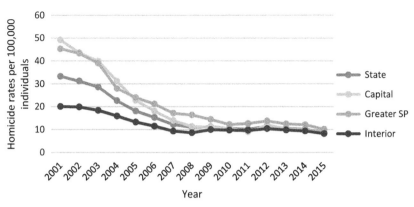

FIGURE 6.6. Homicide rates in São Paulo by region (2001–2015)
Source: Author's elaboration with data from the SSP-SP.

individuals in 1999 to 9 per 100,000 in 2015.[58] By contrast, the most important increase in violence came in 2012, when the truce between the state and the PCC was temporarily broken. I will analyze this period in the next subsection.

Although the PCC is not entirely responsible for the homicide decline in São Paulo, experts and politicians admit their influence. Security expert Guaracy Mingardi attributed the decrease in violence to the PCC's avoidance of conflict with the police to preserve their business operations. He explained, "The guy responsible for the *biqueira* (drug selling point) doesn't want complications; he wants to sell. If he starts to let people get killed there, the (PM) captain will be held responsible and the (PC) delegate will get on him. He wants the business but without the deaths. There is a very clear rule. The PCC has some influence."[59]

Various PT legislators, whose electoral strongholds are in neighborhoods controlled by the PCC, explained how the gang reduced violence in these areas. The following dialogue from an interview I had with a councilmember illustrates this dynamic:

[58] The PSDB government's promotion of alternative policing strategies to control crime, such as endorsing community policing, restricting access to firearms and instituting alcohol curfews, also contributed to this major decrease in criminal violence. Other scholars claim that socioeconomic and demographic factors are the main driver behind this decrease (Peres et al. 2011).

[59] Interview by author with security expert, Guaracy Mingardi, São Paulo, November 3, 2014.

Q: The PCC controls crime in the periphery?

A: Controls, disciplines, organizes.

Q: How do they do that?

A: It is a local action. They break up small (drug) organizations and reduce local conflicts. They help the community [by organizing] parties; they create a policy to avoid problems with the community. They even go as far as disciplining a young boy who breaks into a house to steal.[60]

Representatives from a human rights NGO in a poor neighborhood in the Eastern Zone of the City of São Paulo recounted one such example of the PCC's crime regulation. After two kids from a "troubled family" in the neighborhood broke into and burglarized their locale, the community turned in the kids and the traffickers made them return the stolen goods.[61] These testimonies show how the PCC meted out justice, delivered security and exercised governance – with the state's acquiescence – in the urban periphery. In short, the gang's containment of criminal violence is another key ingredient of coordinated coexistence. While the PCC's motto is, "War with the state, peace among thieves," its leaders have sought to maintain peace with the state as well.

A Temporary Lapse of Peace: The Breaking of the Truce in 2012

The truce between the São Paulo state and the PCC was interrupted between May and November 2012. The crucial factor behind this temporary break was Security Secretary Ferreira Pinto's decision to rely on the ROTA, as opposed to specialized divisions in the Civil Police, to investigate organized crime.[62] According to then PM Commander General Colonel Camilo, Ferreira Pinto was able to make this decision once Camilo exited his post:

We had an increase [in conflict] from 2012 until now, in my opinion, because there was a misguided steering of security toward confrontation. [Ferreira Pinto] had the idea that you had to be hard and rigid with crime. During the years I was

[60] Interview by author with council member, Jair Tatto, São Paulo, November 11, 2014. Similar narrations appeared in interviews with PT council member, José Américo, and PT State Deputy Donato (both in São Paulo, November 11, 2014). These legislators admitted that they needed the approval of gang members to campaign in certain neighborhoods.

[61] Interview by author with representatives of community-based NGO in Southeastern zone of São Paulo, November 25, 2014.

[62] Technically, the Civil Police investigate crimes, but the Military Police also have special investigative units.

in command, I did not always let that happen. There was a balance. With my exit, he did what he always wanted to do: use special troops [ROTA] in fighting crime.[63]

This quote and the next one highlight that confronting the PCC was a political decision and not an autonomous police initiative. The ROTA commander at the time, Colonel Telhada, praised the same aspects of the secretary's strategy that PM Commander Camilo criticized:

[Secretary] Antônio Ferreira Pinto fought hard against organized crime. He brought me to the ROTA. We fought every day, seized weapons, money, [arrested] the heads of crime. Hardly a week went by without two or three operations. When I left the ROTA, and he left the Security Department that ended. Fighting now is minimal, it's nothing, it's embarrassing.[64]

The results of the initial shift were immediately apparent. The ROTA killed twice as many individuals during the first semester of 2012 (45) than in the same period in 2010 (22). After one operation ended up with several PCC members killed, the gang vowed to kill six police officers for every dead gang member and police casualties piled up. During 2012, 106 policemen were killed, nearly twice as many as in the previous year (56).[65] The police, in turn, killed between 100 and 200 more people than in the previous year. The murder rampage, particularly the large number of police victims, eventually led Ferreira Pinto to resign in November 2012.

Ferreira Pinto's successor, Fernando Grella Vieira,[66] a former head state prosecutor, promised a police force more respectful of human rights, and halted the police's violent approach.[67] In the first eight months of 2013, the government expelled 398 police officers – the highest monthly average during Alckmin's government – and arrested 237.[68] At the end of 2013, the number of victims of police violence decreased back to 2011

---

[63] Interview by author with Colonel Camilo, October 30, 2014.

[64] Interview by author with former ROTA commander and current council member, Colonel Telhada, São Paulo, November 6, 2014.

[65] www.terra.com.br/noticias/infograficos/ataques-a-pms. See also, "What's killing Brazil's police?" Graham Denyer Willis, *New York Times*, December 1, 2012. Only three of these police officers were killed on duty; the rest were either off-duty or retired.

[66] Neither Grella nor his deputy secretary returned requests for an interview.

[67] See "Novo secretário de Segurança assume prometendo mudanças e respeito aos direitos humanos," *UOL notícias*, November 22, 2012.

[68] "Média de policiais presos e demitidos em 2013 é a maior da era Alckmin em SP," *R7 Notícias*, October 15, 2013.

levels.[69] This change in office restored the coordinated coexistence arrangement that the previous secretary had disrupted.

EPILOGUE

When São Paulo began the new democratic period in the 1980s, high political competition obstructed the Montoro administration's initiatives to reform the police and paved the way for his successors to engage in overt penal populism. Nearly forty years later, PSDB governor João Doria will conclude his first term (2019–2022), which will mark twenty-eight years of consecutive *tucano* rule since Mário Covas took office in January 1995.[70] During his term, the governor has kept various of the security policies of his predecessors, as well as the low homicide rates in the state. Police violence has also remained stable, well below the alarming rates observed in Rio de Janeiro. The implicit yet recognized pact with the PCC is still in place. In short, coordinated coexistence with drug trafficking continues.

This chapter has shown how the PSDB's entrenchment in power allowed it to maintain policy initiatives that reduced the autonomy of the state police. The government's professionalization of both the Civil and Military Police enabled regulation of drug trafficking through coordinated coexistence. The state's security policy contributed to the PCC's growth as the primary drug gang in São Paulo – and ultimately Brazil – expanding from the prison into the urban periphery. Police restricted their confrontation against, and rent extraction from, the hegemonic drug gang. Unlike what occurred in Rio de Janeiro for most of the democratic period (Chapter 3), São Paulo conveys the importance of sustaining initiatives over several administrations to professionalize the police.

The São Paulo experience also compels us to reexamine how nonaggression agreements between state and criminal actors can emerge and persist. On the one hand, governments need to remain in office for sufficiently long periods to implement significant changes to police organizational procedures and crime-fighting strategies that enable these agreements. On the other hand, this coordinated arrangement involves the

---

[69] http://ponte.org/pms-de-São-paulo-matam-uma-pessoa-a-cada-10-horas. According to this organization, the police killed 715 people in 2012 and 574 in 2013. Official records from the SSP are: 535 (2011), 619 (2012) and 505 (2013).

[70] Doria was the first PSDB governor to win in the second round since Mário Covas, having obtained only 31 percent of the vote in the first round, a sizable drop from Alckmin's 57 percent four years prior.

state ceding part of its authority to non-state armed actors, who often enjoy greater legitimacy in marginalized neighborhoods than the police itself, given the latter's historical mistreatment of the poor. Moreover, police tolerance of drug trafficking surely does not increase its legitimacy among most urban residents. While this informal regulatory arrangement is more peaceful than the other regimes examined in this book, it is far from optimal.

Furthermore, this case shows that reducing police autonomy is not exclusive to progressive or left-of-center governments. Like Cabral's PMDB in Rio de Janeiro, which managed to curb police violence during the initial implementation of the UPP program, the PSDB in São Paulo, while initially considered more progressive, is now indisputably a conservative, center-right party. However, both have succeeded in reducing police autonomy more than center-left governors like Brizola (Rio de Janeiro) or Montoro (São Paulo), in part because the latter generate more rejection and resistance from the police.

Finally, this case is another illustration of how political decisions shape drug markets. The government's violent treatment of prisoners, criminals and marginalized sectors in general, contributed to the emergence of the most powerful drug gang in the state, the PCC. Meanwhile, its subsequent decisions in security and penitentiary policy allowed the gang to consolidate its monopoly on drug trafficking in São Paulo. While this enabled the peace agreement to persist, it also strengthened a rival with the potential to gun down police officers and paralyze the city.

The following, concluding chapter summarizes the evolution of the four informal regulatory arrangements (particularistic confrontation, negotiation, protection rackets and coordinated coexistence), not just within each case but across the cases as well. I also discuss the theoretical and policy implications of these findings and suggest avenues for further research on illicit markets and criminal violence.

7

Regulation of Criminal Markets in Weak Institutional Contexts

Drug trafficking is the most profitable illicit activity in the world and a major source of criminal violence in Latin America. Despite, or precisely because of its size and complexity, this illicit market is ripe for state regulation. As this book has shown, drug regulation exceeds the enforcement of domestic statutes based on international conventions that prohibit the commercialization of controlled substances. State actors also tolerate, protect or prey upon domestic drug dealing to achieve order, financial gain, or both. The "war on drugs" is only part of how states respond to drug trafficking.

Governing politicians rely heavily on police to regulate this illicit activity. While politicians *de jure* control police forces, police often have *de facto* autonomy from the government. Police corruption and extralegal violence, a primary consequence of such autonomy, can often jeopardize the government's electoral prospects. Furthermore, police have often challenged political authorities, sometimes even through protests, threats and actual attempts on their lives. Politicians must, then, first control their police to benefit (electorally and/or materially) from the regulation of illicit markets. Most studies on criminal violence overlook the necessary but often tumultuous relationship between the politicians who design security policies and the law enforcement agencies that implement them. Meanwhile, studies on police politics rarely focus on how police shape illicit markets and criminal violence. This book has shed light on these two aspects.

Through the concept of informal regulatory regimes, I have described the various ways in which state law enforcement agencies interact with drug traffickers. State actors do not only fight or obtain bribes from criminals. These practices are part of broader regulatory arrangements. The informal regulatory regimes I specify also include the possibility of toleration (coordinated coexistence), distinguish between coordinated or uncoordinated corruption and violence, and link police lethality, corruption and criminal violence.

By analyzing variation in police autonomy, I have underscored the distinct incentives of, and multiple tensions between, police and politicians in democracies with weak institutions. Unlike in developed democracies, where politicians typically respect and benefit from bureaucratic autonomy, in developing democracies autonomy can be a liability – or even a threat – for governing officials. Thus, politicians need to reduce police autonomy, whether through professionalization or politicization, to obtain peace in their districts or money in their pockets.

Finally, this book has highlighted the complex entanglement of democracy, policing and illicit markets. Political turnover and fragmentation outline the limits of incumbents' power and reveal them to other political actors, including the police. Police perceptions of incumbents' strength influences their compliance with the administration, including in how they regulate drug markets.

Throughout the previous chapters, I have focused on the variation *within* each case to leverage my argument. In this concluding chapter, I compare *across* cases to show the analytical generalizability of my findings. I then discuss potential extensions of this argument to other Global South countries. Finally, I discuss theoretical and policy implications and different directions for future research.

SUMMARY OF VARIATION ACROSS AND WITHIN CASES

The subnational governments analyzed in this book shifted over time from displaying uncoordinated regulatory regimes to exhibiting coordinated ones (or vice versa) primarily due to the decrease (or increase) of political turnover. High political turnover implies greater policy instability. The extreme version of this has been the political pendulum between "pro-human rights" and "law and order" governments seen in all cases. In Rio de Janeiro, hardliners Moreira Franco and Alencar succeeded progressive Brizola. In Santa Fe, starting in the mid-1990s, reformist Obeid ceded office to conservative Reutemann, came back and was replaced by socialist Binner, who, despite his general progressive agenda, made little headway on police professionalization. In Buenos Aires, in the late 1990s, exiting governors appointed successors who broke with their faction soon after taking office, such as the right-wing Ruckauf and the moderate Solá (who succeeded each other). Finally, in São Paulo in the 1980s, conservative PMDB member Quércia replaced progressive Montoro and then handed the governorship to his even further right-leaning security secretary, Fleury, in turn succeeded by the progressive Covas, who kickstarted the uninterrupted tenure of the PSDB.

In each of these cases, the new incumbents upturned the security policies of their predecessors. Rio's case was the most extreme. Moreira Franco reversed Brizola's order to halt police intrusions in favelas. Alencar instituted Faroeste to reward officers who used lethal force, contrary to Brizola and Cerqueira's indications. In Santa Fe, Reutemann's security minister declared Obeid's reform "buried." Buenos Aires governor-elect, Ruckauf informed the sitting security minister he would not continue his reform while his vice-governor (and successor) Solá spearheaded a new reformist initiative. Finally, in São Paulo, Quércia and Fleury eliminated the small gains made by Montoro in reforming the Civil Police and constraining the brutal ROTA, the elite squad of São Paulo's Military Police. Incoming governors shifted previous security ministers, staff and police authorities as well. Turnover thus also implied high transition costs as new incumbents renewed relations with police and stumbled upon the roadblocks left by their predecessors. Entrant administrations encountered not just heightened security problems but also few administrative resources to tackle them.

High turnover not only impeded the consolidation of police reforms; it also fostered internal dissent within the police and reduced their incentives to comply with elected officials. Politicians' urge to make important policy changes early in their terms clashed with police inertia and foot dragging. Administrations in all four districts faced police protests. In some cases, police chose more violent means of resistance. Argentine police threatened governors and security ministers, sometimes even tried to kill them, as the assassination attempt against Santa Fe governor, Bonfatti, crudely revealed. Brazilian police, meanwhile, let homicides occur (or even committed them) to destabilize administrations, as recounted by officials in the administrations of Brizola and Garotinho in Rio and Montoro in São Paulo. The impasse in security politics meant that police capacity or accountability did not increase during these periods; in other words, police retained or expanded their autonomy.

Autonomous police were more likely to regulate drug trafficking through unchecked corruption and, in some cases, violence. They enforced *particularistic* regulatory arrangements, either centered on *confrontations* – dispersed attacks by police against drug gangs, or *negotiations* – segmented pacts in which each police unit, division or officer tried to cut a deal for himself. These patterns prevailed for most of the last forty years in Rio de Janeiro – with a brief interval of coordinated coexistence during the successful years of Pacification (2008–2013) – and in the last decade in Santa Fe (2007–2015), respectively. In Santa Fe, reform cycles during the preceding Peronist administrations (1997–2006) nurtured the police upheaval that erupted during the Socialist tenure. There were also shorter stretches of particularistic confrontation in São Paulo in the initial democratic years (1982–1994) and of particularistic negotiation in Buenos Aires during the late 1990s and early 2000s. In each case, police corruption ran rampant and criminal violence increased.

By contrast, low turnover reduced police autonomy by consolidating formal or informal policies to control the police. It convinced police commanders that the incumbent was the "only game in town" and increased their compliance with the administration. The effect of low turnover on police autonomy and informal regulation varied with political fragmentation. With greater concentration of power, entrenched governments in Buenos Aires, and initially in Santa Fe, appropriated police rents from illicit activities. These districts' trajectories initially ran parallel and then diverged significantly. Both began the democratic period implementing *protection rackets*. This strategy posed few political costs since it sidelined reform and deterred police backlash, while police malfeasance remained hidden from public view. It also benefited incumbents with illicit rents and relative order, as criminal violence remained low. These administrations did not increase police budgets, improve officers' working conditions or clean up corrupt internal procedures. Moreover, they made police career advancement contingent on monetary contributions. Politicization made police subservient to the party in power but not accountable to the rule of law. Police thus turned to illicit market rents – initially, gambling and prostitution and, later, drug trafficking – for internal financing and leverage for political favors. Protection rackets prevailed in Buenos Aires for most of this period, but were especially salient after 2007, when the Scioli administration restored them in an augmented version, and in Santa Fe until the mid-1990s. During these periods, police corruption was high yet centralized while criminal violence remained low.

With high fragmentation, by contrast, politicians faced stronger barriers to appropriate rents extracted by the police because credible political rivals either denounced corruption or competed for the same illicit funds. This combination motivated political incumbents to promote police professionalization, as in the cases of São Paulo since the mid-1990s and Rio de Janeiro during Pacification. These governments improved police training and promotion procedures, established performance criteria to evaluate the police, postulated clear operational guidelines and supervised police interventions in marginalized neighborhoods. In São Paulo, the administration also instated stronger mechanisms to hold police accountable, like the Ombudsperson's Office. Professionalization stymied rampant police brutality and corruption and thus enabled the regulation of illicit markets through *coordinated coexistence*. Police violence in Rio and São Paulo became more selective, averting the spirals of violence that had previously spiked up homicide rates in these districts.

Beyond this within-case variation, there are country-level differences between Argentina and Brazil. When regulatory arrangements break down, Brazilian cases tend toward particularistic confrontation, exhibiting greater levels of police violence, while Argentine cases tend toward particularistic negotiations, which possess greater police corruption. On the one hand, this contrast reflects the continuing gap in strength of their respective criminal organizations and the violence they can exert against the police. On the other hand, it also reflects the different political trajectories in each case predicted by this theory. Argentine state-level governments were able to concentrate power and politicize the police, who developed a particular skill of extracting rents from illicit markets. When this arrangement broke down, police were more likely to continue this extraction while hoarding rents for themselves instead of sharing them with incumbents. Meanwhile, Brazilian parties were never able to reach such levels of political dominance. This inhibited them from not just centralizing police corruption but also from correcting traits leading to police violence inherited from the dictatorship. Police violence thus grew rampant in Brazil, partly to resist – and undermine – reformist administrations.

Table 7.1 summarizes the different case trajectories in terms of political competition, police autonomy and drug trafficking regulation. These cases illustrate my theory that low political turnover reduces police autonomy and produces coordinated drug regulation regimes, while high alternation in power increases police autonomy and generates uncoordinated regulatory arrangements. I have also shown that political fragmentation obstructs policy implementation and decreases the internal coherence governments need to control the police under high turnover,

TABLE 7.1. *Summary of variation across the different cases*

	High political turnover and fragmentation		*Low political turnover and fragmentation*	*Low political turnover, high fragmentation*
Political competition	Policy instability; transition costs Policy incoherence and obstruction		Informal policy stability; only game in town No checks on or competition for rent capture	Formal policy stability, only game in town Stronger checks on or competition for rent capture
Police autonomy	*High* No professionalization or centralization of rents Low capacity and accountability		*Low (Politicization)* No reform; centralization of illicit rents Low capacity and personal accountability to ruler	*Low (Professionalization)* Implemented reforms Higher capacity and accountability
Regulatory regimes	*Particularistic confrontation* High police violence and high uncoordinated police corruption High criminal violence	*Particularistic negotiation* High uncoordinated police corruption, low police violence High criminal violence	*Protection racket* High and coordinated police corruption, low police violence Low criminal violence	*Coordinated coexistence* Low police violence; low uncoordinated corruption Low criminal violence
Cases	Rio de Janeiro (1983–2007; 2014–) São Paulo (1983–1994)	Rosario (1997–2019) Buenos Aires (1997–2003)	Buenos Aires (1983–1996; 2004–2015) Rosario (1983–1996)	São Paulo (1995–2015) Rio de Janeiro (2008–2013)

Source: Author's elaboration

while influencing whether politicians restrict or appropriate police rents in entrenched governments, leading to coordinated coexistence and protection rackets, respectively. The next sections extend this argument to other Global South cases and explore the theoretical and policy implications of these findings.

EXTENSIONS OF THE ARGUMENT: DRUG TRAFFICKING REGULATION IN OTHER CASES

A cursory look at different Latin American urban areas offers multiple extensions for this book's argument.[1] In terms of outcomes, the regulation through particularistic confrontation we saw in Rio de Janeiro closely resembles the militaristic approach applied against drug trafficking in Colombia, especially in Medellín, in the mid-1980s and early 1990s and in México since the mid-2000s. These three cases display the destabilizing effect of state fragmentation in containing drug-related violence and the failure of non-conditional repression of drug trafficking (Durán-Martínez 2017; Lessing 2017). However, there is significant within-case variation in each of them. The Colombian cities of Cali, or even Medellín following the fall of Pablo Escobar, exhibit features of coordinated coexistence, with greater political cohesion, police professionalization and significant reductions in levels of violence (Durán-Martínez 2017). México, meanwhile, was the paradigmatic example of protection rackets during the PRI hegemony, with null political competition, police politicization, centralized corruption and restrained violence. In general, the country has shifted toward particularistic arrangements following increases in political competition, the collapse of preexisting protection networks and the spread of police corruption (Trejo and Ley 2020).

The variation between the main four Central American countries (El Salvador, Guatemala, Honduras and Nicaragua) partially aligns with this book's main theoretical claims. Of these four, Nicaragua most closely resembles a coordinated coexistence regime. After many years of continuous Sandinista rule, it had one of the most professionalized police in Latin America and its homicide rates paled in comparison to those of its neighbors. Although one might reasonably argue against its present democratic credentials, it is worth noting that the professionalization of

---

[1] Argentina, Brazil, Mexico and Venezuela are the only four federal countries in the region. The rest all have a singular national police force. Mexico is the only country with autonomous local police.

the National Police was a political arrangement between the exiting
Sandinistas and their rivals in the early 1990s, when greater political
competition existed. By contrast, El Salvador,[2] Guatemala and
Honduras have failed to advance police professionalization, partly
because of policy instability resulting from electoral turnover, partly due
to police resistance to the reforms instituted as part of the peace accords
to end their respective civil wars (Bailey and Dammert 2006).
Governments in these countries typically employed particularistic confrontation against gangs involved in drug dealing, combining high levels
of anarchic police violence and corruption to regulate this enterprise
(Cruz 2011; Martínez 2016; Yashar 2018).

In South America, the urban areas of Chile and Perú also show signs of
coordinated coexistence.[3] The Santiago, Chile, case is straightforward
since it hosts the strongest political institutions, the most professionalized
police forces, as well as the lowest homicides in any city in the region,
about 5 per 100,000 people.[4] At the national level – which manages the
police – Chile long qualified as a case of low turnover and high fragmentation. Despite their continuous twenty years in power (1989–2009), the
social democratic coalition Concertación faced numerous policy roadblocks erected by the authoritarian constitution of 1980. While this might
have impeded the politicization of the police, it also carried the cost of
maintaining their association with the previous dictatorship.

The case of Lima, Perú is more puzzling. State capacity in Perú is
weaker than in Chile or most of Latin America. Yet despite being the
capital of one of the main cocaine producers in the world, Lima has far
lower violence than one would expect, with 6.2 homicides per 100,000
people in 2018.[5] Despite its chaotic political system, or perhaps because
of it, no Peruvian government has been able to politicize the national
police since the Fujimori regime employed it to spy and repress the
opposition. Holland's analysis of forbearance also shows that Peruvian
municipal governments are capable of employing the police to evict

---

[2] In El Salvador, the brief truce between rival gangs sponsored by the Funes administration
(2009–2014) in 2012 collapsed after his term ended and his vice-president, Sánchez Cerén,
came to power (Cruz and Durán-Martínez 2016).
[3] Their rural areas, especially in Perú, have much weaker state presence and are outside the
scope conditions of this book.
[4] This is higher than the national rate, which is around 3 homicides per 100,000 individuals (2018).
[5] The national homicide rate in Perú in 2018 was 7.8 per 100,000, a bit higher but still quite
low for Latin American standards.

squatters but mostly choose not to do so because of fear of political backlash (Holland 2017). The Peruvian state could also have the capacity to regulate drug markets such that they do not produce overt violence in metropolitan areas.

Beyond Latin America, weakly institutionalized democracies in other regions also implement these drug regulatory regimes. The Philippines might be the most illustrative example of particularistic confrontation. Since taking power in 2016, President Rodrigo Duterte has proclaimed a war on drugs that resulted in mass summary executions of low-level dealers and couriers. The most conservative estimate is that, between 2017 and June 2019, the police have killed 5,532 people.[6] Like in Rio de Janeiro, police violence in the Philippines is used to extort and intimidate criminals, and thus is coupled with unbridled corruption (Jensen and Hapal 2018). South Africa and India, two other key representatives of the Global South, exhibit different patterns of police–government relations and crime regulation. The South Africa's African National Congress party (ANC), the dominant party for the last two decades, initially tried to reform the police to make it more representative of the nation, but increasingly politicized it (Altbeker 2009). The police, in turn, govern drug markets in various regions through protection rackets, often engaging in widespread corruption at the behest of elected officials (Faull 2007). In India, police–government relations and regulatory regimes also vary across states. Extending Wilkinson's argument regarding the policing of ethnic violence, in which greater political competition yields more inclusive (and professionalized) police organizations, one could assume that greater competition could also result in fewer informal compacts with criminal actors for material gain (Wilkinson 2006).

THEORETICAL AND POLICY IMPLICATIONS

In this book, I have presented a theoretical framework relating democratic competition, police–government relations and state responses to illicit markets. My findings have theoretical and policy implications for these issues as well as for institutional stability and change, political agency and the political economy of illicit markets in developing democracies.

---

[6] See   www.reuters.com/article/us-philippines-drugs-performance-exclusi/exclusive-shock-and-awe-has-failed-in-philippines-drug-war-enforcement-chief-says-idUSKBN2010IL.

Democracy and Policing

This book has shown that high turnover impedes politicians from reducing police autonomy while police have stronger incentives to comply with entrenched administrations. The troubling implication is that parties' alternation in power – a desirable, if not necessary, condition for democracy – can be detrimental to drug market regulation and security policy in general. From a top-down perspective, the policy implication is not to annul turnover but to neutralize the mechanisms through which it increases police autonomy, in other words, policy instability and transition costs. Different parties could, for instance, agree to maintain certain core security policies even if they replace each other in power. Mechanisms for ensuring greater participation by the opposition in policy design or implementation could also reduce transition costs. Governments could also amend bureaucratic procedures to ensure the stability of mid-level political appointees and make police commanders' tenure depend on partisan consensus and overlap between governments.[7]

From a bottom-up perspective, turnover depends on voters' choices. Citizens might be lured by populist promises to "end violence in six months" (Moreira Franco in Rio de Janeiro), "shoot up criminals" (Ruckauf in Buenos Aires) or similar "mano dura" initiatives to elect candidates who undermine police professionalization and legitimacy (Ungar 2009; Holland 2013; Bonner 2019). However, this peril of democratic competition can carry its own remedy. These politicians not only failed to deliver their promise of greater security, but their exacerbation of police violence and consequent increase of criminal violence thwarted their reelection prospects, whether for themselves or their party. "Tough-on-crime" can be popular politics, especially at first, but it rarely makes good policy.[8] Politicians from all parties as well as the media and NGOs should inquire aspiring candidates about their concrete security proposals and government outcomes, not just during elections but through the entire administration.

Political fragmentation also poses a dilemma for institutional design. On the one hand, it can obstruct necessary policy changes and undermine

---

[7] As in many other examples described in this book, it is not enough that the formal rule should be in place but that political actors have actual incentives to abide by them and do not instate parallel or supplementary *informal* institutions (Helmke and Levitsky 2004).

[8] Other policy implications of punitivism, such as increased incarceration, are much less politically costly (Flom and Post 2016).

incumbents' momentum. On the other, it can prevent incumbents from engaging in police politicization, predatory rent-seeking and other abuses of power. Furthermore, when incumbents can overcome hurdles of high fragmentation, policy stability is more likely, as in the case of São Paulo's reformist initiatives in the late 1990s or Rio de Janeiro's Pacification program between 2008 and 2014. This book thus questions the idea of a straightforward tradeoff between political competition and criminal conflict in developing democracies, a common argument in the political violence literature. It also problematizes the notion that greater fragmentation is either inherently healthy or damaging for policymaking in democracy. Rather, its findings stress the intricate and nonlinear relationship between (in)security and democracy. As Arias and Goldstein commented, violence, whether carried out by the state or criminals, is not a sign of partial, illiberal, incomplete or disjunctive democratization, but rather a feature of democratic regimes themselves (Arias and Goldstein 2010, 4). The same applies to the types of policies that either accelerate or dampen these types of violence.

This study also has theoretical and practical implications for police autonomy. One of its findings is that, in weak institutional contexts, reducing police autonomy, whether through professionalization or politicization, yields better security outcomes than police self-government, which often leads to rampant corruption and abuse of force. While most agencies in developed countries, and some "pockets of efficiency" in developing countries,[9] have sufficient standing to demand high autonomy from elected politicians, most bureaucracies in developing democracies require some political supervision to fulfill their stated missions. A policy implication is that states need mechanisms through which politicians can supervise agencies without manipulating them for their own partisan or personal benefit. In short, in addition to the risks of politicization, scholars and policymakers should also be aware of the risks of high bureaucratic autonomy.

Political Agency, Institutional Stability and Change

The evolution of drug trafficking regulation involves a two-part paradox. The first part is that, while in weak institutional contexts many things change frequently, such as governing incumbents, security staffs, formal

---

[9] Schneider 1992; Geddes 1994; Evans 1995.

institutional rules, security policies and levels of crime, most regulatory regimes endure for years, even decades. This motivates two additional reflections. First, that institutional serial replacement, in other words, "radical and recurrent change" (Levitsky and Murillo 2013), applies primarily to *formal* institutions and policies. *Informal* institutions, by contrast, such as uncodified drug trafficking regulatory regimes, can be more stable, if not in design at least in their enforcement.

Second, individual agency is necessary yet insufficient to reduce police autonomy and shape regulatory arrangements when dynamics of political competition are unfavorable, as the cases of uncoordinated regulatory regimes in Rio de Janeiro and Santa Fe illustrate. Many committed reformers in these districts failed to implement their preferred policies. In Rio, Brizola made reform a core component of his first gubernatorial campaign, riding the optimistic wave of re-democratization. Brizola even had an ally as the head of the Military Police, Colonel Cerqueira. None of this mattered. Political fragmentation obstructed the governor's initiatives and political turnover – the election of PMDB candidate Moreira Franco in 1986 – undid what little remained of his work. In Santa Fe, Governor Obeid also dedicated himself to the cause of police professionalization, yet he belonged to a party that typically profited from police illicit rent extraction. Factional disputes undercut his reformist efforts. His replacement, first by Reutemann, a Peronist conservative, and then by Binner, a democratic socialist, obliterated his reforms. Binner, and the Progressive Front governors who succeeded him, constitute a tragic case of honest politicians – no Socialist governor or their ministers has been credibly accused of corruption, even by their rivals – who, while not profiting from police illicit rent extraction, did not curtail it either.

The stability of informal regulatory regimes sometimes implies that governments get stuck in a public security perverse equilibrium (Flom and Post 2016), a situation both politicians and the police know is deficient but are unable or unwilling to change. Political incumbents realize the security problems they face, including the lack of professionalized police departments, but abjure necessary reforms for fear of police backlash or the enticement of illicit rents. They only shift gears when worsening security outcomes undermines their electoral prospects but then lose the political power (or the time in office) needed to see the reforms through. Police, meanwhile, often complain of societal mistrust, yet maintain the corrupt and violent practices that decrease their social legitimacy and discourage citizens' cooperation, which further undermines their capacity to prevent crime and spurs hasty interventions by anxious politicians.

Commanders often reject these projects, even when they could reduce officers' occupational hazards and bolster their standing.[10] Citizens, meanwhile, continue to suffer from high insecurity (by the hands of the police as well as from criminals) and police corruption, further motivating politicians to reduce police autonomy and endure police resistance. In sum, police and politicians persist in a tumultuous principal–agent relationship in which the state provides deficient public security responses to most citizens – but especially to the poor – and cements distrust in the rule of law (O'Donnell 1993; Méndez et al. 1999; Auyero and Sobering 2019).

The second part of the paradox regarding regulatory arrangements is that they might last for decades but can collapse quite rapidly. In Santa Fe and Buenos Aires, for instance, entrenched protection rackets evaporated swiftly, sending public security in a downward spiral. In São Paulo, Ferreira Pinto's policy switch to use the ROTA against the PCC drug gang shook up coordinated coexistence during 2012, although the PCC and the government promptly renewed their *acordo*. In Rio, Pacification covered only 38 of the 1,000 favelas only in the city of Rio, never mind the whole state. For all its impact on reducing police violence, this program was limited in scope and depth. Hence, this coordinated coexistence arrangement collapsed rapidly due to fiscal scarcity and political turmoil. The fragility of these arrangements is a cautionary tale both for the entrenched governments that instate them and for the new incumbents resolved to "cleaning up the police" or "ending state deals with criminals."

The rare successes in reducing the autonomy of Latin American police compel us to examine the sources and shapes of such institutional changes. In terms of sources, external prompts were only relevant in a few cases. The most important example is the preparation for international events, such as the 2014 World Cup and the 2016 Summer Olympic Games in Rio de Janeiro, which incentivized the government to foster an alternative regulation of crime and violence in the city. In the remaining positive transitions, prompts were endogenous. In São Paulo, the Carandiru prison massacre in 1992, the Favela Naval killings in 1997 and the May 2006 attacks, which accelerated police professionalization and coordinated coexistence with the PCC, sprung from the police's previously high autonomy and regulation of crime through

---

[10] As we have seen, officers have good reasons to distrust politicians, given that several governors proclaim police reforms merely to benefit from police illicit rent extraction or political repression.

particularistic confrontation. In Buenos Aires, grotesque scandals of police involvement with crimes such as the AMIA terrorist attack – later proven false – and the murders of news photographer José Luis Cabezas and student Axel Blumberg triggered police reforms and regulatory regime changes in the late 1990s and early 2000s.

Finally, in terms of speed and scope, incremental changes were more successful than encompassing reform initiatives, which backfired and led to particularistic arrangements. The PSDB in São Paulo gradually introduced multiple statutes to monitor police violence and new crime control programs. Cabral and Beltrame in Rio de Janeiro began installing UPPs in more "tranquil" favelas to generate societal and political support for Pacification. The program then spread into more dangerous areas of the city and altered police internal governance to reduce corruption and brutality. A problem in the policy realm is the time it takes for politicians and police to see enough increasing returns from professionalization such that deviating toward opportunistic corruption or crowd-pleasing "tough on crime" measures becomes costlier (Pierson 2004). These incremental changes can generate initial support for security policies; however, policy stability is essential to professionalize the police and coordinate regulatory arrangements.

Limits to political agency notwithstanding, politicians are sometimes capable of learning and deviating from the perverse equilibrium path of uncoordinated regulation. Governor Covas' capacity to forge a consensus between political parties and with police on an alternative homicide prevention approach enabled the transformation of São Paulo's police. In Buenos Aires, federal and state-level Peronist leaders temporarily cooperated to control the Bonaerense, realizing that their permissiveness in exchange for illicit rents had made police dangerous, politically, and safety-wise. Despite its shortcomings, Pacification in Rio de Janeiro signaled a change in the government's evaluation of the political and social costs of violent interventions in favelas (at least the most visible ones). Sadly, politicians (and their districts) must often hit rock bottom before acknowledging the costs of the status quo and the need for change.

In short, although political agency is insufficient to modify entrenched police structures and functions, political skill can seize upon different opportunities granted by the distribution of power to ignite these transformations. Politicians can muster windows of opportunity opened by crises to promote incremental reforms that can garner sufficient political and police support to persist regardless of partisan turnover (González 2020). Stepping out of perverse equilibria is daunting but possible, provided incumbents, opposition politicians and police collaborate. A first step toward that goal is understanding each other's interests and the risks of different strategies. This book has shed light on both of these aspects.

Political Economy of Illicit Markets

Finally, this book has at least two interrelated implications for the political economy of drug markets. First, it has shown how informal politics and policies shape illicit as well as formal markets. Informal aspects of policies can affect how criminals organize. In Rio de Janeiro, violent police corruption against the CV splintered it into different factions and fostered cartel-state violence (Lessing 2017), while in São Paulo, several administrations' penitentiary and security policies contributed to the PCC's monopoly, which facilitated the *acordo* brokered in 2006.

Second, this book has recast the relevance of market centralization for variation in criminal violence. Violence results from shifts not just in market *fragmentation* but also in market *stability*. In the late 1980s, Rio's government chose to confront rather than tolerate a hegemonic criminal actor (the CV); it subsequently destabilized and fragmented the drug market, with catastrophic results. In Santa Fe, decentralized police corruption enticed drug dealers to expand their territorial and market share, while in Buenos Aires, centralized police corruption inhibited gangs' expansion and stabilized the fragmented drug market. Governments in São Paulo and Buenos Aires have been able to broker peaceful arrangements with a hegemonic drug gang and small drug dealing outfits, respectively. Drug market concentration is not a necessary condition for low levels of criminal violence.

One last clarification is in order. This book does not advocate for a police-centered regulation of drug trafficking. However, I do argue that, because drug trafficking remains illegal – and will likely remain so for the foreseeable future – police and other criminal justice institutions should be better qualified to deal with it in ways that both advance security and respect human rights. Therefore, politicians should exercise intelligent control over the police while providing officers with enough resources to ensure public safety.

The broader debate on the legalization of drug consumption, or even the entire chain of drug production and commercialization, is beyond the scope of this book. However, the cases analyzed – as well as many others in Latin America and other regions – reaffirm the need to reevaluate governments' approaches to this transnational criminal market. Informal regulatory arrangements, even their coordinated versions – coordinated coexistence and protection rackets – while less violent, pose various political and normative problems.

In political terms, for instance, coordinated coexistence is rare and potentially fragile. On the one hand, it might collapse after shifts in power between parties, factions, or even within security cabinets – as the temporary breakdown of the truce in São Paulo during Ferreira Pinto's tenure in 2012 illustrated. On the other hand, entrenched politicians must forgo attempts to appropriate police illicit rents, a temptation both if the opposition loses the power to keep incumbents in check or, conversely, if incumbents are in an electoral bind. Meanwhile, protection rackets are not only fragile but risky, since entrenched politicians might abuse their authority for other purposes rather than illicit rent collection, such as the repression of political opposition or of specific social or ethnic groups.

These arrangements also present normative issues. Protection rackets rely on incumbents' participation in illicit rent collection by police, which hardly fits citizens' expectations of democratic governance. Moreover, protection rackets and coordinated coexistence both imply a state delegation of security and justice provision, and ultimately sovereignty over life and death, to non-state armed actors (Arias 2006a; Denyer Willis 2015). Thus, when state actors with high capacity acknowledge that they do not hold the monopoly of legal violence in the most densely populated metropolitan areas in their territory, prospects for the advancement of equality and the rule of law are troubling (O'Donnell 1993, 1358–59). In short, informal regulatory arrangements are not positive developments, even when they manage to control crime. However, only by understanding their origin and evolution will it be possible to move beyond them.

AVENUES FOR FUTURE RESEARCH

This book has focused on how politicians and police regulate domestic drug dealing. While this is the largest criminal market, many others are relevant. Also, police are not the only agency that regulates illicit markets, even if they are the ones in most frequent contact with criminals. Here I discuss some potential directions for future research on the political economy of illicit markets.

Regarding research on illicit markets, I find three main challenges. The first, and most obvious one, is to move beyond the study of drug trafficking, which has been the primary focus of social scientists yet is hardly the only illicit market which generates immense revenue for criminals and corrupt state officials. Extortion is one of the most common activities of criminal groups, from rudimentary street gangs to organized crime syndicates (Moncada 2021). The exploitation of human trafficking victims for sexual or commercial purposes also requires the passivity, if not corruption, of different state agencies to ignore the sweatshops, massage parlors and cabarets where women and girls are exploited (Shelley 2010). Victims of human trafficking often manufacture the products sold in second-hand stores, as well as in many premium outlets. Millions of smartphones are stolen every year and resold in informal markets, sometimes travelling across continents. So far, there is little systematic study of the formal and informal responses of state actors to these and other illicit markets (but see Beckert and Dewey 2017).

The two remaining directions are more challenging. The first move involves analyzing nonterritorially as well as territorially based illicit economies. Money laundering, for example, does not require criminal actors to control territories or confront police yet is an essential facet of transnational organized crime (Levi and Reuter 2006). Criminals often use political campaigns to launder their profits. Additionally, digital or cybercrime is growing exponentially, both in terms of the acquisition of illicit products online and in terms of the crimes perpetrated exclusively via the Internet, such as phishing, denial of service and cyber-ransom. Deterritorialized, organized crimes typically involve more fluid networks and different linkages between states and economic actors.

The second challenge is moving from an analysis centered on violence to focus on other aspects of illicit markets and organized crime. While there are good reasons for studying homicides, other features of illicit markets are also worth exploring, such as the different ways in which criminal actors seek to immerse themselves in the formal political and economic systems (Godson 2003; Albarracín 2018). Relatedly, we have much less knowledge about how criminals embed themselves in formal businesses and markets than in electoral politics. The nonterritorial markets mentioned above typically do not involve violence, which should motivate us to rethink our analytical framework. Even when studying violence, our definition should broaden to include other types of harm, including sexual and gender violence – attributable to both state and criminal actors – child exploitation and the psychological consequences of living in areas with distinct levels of violence and criminal activities.

On the other side of the equation, there are still multiple unexplored avenues on the politics of the police as well as other state agencies who regulate illicit markets. Latin American countries are increasingly relying on their military forces in the fight against drug trafficking, which follow different external operations and internal procedures than the police. Intelligence agencies also participate in this métier, supplying information to state agencies – and sometimes to criminals; theirs is, obviously, a more secretive environment rarely explored by social scientists. Customs and immigration officials are often the first line of defense against transnational criminal activities as well as countries' international commercial exchanges with the rest of the world, yet the dreariness and intricacy of their work has spawned neglect from the academic community. Social scientists focus more on the abject living conditions and criminal governance of penitentiary systems than on how state actors implement formal and informal penitentiary policies. While all these bureaucratic agencies are under the loop of the executive, other state actors are not, the most important being the judiciary. In most Latin American countries, judges and prosecutors, who are formally independent from the executive branch, direct investigations on serious or organized crime. So far, however, there are few systematic studies of the role any of these agencies play in terms of the state's response to illicit markets and organized crime, as well as of their respective politics.

Finally, there are still multiple research pathways within the police itself. Political scientists have still only cursorily explored various internal procedures that are key to police organizational life. For instance, police recruitment is fundamental, given that police departments devote around 80 percent of their budgets to paying salaries. Relatedly, there are few if any studies that closely examine police formal (and informal) budgets and the extent to which political decisions affect them.

Most Latin Americans live in regions affected by criminal markets and by state violence or corruption. This situation, however, is not fixed. Politicians, even within the constrained realm of informal criminal justice policies, can alter how they approach drug trafficking and other criminal markets. A crucial step is whether they take the necessary measures to professionalize their police departments. So far, many governments in the region have ignored this necessity, often at their own peril; many have, contrarily, fueled violence and corruption by police. They tend to find themselves in the same quandaries after many years – or even decades. This book has shown how political competition helps explain these changing dynamics. Advancing any reform requires recognizing the importance of power balances between the relevant actors. It is not simply about getting the policies right. Politics also matters.

Political science research has largely neglected the police, especially in its regulation of criminal markets. This book has captured the importance of not just the police but also politicians, and the state more generally, in regulating these illicit exchanges. How this regulation occurs affects levels of violence, which, beyond its direct human costs, disrupt social life, hamper economic activities, stigmatize neighborhoods and heighten cynicism toward, if not fear of, the state. This book has shown not just how subnational governments get themselves into the worst of these predicaments, but also what they need to get out of them. Democracy, policing and illicit markets are currently intrinsically linked, in the worst cases, through rampant corruption and violence. State actors and citizens in general have the responsibility to ease and ultimately untie this toxic knot. Peace in the region largely depends on it.

Appendix 1

INTERVIEWS

Rio de Janeiro[1]

RJ01 Colonel Paulo Ricardo Paúl, former Military Police, August 25, 2014.

RJ02 Andréa Pachá, civil judge, State of Rio de Janeiro, August 28, 2014.

RJ03/4 Two social movement activists from NGO #1 working with favela youth, August 28, 2014.

RJ05 Flávio Bolsonaro, state deputy, Legislative Assembly of Rio de Janeiro (ALERJ), August 29, 2014.

RJ06 Military Police coronel, PMERJ headquarters, September 1, 2014.

RJ07 Ignácio Cano, professor and researcher, State University of Rio de Janeiro (UERJ), September 1, 2014.

RJ08 Former BOPE officer (rank of captain), September 1, 2014.

RJ09 Municipal Guard official, September 3, 2014.

RJ10 Michel Misse, professor and researcher, Urban Violence Study Nucleus-Federal University of Rio de Janeiro (NECVU/UFRJ), September 3, 2014.

---

[1] All interviews conducted in the City of Rio de Janeiro, unless noted otherwise. The positions of interviewees refer to the moment when the interview was conducted.

RJ11/12 Capitão (Captain) Sandro Costa and Coronel Ubiratan D'Angelo – former Military Police high officials, members of Viva Rio NGO, September 4, 2014.

RJ13 Reimont, city councilman, *Partido Trabalhista* (PT, Workers party), September 4, 2014.

RJ14 Member of Comissão Estadual da Verdade (State Truth Commission), September 4, 2014.

RJ15 Director of NGO #2 (favela youth), municipality located in the periphery of Rio de Janeiro, September 5, 2014. (Name of location also preserved for confidentiality purposes.)

RJ16 Marcus Ianoni, professor at Federal Fluminense University, September 7, 2014.

RJ17 Rodrigo Pimentel, former BOPE captain and current reporter for Globo TV, September 8, 2014.

RJ18 Former delegate Civil Police, September 8, 2014.

RJ19 Luciana Boiteux, penitentiary council of Rio de Janeiro, September 9, 2014.

RJ20 Rubens Casara, criminal court judge, state judicial system, September 9, 2014.

RJ21 João Trajano Sento-Sé, professor and researcher, *Universidade Estadual do Rio de Janeiro*, September 9, 2014.

RJ22 Journalist from *Jornal do Brasil*, September 10, 2014.

RJ23 Jorge Manaia, city councilman, *Partido Verde* (PV, Green party), September 11, 2014.

RJ24 State Penitentiary Administration Secretary, high official, September 12, 2014.

RJ25 Former Military Police colonel, September 16, 2014.

RJ26/27 NGO #3 activists (one former drug trafficker – former trafficker I), September 16, 2014.

RJ28 NGO #4 director (favelas), September 17, 2014.

RJ29 Former high-ranking Civil Police delegate, September 17, 2014.

RJ30-RJ32 Three former drug traffickers, II, III and IV, working with NGO #3, September 18, 2014.

RJ33 Former militia member working with NGO #3, September 18, 2014.

RJ34 Leila do Flamengo, city councilwoman (PMDB), September 18, 2014.

RJ35 Secretary of security mid-level official, September 19, 2014.

RJ36 Jorge da Silva, former Military Police colonel, Niterói, September 19, 2014.

RJ37/42 Rocinha local representatives, December 1–2, 2014.
RJ43 UPP commander, Rocinha, December 2, 2014.
RJ44 Civil Police delegate, Rocinha, December 4, 2014.

Santa Fe[2]

SF01 Fernando "Chino" Rosúa, November 7, 2013, former high-ranking political officer, Obeid administration. Rosario.
SF02 Alberto Martínez, November 7, 2013, former police officer and president of APROPOL police union. Rosario.
SF03 Pablo Venturi, Pitu Salinas, November 7, 2013, activists in *Movimiento 26 de Junio* (social movement based in Villa Moreno). Rosario.
SF04 Maximiliano Pullaro, November 8, 2013, provincial deputy (FPCS). Rosario.
SF05 Oscar Urruty, November 8, 2013, provincial deputy (FPV-PJ). Rosario.
SF06 Alberto Cortés, November 8, 2013, councilmember Rosario (Socialist). Rosario.
SF07 José Luis Giacometti, November 8, 2013, former high-ranking police officer. Rosario.
SF08 Gonzalo Del Cerro, November 11, 2013, Rosario councilmember (UCR). Rosario.
SF09 Mariano Savia, November 11, 2013, former provincial police chief. Rosario.
SF10 Lisandro Enrico, November 11, 2013, provincial senator (UCR-FPCS). Rosario.
SF11 Alicia Gutiérrez, November 12, 2013, state deputy (FPCS). Rosario.
SF12 Eduardo Toniolli, November 12, 2013, provincial deputy (FPV). Rosario.
SF13 Former high-ranking police officer, Rosario unit, November 12, 2013. Rosario.
SF14 Juan Murray, November 12, 2013, federal prosecutor. Rosario.
SF15 Roberto Bruera, November 13, 2013, councilmember of Rosario (PDP-FPCS). Rosario.
SF16 Gabriel Ganon, November 13, 2013, general public defender of the province of Santa Fe. City of Santa Fe.

[2] The positions of interviewees refer to the moment when the interview was conducted.

SF17 Diego Poretti, November 14, 2013, provincial undersecretary of security. City of Santa Fe.

SF18 Leandro Corti, November 14, 2013, former provincial security minister. City of Santa Fe.

SF19 Matías Drivet, November 15, 2013, provincial secretary of public security. City of Santa Fe.

SF20 Ana Viglione, November 15, 2013, provincial secretary of complex crimes. City of Santa Fe.

SF21 Héctor Aguiar, November 15, 2013, police officer and delegate of ULTRAPOL (police union). City of Santa Fe.

SF22 Luis Acuña, November 18, 2013, provincial deputy (FPV-PJ). Provincial legislature. City of Santa Fe.

SF23 Máximo Sozzo, November 18, 2013, university professor, specializing in police reform. City of Santa Fe.

SF24 Pablo Cococcioni, November 18, 2013, provincial undersecretary of penitentiary affairs. City of Santa Fe.

SF25 Raúl Lamberto, November 19, 2013, provincial security minister.

SF26 Paula Ballesteros, November 19, 2013, Center for Municipal and Provincial Studies (CEMUPRO). Rosario.

SF27 Luis Caterina, November 19, 2013, provincial judge. Rosario.

SF28 Jorge Barraguirre, November 19, 2013, provincial prosecutor before the state supreme court. Rosario.

SF29 Jorge Pérez de Urrechu, November 20, 2013, provincial judge. Rosario.

SF30 Daniel Cuenca, November 20, 2013, former provincial security minister. Rosario.

SF31 Francisco Broglia, November 20, 2013, former member of the secretary of community prevention. Rosario.

SF32 Guillermo Camporini, June 24, 2014, provincial prosecutor. Rosario.

SF33 Héctor Vera Barros, June 24, 2014, federal Judge. Rosario.

SF34 Hernán Lascano, June 24, journalist for *La Capital* newspaper. Rosario.

SF35 Three members of *Red Antimafia* (AntiMafia network), June 24, 2014. Rosario.

SF36 Juan Carlos Vienna, June 25, 2014, provincial judge. Rosario.

SF37 Fernando Asegurado, June 25, 2014, secretary of government, municipal government of Rosario.

Buenos Aires[3]

BA01 Felipe Solá, former governor, July 3, 2011, City of Buenos Aires.

BA02 León Carlos Arslanian, former provincial security minister, July 4, 2011, City of Buenos Aires.

BA03 Alberto Piotti, former provincial security secretary, July 4, 2011, City of Buenos Aires.

BA04 Eduardo de Lázzari, former provincial security secretary, June 2012, La Plata.

BA05 Marcelo Sain, provincial deputy and former provincial deputy security minister, July 20, 2013.

BA06 Federico Suñer, security secretary of San Isidro municipality, September 27, 2013

BA07 Raúl Maza, National Military Police officer, September 27, 2013.

BA08 Gustavo Sibilla, former director of planning, national security ministry, October 1, 2013, City of Buenos Aires.

BA09 Claudio Izaguirre, president of Argentina Antidrug Association, October 2, 2013, Malvinas Argentinas.

BA10 Laura Piana and Norberto Tirendi, deputy directors of external auditing office, provincial security ministry, October 3, 2013, La Plata.

BA11 Alberto Giordano, advisor for *Frente Renovador* senator, October 3, 2013, La Plata.

BA12 Carlos del Frade, journalist, October 5, 2013, La Plata.

BA13 Marcelo "Oso" Díaz, state deputy, October 8, 2013, La Plata.

BA14 Julio César Frutos, former high-ranking officer, provincial police, October 8, 2013, La Plata.

BA15 Rodrigo Pomares and Ángela Oyhandy, State Memory Commission (NGO) directors, October 8, 2013, La Plata.

BA16 Mirta Juárez and Mario Santillán, municipal directors of community security (San Martín) October 11, 2013, San Martín.

BA17 José María Fernández, secretary of security, Municipality of San Martín, October 11, 2013, San Martín.

BA18 Norberto Emmerich, expert on drug trafficking, October 15, 2013, City of Buenos Aires.

---

[3] All interviews took place in Buenos Aires province unless otherwise indicated. The positions of interviewees refer to the moment when the interview was conducted.

BA19 Local neighborhood NGO director, Greater BA municipality, October 2013.

BA20 Alfredo Meckievi, provincial senator, October 15, 2013, La Plata.

BA21 Eduardo Amadeo, national deputy, October 16, 2013, City of Buenos Aires.

BA22 Prosecutor, anti-drug prosecution office of San Martín, October 18, 2013, San Martín.

BA23 Roberto Siminián, San Martín municipal councilmember, October 18, 2013, San Martín.

BA24 Natalia Gambaro, national deputy, October 24, 2013, City of Buenos Aires.

BA25 Iván Budassi, provincial deputy, October 30, 2013, La Plata.

BA26 Ana Museri, researcher with Center for Legal and Social Studies (CELS) November 21, City of Buenos Aires.

BA27 Virginia Messi, journalist, November 30, 2013, City of Buenos Aires.

BA28 Judicial official, Federal Judiciary Office of San Isidro, December 16, 2013, San Isidro.

BA29 High-ranking officer in the Drug Trafficking Division, Federal Police, December 16, 2013, City of Buenos Aires.

BA30 Héctor D'Aquino, Florencio Varela municipal council member, December 11, 2013, Florencio Varela.

BA31 Laura Vivas, municipal under-secretary of security (Florencio Varela), December 11, 2013, Florencio Varela.

BA32 Dardo Ottonello, Florencio Varela municipal council member, December 11, 2013, Florencio Varela.

BA33 Sergio Torres, federal judge, December 12, 2013, City of Buenos Aires.

BA34 Silvio Álvarez, Florencio Varela municipal council member, December 13, 2013, Florencio Varela.

BA35 Andrés Watson, Florencio Varela council member and former secretary of government, December 13, 2013, Florencio Varela.

BA36 Director of Varela Center for Social Rehabilitation (CEVARESO), December 13, 2013, Florencio Varela.

BA37 Jorge Sica, federal prosecutor, San Martín, December 16, 2013, San Martín.

BA38 Police union representatives (3), December 17, 2013, La Plata.

BA39 Parish priest in a poor neighborhood of the City of Buenos Aires, December 18, 2013, City of Buenos Aires.

BA40 Daniel Ivoskus, San Martín municipal council member and former secretary of government, December 20, 2013, San Martín.

BA41 Police district chief, San Martín municipality, December 23, 2013, San Martín.

BA42 Ricardo Casal, former provincial security minister, January 16, 2014, La Plata.

BA43 Eugenio Burzaco, former chief of Metropolitan Police of the City of Buenos Aires, June 12, 2014, City of Buenos Aires.

BA44 Salvador Baratta, former deputy chief of the provincial police, June 16, 2014, Lanús.

BA45 César Albarracín, provincial secretary of crime policy, June 17, 2014, La Plata.

BA46 Eduardo Duhalde, former governor, July 3, 2014, City of Buenos Aires.

BA47 Jesús Celis, Florencio Varela municipal security secretary, August 6, 2014, Florencio Varela.

BA48 Neighborhood political and social worker, municipality of Greater Buenos Aires, August 11, 2014.

BA49 Ricardo Ivoskus, former San Martín municipal mayor, August 12, 2014, San Martín.

BA50 Jorge D'Onofrio, provincial senator (*Frente Renovador*), August 13, 2014, La Plata.

BA51 Pablo Wuhsagk, state prosecutor's office, August 13, 2014.

São Paulo[4]

SP01 Former Military Police soldier, October 22, 2014.

SP02 Military Police corporal, October 23, 2014.

SP03 Conte Lopes, former ROTA colonel, city council member, October 23, 2014.

SP04 Mário Covas Neto, city council member (PSDB), October 23, 2014.

SP05 Orlando Bolçone, state deputy (PSDB), October 29, 2014.

SP06 Reis, former Civil and Military Police officer, city councilman, October 29, 2014.

SP07 Military Police lieutenant, Santana, São Paulo, October 30, 2014.

---

[4] All interviews conducted in the city of São Paulo unless specifically indicated. The positions of interviewees refer to the moment when the interview was conducted.

SP08 Colonel Camilo, former head of the Military Police, city council member, October 30, 2014.

SP09 Guaracy Mingardi, professor and security expert, University of São Paulo, November 3, 2014.

SP10 Arnaldo Hossepian Jr., former deputy secretary of security, November 3, 2014.

SP11 Antônio Assunção "Delegado" de Olim, civil police investigator, November 4, 2014.

SP12 Military Police captain, Transit Division, November 5, 2014.

SP13 Marco Antônio Desgualdo, former chief of Civil Police, head of Administrative Crimes Division, November 5, 2014.

SP14 Military Police captain, Eastern Zone precinct, November 6, 2014.

SP15–17 Military Police soldiers (3), Eastern Zone precinct, November 6, 2014.

SP18 Colonel Telhada, former head of ROTA (Military Police), current council member, November 6, 2014.

SP19 Lieutenant, Military Police, Western Zone precinct, November 7, 2014.

SP20 José Américo, council member (PT), November 10, 2014.

SP21 Donato, council member (PT), November 11, 2014.

SP22 Jair Tatto, council member (PT), November 11, 2014.

SP23 Hamilton Pereira, state deputy (PT), November 11, 2014.

SP24 Marco Petrelluzzi, former state security secretary, November 12, 2014.

SP25 Domingos Paulo Neto, former chief of Civil Police, head of Capital Department of PC, November 12, 2014.

SP26 Ronaldo Marzagão, former state secretary of security, November 13, 2014.

SP27 Military Police soldier, Guarulhos, November 14, 2014.

SP28 Civil Police station delegate, Southern Zone precinct, November 18, 2014.

SP29 Adriano Diogo, state deputy (PT), November18, 2014.

SP30 Mayor in ROTA (Military Police), November 21, 2014.

SP31 Colonel in Military Police, Capital Department, November 24, 2014.

SP32 Fernando Capez, State deputy (PSDB), November 24, 2014.

SP33–35 Community-based human rights NGO activists (3), November 25, 2014.

SP36 Wagner Fontes, director of Division of Organized Crime, Civil Police, November 26, 2014.

SP37 Investigator in Drug Trafficking Division, Civil Police, November 26, 2014.

SP-38 Rodrigo Moraes, state deputy, November 27, 2014.
SP39 Colonel Levi, director of Military Police internal affairs division, November 28, 2014.

OTHER SOURCES

Rio de Janeiro

Newspapers
National:
O Globo
Jornal do Brasil
Veja
Isto É
Folha de São Paulo
International
Rio Times
Los Angeles Times
The Economist

Government Agencies
Instituto de Segurança Pública-Rio de Janeiro (ISP-RJ, Secretaria de Segurança Pública)
Unidade de Polícia Pacificadora: www.upprj.com

Non-Governmental Organizations
Núcleo de Estudos da Violência – Universidade de São Paulo (NEV-USP, Center for the Study of Violence – University of São Paulo)
Viva Rio

Santa Fe

Newspapers
National:
La Nación
Clarín
Página12
La Política Online
Provincial:
La Capital

El Litoral
El Ciudadano
Periódico Pausa
Rosario3

Government Agencies
Ministerio de Seguridad de la Provincia de Santa Fe
Tribunales provinciales de Santa Fe
Sistema Nacional de Información Criminal (SNIC, National Criminal
Information System)

Non-Governmental Organizations
Red Antimafia
Universidad Nacional del Rosario – proyecto Calles

Buenos Aires

Newspapers
La Nación
Clarín
Página12
La Política Online
Perfil

Government Agencies
Ministerio de Seguridad de la Provincia de Buenos Aires (Buenos Aires
provincial security ministry): www.minseg.gob.ar
Procuración General de la Provincia de Buenos Aires (Buenos Aires
General Attorney's Office)
Auditoría de Asuntos Internos de la Provincia de Buenos Aires (Internal
Affairs Office)
Sistema Nacional de Información Criminal (SNIC, National Criminal
Information System)

Non-Governmental Organizations
Centro de Estudios Legales y Sociales (CELS, Center of Legal and
Social Studies)
Comisión Provincial por la Memoria (Provincial Memory Commission)
Coordinadora contra la Represión Policial e Institucional (CORREPI,
Association Against Police and Institutional Repression)

São Paulo

Newspapers
  Folha de São Paulo
  Estado de São Paulo (Estadão)
  O Globo
  iG.com.br

Government agencies
  Secretaria de Segurança Pública – São Paulo: www.ssp-sp.gov.br

Non-Governmental Organizations
  Núcleo de Estudos da Violência, Universidade de São Paulo (NEV-USP,
    Violence Studies Nucleus, University of São Paulo)
  Human Rights Watch (HRW)
  Local neighborhood association in Eastern Zone of São Paulo

Appendix 2

TABLE A.1. *Rio de Janeiro security secretaries, 1995–2014*

Governor	Security Secretary	Former position	Period	Months in office
Marcello Alencar (1995–1998)	Dulcimer Lima da Silva	Federal Army General	January–May 1995	4
	Nílton de Albuquerque Cerqueira	Federal Army General	May 1995–April 1998	35
	Noaldo Alves Silva	Federal Army Colonel	April 1998–December 1998	9
Anthony Garotinho (1999–2002)	José Siqueira Silva	Federal Army General	January–April 1999	4
	Josias Quintal de Oliveira	Former Military Police	April 1999–April 2002	36
Benedita da Silva (2002–2003)	Roberto Armando Ramos de Aguiar	Lawyer and university professor	April–December 2002	8
Rosinha Garotinho (2003–2006)	Josias Quintal de Oliveira	Federal senator	January–April 2003	4
	Anthony Garotinho	State governor	April 2003–September 2004	17

Governor	Security Secretary	Former position	Period	Months in office
	Marcelo Zaturansky Nogueira Itagiba	Federal police delegate	December 2004– March 2006	18
	Roberto Precioso Júnior	Federal police delegate	March– December 2006	9
Sérgio Cabral (2006–2013)	José Mariano Beltrame	Federal police delegate	January 2007– December 2014	118
Luis Fernando Pezão (2013–2018)			January 2015– October 2016	

Source: Author's elaboration from https://pt.wikipedia.org/wiki/Lista_de_secret%C3%A1rios_de_seguran%C3%A7a_p%C3%BAblica_do_Rio_de_Janeiro

TABLE A.2. *Police pacifications units by date of establishment, 2008–2013*

Date UPP established	Unit (Unidade)	UPP name	Zone within Rio
November 28, 2008	1st UPP	Santa Marta	South Zone
February 16, 2009	2nd UPP	Cidade de Deus	West Zone
February 18, 2009	3rd UPP	Batan	West Zone
June 10, 2009	4th UPP	Babilônia and Chapéu-Mangueira	South Zone
December 23, 2009	5th UPP	Pavão-Pavãozinho	South Zone
January 14, 2010	6th UPP	Tabajaras/Cabritos	South Zone
April 25, 2010	7th UPP	Providência	Centro
June 2010	8th UPP	Borel	North Zone
July 2010	9th UPP	Formiga	North Zone
July 28, 2010	10th UPP	Andaraí	North Zone
September 17, 2010	11th UPP	Salgueiro	North Zone
September 30, 2010	12th UPP	Morro do Turano	North Zone
November 30, 2010	13th UPP	Macacos	North Zone
January 28, 2011	14th UPP	São João, Matriz and Quieto	North Zone
February 25, 2011	15th UPP	Coroa, Fallet and Fogueteiro	Centro
February 25, 2011	16th UPP	Escondidinho/Prazeres	Centro
May 17, 2011	17th UPP	São Carlos	Centro

(*continued*)

TABLE A.2. (*continued*)

Date UPP established	Unit (Unidade)	UPP name	Zone within Rio
November 3, 2011	18th UPP	Mangueira	North Zone
January 18, 2012	19th UPP	Vidigal	South Zone
April 18, 2012	20th UPP	Fazendinha	North Zone
April 18, 2012	21st UPP	Nova Brasília	North Zone
May 11, 2012	22nd UPP	Adeus/Baiana	North Zone
May 30, 2012	23rd UPP	Alemão	North Zone
June 27, 2012	24th UPP	Fé/Sereno	North Zone
June 2012	25th UPP	Chatuba	North Zone
August 2012	26th UPP	Parque Proletário	North Zone
August 28, 2012	27th UPP	Vila Cruzeiro	North Zone
September 20, 2012	28th UPP	Rocinha	South Zone
January 16, 2013	29th UPP	Manguinhos	North Zone
January 16, 2013	30th UPP	Jacarezinho	North Zone
April 12, 2013	31st UPP	Caju	North Zone
April 12, 2013	32nd UPP	Barreira and Tuiuti	Centro
May 2013	33rd UPP	Cerro-Corá	South Zone
September 2013	34th UPP	Parque Arará/Mandela	North Zone
December 2, 2013	35th UPP	Lins	North Zone
December 2, 2013	36th UPP	Camarista Méier	North Zone

Source: Author's elaboration from www.upprj.com/index.php/historico

TABLE A.3. *List of provincial security ministers (2007–2015) since the official creation of the ministry (Santa Fe, Argentina)*

Governor (party, period)	Security minister	Previous position	Period in office	Months in office
Hermes Binner (Socialist party, 2007–2011)	Daniel Cuenca	University professor and private lawyer	December 2007–December 2009	24
	Álvaro Gaviola	Director of the Provincial Civil registry	December 2009–December 2011	24
Antonio Bonfatti (Socialist party, 2011–2015)	Leandro Corti	Undersecretary of Penitentiary Affairs	December 2011–June 2012	6
	Raúl Lamberto	Provincial deputy (Socialists)	June 2012–December 2015	42

Source: Author's elaboration from *La Capital*

TABLE A.4. *List and tenure of provincial security ministers per governor in the province of Buenos Aires, 1992–2015*

Governor (party, period)	Security secretary/ minister	Period	Months in office
Eduardo Duhalde (PJ, 1991–1999)	Eduardo Pettigiani	January 1992–December 1993	23
	Alberto Piotti	January 1994–September 1996	32
	Eduardo de Lázzari	October 1996–March 1997	5
	Carlos Brown	March–December 1997	9
	Luis Lugones	December 1997–April 1998	4
	León Arslanian	April 1998–August 1999	16
	Osvaldo Lorenzo	August–October 1999	2
	Carlos Soria	October–December 1999	2
Carlos Ruckauf (PJ, 1999–2001)	Aldo Rico	December 1999–February 2000	3
	Ramón Verón	February 2000–September 2001	19
	Juan José Álvarez	October–December 2001	3
	Alberto Descalzo	January 2002	0
Felipe Solá (PJ, 2002–2007)	Luis Genoud	January–July 2002	6
	Juan Pablo Cafiero	July 2002–September 2003	14
	Juan José Álvarez	September–November 2003	2
	Raúl Rivara	November 2003–April 2004	4
	León Arslanian	April 2004–December 2007	44
Daniel Scioli (FPV-PJ, 2007–2015)	Carlos Stornelli	December 2007–May 2010	29
	Ricardo Casal	May 2010–September 2013	40
	Alejandro Granados	September 2013–December 2015	27

Source: Author's elaboration from various sources

TABLE A.5. *List and tenure of state security secretaries in São Paulo,*
1983–2014

Governor (party, period)	Security Secretary	Period	Months in office
André Franco Montoro (PMDB, 1983–1986)	Manoel Pedro Pimentel	March–September 1983	6
	Miguel Reale Jr.	September 1983– January 1984	5
	Michel Temer	February 1984– February 1986	24
	Eduardo Muylaert	February 1986– March 1987	13
Orestes Quércia (PMDB, 1987–1990)	Luiz Fleury	March 1987– March 1990	37
	Antônio Mariz de Oliveira	March 1990– March 1991	12
Luiz Fleury (PMDB, 1991–1994)	Pedro Franco de Campos	March 1991– August 1992	19
	Michel Temer	August 1992– November 1993	14
	Odyr Pinto Porto	January– September 1994	9
	Antônio de Souza Correa	September– December 1994	3
Mário Covas/Geraldo Alckmin (PSDB, 1994–2002)	José Afonso Silva	January 1995– February 1999	50
	Marco Petrelluzzi	February 1999– January 2002	36
Geraldo Alckmin (PSDB, 2003–2006)	Saulo de Castro Abreu	January 2002– December 2006	60
José Serra (PSDB, 2007–2010)	Ronaldo Marzagão	January 2007– March 2009	27
	Antônio Ferreira Pinto	March 2009– December 2010	22
Geraldo Alckmin (PSDB, 2011–2014)	Antônio Ferreira Pinto	January 2011– November 2012	23
	Fernando Grella Vieira	November 2012– December 2014	25

Source: Author's elaboration from www.ssp.sp.gov.br/institucional/historico/secretarios
.aspx

References

Adorno, Sérgio, and Fernando Salla. 2007. "Criminalidade organizada nas prisões e os ataques do PCC." *Estudos Avançados*, 21: 7–29.

Albarracín, Juan. 2018. "Criminalized Electoral Politics in Brazilian Urban Peripheries." *Crime, Law and Social Change* 69 (4): 553–75.

Alexander, Michelle. 2020. *The New Jim Crow: Mass Incarceration in the Age of Colorblindness*. Tenth anniversary edition. New York and London: The New Press.

Alpert, Geoffrey P., and Roger G. Dunham. 2004. *Understanding Police Use of Force: Officers, Suspects, and Reciprocity*. Cambridge: Cambridge University Press.

Altbeker, Antony. 2009. "The Building of a New South African Police Service: The Dynamics of Police Reform in a Changing (and Violent) Country." In *Policing Developing Democracies*, 260–79. London: Routledge.

Alves, Jaime Amparo. 2018. *The Anti-Black City: Police Terror and Black Urban Life in Brazil*. Minneapolis, MN: University of Minnesota Press.

Alves, Maria Helena Moreira, and Philip Evanson. 2011. *Living in the Crossfire: Favela Residents, Drug Dealers, and Police Violence in Rio de Janeiro*. Philadelphia, PA: Temple University Press.

Amorim, Carlos. 1993. *Comando Vermelho, a História Secreta do Crime Organizado*. Rio de Janeiro: Editora Record.

Arias, Enrique D. 2006a. *Drugs and Democracy in Rio de Janeiro: Trafficking, Social Networks, and Public Security*. Chapel Hill, NC: University of North Carolina Press.

2006b. "The Dynamics of Criminal Governance: Networks and Social Order in Rio de Janeiro." *Journal of Latin American Studies* 38 (02): 293–325.

2013. "The Impacts of Differential Armed Dominance of Politics in Rio de Janeiro, Brazil." *Studies in Comparative International Development* 48 (3): 263–84.

Arias, Enrique D., and Daniel M. Goldstein, eds. 2010. *Violent Democracies in Latin America*. Durham, NC: Duke University Press.

Arias, Enrique D., and Mark Ungar. 2009. "Community Policing and Latin America's Citizen Security Crisis." *Comparative Politics* 41 (4): 409–29.

Arias, Enrique D. 2017. *Criminal Enterprises and Governance in Latin America and the Caribbean*. New York: Cambridge University Press.

Arjona, Ana. 2016. *Rebelocracy*. New York: Cambridge University Press.

Arslanian, Léon Carlos. 2008. *Un Cambio Posible: Delito, Inseguridad y Reforma Policial En La Provincia de Buenos Aires*. First edition. Buenos Aires: Edhasa.

Auyero, Javier. 2001. *Poor People's Politics: Peronist Survival Networks and the Legacy of Evita*. Durham, NC: Duke University Press.

2007. *La Zona Gris: Violencia Colectiva y Política Partidaria en la Argentina Contemporánea*. Buenos Aires and Mexico City. Siglo Veintiuno ed.

Auyero, Javier, and María Fernanda Berti. 2013. *La Violencia En Los Márgenes: Una Maestra y Un Sociólogo En El Conurbano Bonaerense*. Buenos Aires: Katz Editores.

2015. *In Harm's Way: The Dynamics of Urban Violence*. Princeton, NJ: Princeton University Press.

Auyero, Javier, and Katherine Sobering. 2019. *The Ambivalent State: Police-Criminal Collusion at the Urban Margins*. New York: Oxford University Press.

Azaola, Elena. 2009. "The Weaknesses of Public Security Forces in Mexico City." In *Criminality, Public Security, and the Challenge to Democracy in Latin America*. Notre Dame, IN: University of Notre Dame Press.

Bagley, Bruce. 2012. "Drug Trafficking and Organized Crime in the Americas: Major Trends in the Twenty-First Century." Washington, DC: Woodrow Wilson Center, Latin American Program.

Bailey, John, and Lucía Dammert, eds. 2006. *Public Security and Police Reform in the Americas*. Pittsburgh, PA: University of Pittsburgh Press.

Baldwin, Robert, Martin Cave and Martin Lodge. 2012. *Understanding Regulation: Theory, Strategy, and Practice*. 2nd ed. New York: Oxford University Press.

Barcellos, Caco. 2005. *Rota 66: A História da Polícia Que Mata*. Rio de Janeiro: Editora Record.

Bates, Robert. 2008. "Probing the Sources of Political Order." In *Order, Conflict and Violence*, 17–42. Cambridge and New York: Cambridge University Press.

Bayley, David H. 1985. *Patterns of Policing: A Comparative International Analysis*. Crime, Law, and Deviance Series. New Brunswick, NJ: Rutgers University Press.

2006. *Changing the Guard: Developing Democratic Police Abroad*. Studies in Crime and Public Policy. New York: Oxford University Press.

Beare, Margaret E., and Tonita Murray, eds. 2007. *Police and Government Relations: Who's Calling the Shots?* Toronto: University of Toronto Press.

Beckert, Jens, and Matías Dewey. 2017. *The Architecture of Illegal Markets: Towards an Economic Sociology of Illegality in the Economy*. Oxford: Oxford University Press.

Beltrame, José Mariano. 2014. *Todo Dia é Degunda-Feira*. Rio de Janeiro: Sextante.

Bennett, Andrew, and Jeffrey T. Checkel, eds. 2015. *Process Tracing: From Metaphor to Analytic Tool*. Strategies for Social Inquiry. Cambridge and New York: Cambridge University Press.

Bergman, Marcelo. 2018. *More Money, More Crime: Prosperity and Rising Crime in Latin America*. New York: Oxford University Press.

Bertram, Eva, Morris Blachman, Kenneth Sharpe and Peter Andreas. 1996. *Drug War Politics: The Price of Denial*. Berkeley, CA: University of California Press.

Bicudo, Hélio. 2002. *Meu Depoimento Sobre o Esquadrão da Morte*. São Paulo: Martins Fontes.

Binder, Alberto. 2004. *Policías y Ladrones: La Inseguridad en Cuestión*. Buenos Aires: Capital Intelectual.

Biondi, Karina. 2016. *Sharing This Walk: An Ethnography of Prison Life and the PCC in Brazil*. Chapel Hill, NC: University of North Carolina Press Books.

Bittner, Egon. 1970. "The Functions of the Police in Modern Society: A Review of Background Factors, Current Practices, and Possible Role Models." Chevy Chase, MD: National Institute of Mental Health, Center for Studies of Crime and Delinquency.

Black, Julia. 2001. "Decentring Regulation: Understanding the Role of Regulation and Self-Regulation in a 'Post-Regulatory' World." *Current Legal Problems* 54 (1): 103–46.

Bonasso, Miguel. 1999. *Don Alfredo*. Buenos Aires: Editorial Planeta.

Bonner, Michelle D. 2019. *Tough on Crime: The Rise of Punitive Populism in Latin America*. Pittsburgh, PA: University of Pittsburgh Press.

Bowden, Mark. 2002. *Killing Pablo: The Hunt for the World's Greatest Outlaw*. New York: Penguin Books.

Brady, Henry E., and David Collier, eds. 2010. *Rethinking Social Inquiry Diverse Tools, Shared Standards*. Lanham, MD: Rowman and Littlefield Publishers.

Brinks, Daniel M. 2003. "Informal Institutions and the Rule of Law: The Judicial Response to State Killings in Buenos Aires and São Paulo in the 1990s." *Comparative Politics* 36 (1): 1–19.

2008. *The Judicial Response to Police Killings in Latin America*. Cambridge and New York: Cambridge University Press.

Burzaco, Eugenio, and Sergio Berensztein. 2014. *El Poder Narco: Drogas, Inseguridad y Violencia En La Argentina*. Buenos Aires: Sudamericana.

Caldeira, Teresa P. R. 2000. *City of Walls: Crime, Segregation, and Citizenship in São Paulo*. Berkeley, CA: University of California Press.

Calderón, G., G. Robles, A. Diaz-Cayeros and B. Magaloni. 2015. "The Beheading of Criminal Organizations and the Dynamics of Violence in Mexico." *Journal of Conflict Resolution* 59 (8): 1455–85. https://doi.org/10 .1177/0022002715587053.

Cano, Ignacio. 1997. *Letalidade Da Ação Policial No Rio de Janeiro*. Rio de Janeiro: Instituto de Estudos da Religião.

Cano, Ignacio, Doriam Borges and Eduardo Ribeiro. 2012. "O Impacto Das Unidades de Polícia Pacificadora (UPPs) No Rio de Janeiro." *Forum Brasileiro de Segurança Pública - Laboratório de Análise Da Violência (LAV)*.

Carpenter, Daniel P. 2001. *The Forging of Bureaucratic Autonomy: Reputations, Networks, and Policy Innovation in Executive Agencies, 1862–1928.* Princeton, NJ: Princeton University Press.

Carrion Jr., Francisco Machado. 1989. *Brizola: Momentos de Decisão.* Porto Alegre: L & PM Editores.

Casas, Kevin, Paola González and Liliana Mesías. 2018. "La Transformación Policial Para El 2030 En América Latina." www.thedialogue.org/wp-content/uploads/2018/11/kcasas_transformacionpolicial_fi-nal.pdf.

Caulkins, Jonathan P., Peter Reuter and Lowell J. Taylor. 2006. "Can Supply Restrictions Lower Price? Violence, Drug Dealing and Positional Advantage." *The BE Journal of Economic Analysis & Policy* 5 (1). www.degruyter.com/view/j/bejeap.2005.5.issue-1/bejeap.2006.5.1.1387/bejeap.2006.5.1.1387.xml.

Cavallaro, James, and Anne Manuel. 1997. *Police Brutality in Urban Brazil.* New York: Human Rights Watch.

Cavanagh, Gastón. 2014. "Los Monos: The Drug Gang of Rosario, Argentina's Most Violent City." VICE News. August 28, 2014. www.vice.com/en/article/nemm4d/los-monos-the-drug-gang-of-rosario-argentinas-most-violent-city.

Cerqueira, Carlos Magno Nazareth. 2001. *O Futuro de Uma Ilusão: O Sonho de Uma Nova Polícia.* Coleção Polícia Amanhã 6. Rio de Janeiro: Instituto Carioca de Criminologia: F. Bastos Editora.

Chevigny, Paul. 1995. *Edge of the Knife: Police Violence in the Americas.* New York: New Press, Norton.

Chevigny, Paul, Bell Gale Chevigny and Patricia Pittman. 1991. *Police Violence in Argentina: Torture and Police Killings in Buenos Aires.* New York and Buenos Aires: Human Rights Watch; Centro de Estudios Legales y Sociales.

Colmerauer, Marcio. 2014. *O Pássaro de Ferro: Uma História Dos Bastidores Da Segurança Pública Do Rio de Janeiro.* 1st edition. Rio de Janeiro: Editora Record.

Comisión Provincial por la Memoria (CPM), 2012. "Informe Anual: El Sistema de la Crueldad VII." Buenos Aires: FERROGRAF.

Comisión Provincial por la Memoria (CPM), 2013. "Informe Anual: 10 Años." Buenos Aires: FERROGRAF.

Córdoba, Alejandro Javier. 2007. *Ratonera: La Historia Oculta de La Masacre de Andreani.* Argentina: A. J. Córdoba.

Coronel Paúl. 2011. *Cabral Contra Paúl: A Polícia Militar de Joelhos.* Rio de Janeiro: Livre Expressão.

Cruz, José Miguel. 2009. "Police Abuse in Latin America." *AmericasBarometer Insights* 11.

2011. "Criminal Violence and Democratization in Central America: The Survival of the Violent State." *Latin American Politics and Society* 53 (4): 1–33.

Cruz, José Miguel, and Angélica Durán-Martínez. 2016. "Hiding Violence to Deal with the State: Criminal Pacts in El Salvador and Medellin." *Journal of Peace Research* 53 (2): 197–210. https://doi.org/10.1177/0022343315626239.

Dal Bó, Ernesto, Pedro Dal Bó and Rafael Di Tella. 2006. "Plata o Plomo?: Bribe and Punishment in a Theory of Political Influence." *American Political Science Review* 100 (1): 41–53.

Damianovich, Alejandro. 2001. *A Caballo Del Tigre: Memorias de La Casa Gris: El Gobierno de Jorge Obeid En Santa Fe, 1995–1999.* Rosario: Homo Sapiens Ediciones.

Dammert, Lucía. 2009. "Police and Judicial Reform in Chile." In *Policing Insecurity: Police Reform, Security, and Human Rights in Latin America,* 151–68. Lanham, MD: Rowman and Littlefield Publishers.

Darden, Keith. 2008. "The Integrity of Corrupt States: Graft as an Informal State Institution." *Politics & Society* 36 (1): 35–59. https://doi.org/10.1177/0032329207312183.

Davis, Diane E. 2006. "Undermining the Rule of Law: Democratization and the Dark Side of Police Reform in Mexico." *Latin American Politics and Society* 48 (1): 55–86.

Del Frade, Carlos. 2000. *Ciudad Blanca, Crónica Negra. Historia Política Del Narcotráfico En El Gran Rosario.* Rosario and Santa Fe: Ediciones Letra Libre.

Dell, Melissa. 2015. "Trafficking Networks and the Mexican Drug War." *American Economic Review* 105 (6): 1738–79. https://doi.org/10.1257/aer.20121637.

Denyer Willis, Graham. 2015. *The Killing Consensus: Police, Organized Crime, and the Regulation of Life and Death in Urban Brazil.* Oakland, CA: University of California Press.

Denyer Willis, Graham, and Mariana Mota Prado. 2014. "Process and Pattern in Institutional Reforms: A Case Study of the Police Pacifying Units (UPPs) in Brazil." *World Development* 64 (December): 232–42. https://doi.org/10.1016/j.worlddev.2014.06.006.

Dewey, Matías. 2015. *El Orden Clandestino: Política, Fuerzas de Seguridad y Mercados Ilegales En La Argentina.* Vol. 2045. Buenos Aires: Katz Editores.

Dias, Camila Caldeira Nunes. 2011. "Da Pulverização ao Monopólio da Violência: Expansão e Consolidação do Primeiro Comando da Capital (PCC) No Sistema Carcerário Paulista." Doctoral Dissertation, Universidade de São Paulo.

———. 2013. *PCC: Hegemonia Nas Prisões e Monopólio Da Violência.* Coleção Saberes Monográficos. São Paulo: Editora Saraiva.

Dias, Camila Caldeira Nunes, and Fernando Salla. 2013. "Organized Crime in Brazilian Prisons: The Example of the PCC." *International Journal of Criminology and Sociology* 2: 397–408.

Dowdney, Luke. 2004. *Children of the Drug Trade: A Case of Study in Organised Armed Violence in Rio de Janeiro.* Rio de Janeiro: 7 Letras.

Durán-Martínez, Angélica. 2015. "To Kill and Tell? State Power, Criminal Competition, and Drug Violence." *Journal of Conflict Resolution* 59 (8): 1377–402.

Durán-Martínez, Angélica. 2017. *The Politics of Drug Violence: Criminals, Cops and Politicians in Colombia and Mexico.* New York: Oxford University Press.

Dutil, Carlos, and Ricardo Ragendorfer. 1997. *La Bonaerense: Historia Criminal de la Policía de la Provincia de Buenos Aires.* Buenos Aires: Planeta.

Eaton, Kent. 2008. "Paradoxes of Police Reform: Federalism, Parties, and Civil Society in Argentina's Public Security Crisis." *Latin American Research Review* 43 (3): 5–32.

Evangelista, Helio de Araujo. 2003. *Rio de Janeiro: Violência, Jogo do Bicho e Narcotráfico Segundo Uma Interpretação.* Rio de Janeiro: Revan.

Evans, Peter B. 1989. "Predatory, Developmental, and Other Apparatuses: A Comparative Political Economy Perspective on the Third World State." *Sociological Forum* 4 (4): 561–87.

1995. *Embedded Autonomy: States and Industrial Transformation.* Princeton Paperbacks. Princeton, NJ: Princeton University Press.

Fassin, Didier. 2013. *Enforcing Order: An Ethnography of Urban Policing.* Cambridge: Polity.

Faull, Andrew. 2007. "Corruption and the South African Police Service. A Review and Its Implications." *Institute for Security Studies Papers* 2007 (150): 20–40.

Federico, Mauro. 2008. *País Narco. Tráfico de Droga En Argentina: Del Tránsito a La Producción Propia.* Buenos Aires: Sudamericana.

Feltran, Gabriel de Santis. 2011. *Fronteiras de Tensão: Política e Violência Nas Periferias de São Paulo.* São Paulo: Editora UNESP.

Ferraz, Claudio, and Bruno Vaz. 2013. "The Effects of the Pacification Police on Crime and Violence." Working paper.

Flom, Hernán, and Alison E. Post. 2016. "Blame Avoidance and Policy Stability in Developing Democracies: The Politics of Public Security in Buenos Aires." *Comparative Politics* 49 (1): 23–42.

Fogelson, Robert M. 1977. *Big-City Police. Urban Institute Study.* Cambridge, MA: Harvard University Press.

Freidenberg, Flavia, and Steven Levitsky. 2006. "Informal Institutions and Party Organization in Latin America." In *Informal Institutions and Democracy: Lessons from Latin America,* 178–200. Baltimore, MD: Johns Hopkins University Press.

Freire, Danilo. 2018. "Evaluating the Effect of Homicide Prevention Strategies in São Paulo, Brazil: A Synthetic Control Approach." *Latin American Research Review* 53 (2).

Frühling, Hugo, Joseph S. Tulchin and Heather A. Golding, eds. 2003. *Crime and Violence in Latin America: Citizen Security, Democracy, and the State.* Washington, DC and Baltimore, MD: Woodrow Wilson Center Press and Johns Hopkins University Press.

Fuentes, Claudio. 2005. *Contesting the Iron Fist: Advocacy Networks and Police Violence in Democratic Argentina and Chile. Latin American Studies: Social Sciences and Law.* New York: Routledge.

Gambetta, Diego. 1996. *The Sicilian Mafia: the business of private protection.* Cambridge, MA: Harvard University Press.

Garotinho, Anthony, and Luiz Eduardo Soares. 1998. *Violência e Criminalidade No Estado Do Rio de Janeiro: Diagnóstico e Propostas Para Uma Política Democrática de Segurança Pública.* 1st edition. Rio de Janeiro: Editora Hama.

Gay, Robert. 2005. *Lucia: Testimonies of a Brazilian Drug Dealer's Woman. Voices of Latin American Life.* Philadelphia, PA: Temple University Press.
2015. *Bruno: Conversations with a Brazilian Drug Dealer.* Durham, NC: Duke University Press.

Geddes, Barbara. 1994. *Politician's Dilemma: Building State Capacity in Latin America.* Berkeley, CA: University of California Press.

Gerber, Theodore P., and Sarah E. Mendelson. 2008. "Public Experiences of Police Violence and Corruption in Contemporary Russia: A Case of Predatory Policing?" *Law & Society Review* 42 (1): 1–44.

Giraudy, Agustina, Eduardo Moncada and Richard Snyder. 2019. *Inside Countries: Subnational Research in Comparative Politics.* Cambridge: Cambridge University Press.

Glenny, Misha. 2016. *Nemesis: One Man and the Battle for Rio.* 1st edition. New York: Alfred A. Knopf.

Godson, Roy, ed. 2003. *Menace to Society: Political-Criminal Collaboration around the World.* New Brunswick, NJ: Transaction Publishers.

Goertzel, Ted, and Tulio Kahn. 2009. "The Great São Paulo Homicide Drop." *Homicide Studies* 13 (4): 398–410.

Goldstein, Donna M. 2003. *Laughter out of Place: Race, Class, Violence, and Sexuality in a Rio Shantytown.* Berkeley, CA: University of California Press.

Goldstein, Herman. 1975. *Police Corruption: A Perspective on Its Nature and Control.* Washington, DC: Police Foundation.

Goldstein, Paul J. 1985. "The Drugs/Violence Nexus: A Tripartite Conceptual Framework." *Journal of Drug Issues* 15 (4): 493–506.

González, Gustavo. 2007. "Reforma Policial y Política: Un Complejo Entramado de Compromisos, Resistencias y Condiciones de Posibilidad." *Urvio: Revista Latinoamericana de Seguridad Ciudadana* (2): 154–63.

González, Yanilda María. 2020. *Authoritarian Police in Democracy: Contested Security in Latin America.* Cambridge and New York: Cambridge University Press.

Greene, Kenneth F. 2009. *Why Dominant Parties Lose: Mexico's Democratization in Comparative Perspective.* Cambridge and New York: Cambridge University Press.

Grzymala-Busse, Anna. 2003. "Political Competition and the Politicization of the State in East Central Europe." *Comparative Political Studies* 36 (10): 1123–47.

Gudel, Leonardo. 2009. *Sangue Azul: Morte e Corrupção na PM do Rio.* 1st edition. Belo Horizonte, MG: Geração Editorial.

Helmke, Gretchen, and Steven Levitsky. 2004. "Informal Institutions and Comparative Politics: A Research Agenda." *Perspectives on Politics* 2 (04): 725. https://doi.org/10.1017/S1537592704040472.

Hill, Peter B. E. 2006. *The Japanese Mafia: Yakuza, Law, and the State.* Oxford: Oxford University Press.

Hinton, Mercedes S. 2006. *The State on the Streets: Police and Politics in Argentina and Brazil.* Boulder, CO: Lynne Rienner Publishers.

Hinton, Mercedes S, and Tim Newburn. 2009. *Policing Developing Democracies.* London: Routledge.

Holland, Alisha C. 2013. "Right on Crime? Conservative Party Politics and Mano Dura Policies in El Salvador." *Latin American Research Review* 48 (1).
2016. "Forbearance." *American Political Science Review* 110 (2): 232–46.
2017. *Forbearance as Redistribution: The Politics of Informal Welfare in Latin America*. Cambridge and New York: Cambridge University Press.
Hollanda, Cristina Buarque de. 2005. *Polícia e Direitos Humanos: Política de Segurança Pública No Primeiro Governo Brizola (Rio de Janeiro, 1983–1986)*. Rio de Janeiro: Editora Revan.
Holloway, Thomas H. 1993. *Policing Rio de Janeiro: Repression and Resistance in a 19th-Century City*. Stanford, CA: Stanford University Press.
Hope, Kempe Ronald, ed. 2016. *Police Corruption and Police Reforms in Developing Societies*. Boca Raton, FL: CRC Press, Taylor & Francis Group.
Human Rights Watch. 2009. *Lethal Force: Police Violence and Public Security in Rio de Janeiro and São Paulo*. Human Rights Watch.
Huber, John D, and Charles R Shipan. 2002. *Deliberate Discretion? The Institutional Foundations of Bureaucratic Autonomy*. Cambridge University Press.
Huggins, Martha K., ed. 1991. *Vigilantism and the State in Modern Latin America: Essays on Extralegal Violence*. New York: Praeger.
Huggins, Martha K. 1998. *Political Policing: The United States and Latin America*. Durham, NC: Duke University Press.
Inter-American Drug Abuse Control Commission (CICAD). 2015. "Report on Drug Use in the Americas 2015." Washington, DC: Organization of American States, Secretariat on Multidimensional Security, Inter-American Drug Abuse Control Commission, Inter-American Observatory on Drugs.
Jensen, Steffen, and Karl Hapal. 2018. "Police Violence and Corruption in the Philippines: Violent Exchange and the War on Drugs." *Journal of Current Southeast Asian Affairs* 37 (2): 39–62.
Johnson, Howard, and Christopher Giles. 2019. "Philippines Drug War: Do We Know How Many Have Died?" BBC News, November 12, 2019, sec. Asia. www.bbc.com/news/world-asia-50236481.
Kalyvas, Stathis N. 2006. *The Logic of Violence in Civil War*. Cambridge and New York: Cambridge University Press.
2015. "How Civil Wars Help Explain Organized Crime – And How They Do Not." *Journal of Conflict Resolution* 59 (8): 1517–40. https://doi.org/10.1177/0022002715587101.
Keefer, Philip, Norman Loayza and Rodrigo R. Soares. 2010. "Drug Prohibition and Developing Countries: Uncertain Benefits, Certain Costs." In *Innocent Bystanders: Developing Countries and the War on Drugs*, 9–60. Basingstoke, New York and Washington, DC: Palgrave Macmillan and World Bank.
Kitschelt, Herbert, and Steven Wilkinson, eds. 2007. *Patrons, Clients, and Policies: Patterns of Democratic Accountability and Political Competition*. Cambridge and New York: Cambridge University Press.
Klipphan, Andrés. 2004. *Asuntos Internos: Las Mafias Policiales Contadas Desde Adentro*. 1st edition. Crónica Argentina. Buenos Aires: Aguilar.
Lagos, Marta, and Lucía Dammert. 2012. *"La Seguridad Ciudadana: El Problema Principal de América Latina."* 9: 21–47. Lima: Corporación

Latinobarómetro. www.latinobarometro.org/documentos/LATBD_La_segur idad_ciudadana.pdf.

Leech, Beth L. 2002. "Asking Questions: Techniques for Semistructured Interviews." *Political Science and Politics* 35 (4): 665–68. https://doi.org/10 .1017/S1049096502001129.

Leeds, Elizabeth. 1996. "Cocaine and Parallel Polities in the Brazilian Urban Periphery: Constraints on Local-Level Democratization." *Latin American Research Review* 31 (3): 47–83.

Lessing, Benjamin. 2015. "Logics of Violence in Criminal War." *Journal of Conflict Resolution* 59 (8): 1486–1516. https://doi.org/10.1177/0022002715587100.

2017. *Making Peace in Drug Wars: Crackdowns and Cartels in Latin America.* Cambridge and New York: Cambridge University Press.

Lessing, Benjamin, and Graham Denyer Willis. 2019. "Legitimacy in Criminal Governance: Managing a Drug Empire from behind Bars." *American Political Science Review* 113 (2): 584–606.

Levi, Michael, and Peter Reuter. 2006. "Money Laundering." *Crime and Justice* 34 (1): 289–375.

Levitsky, Steven. 2003. *Transforming Labor-Based Parties in Latin America: Argentine Peronism in Comparative Perspective.* Cambridge and New York: Cambridge University Press.

Levitsky, Steven, and Maria Victoria Murillo. 2013. "Building Institutions on Weak Foundations." *Journal of Democracy* 24 (2): 93–107.

Lipsky, Michael. 2010. *Street-Level Bureaucracy: Dilemmas of the Individual in Public Services.* 30th anniversary expanded edition. New York: Russell Sage Foundation.

López Echagüe, Hernán. 1996. *El otro: una biografía política de Eduardo Duhalde.* 10th edition. Buenos Aires: Planeta.

2000. *El Hombre Que Ríe: Biografía Política de Carlos Federico Ruckauf.* Buenos Aires: Editorial Sudamericana.

Macaulay, Fiona. 2012. "Cycles of Police Reform in Latin America." In *Policing in Africa*, 165–90. New York: Palgrave Macmillan.

Magaloni, Beatriz, Edgar Franco-Vivanco and Vanessa Melo. 2020. "Killing in the Slums: Social Order, Criminal Governance, and Police Violence in Rio de Janeiro." *American Political Science Review* 114 (2): 552–72.

Maggessi, Marina. 2006. *Dura Na Queda.* Rio de Janeiro: Objetiva.

Malone, Mary Fran T., and Lucía Dammert. 2021. "The Police and the Public: Policing Practices and Public Trust in Latin America." *Policing and Society* 31 (4): 418–33.

Manso, Bruno Paes. 2009. "Um Debate Sobre o PCC: Entrevista com Camila Nunes Dias, Gabriel de Santis Feltran, Adalton Marques e Karina Biondi." *Revista de Antropologia Social Dos Alunos Do PPGAS-UFSCar* 1 (2): 154–75.

Martínez, Oscar. 2016. *A History of Violence: Living and Dying in Central America.* London and New York: Verso.

McCann, Bryan. 2014. *Hard Times in the Marvelous City: From Dictatorship to Democracy in the Favelas of Rio de Janeiro.* Durham, NC: Duke University Press.

Méndez, Juan E, Guillermo A. O'Donnell and Paulo Sérgio de M. S Pinheiro, eds. 1999. *The (Un)Rule of Law and the Underprivileged in Latin America*. Notre Dame, IN: University of Notre Dame Press.

Mingardi, Guaracy. 1992. *Tiras, Gansos e Trutas: Cotidiano e Reforma Na Polícia Civil*. 1st edition. São Paulo: Scritta Editorial: Editora Página Aberta.

1999. *Geography of Illicit Drugs in the City of São Paulo*. Management of Social Transformations. www.unesco.org/most/mingardi.doc.

2001. "*Money and the International Drug Trade in São Paulo*." UNESCO.

Misse, Michel. 2007. "Mercados Ilegais, Redes de Proteção e Organização Local Do Crime No Rio de Janeiro." *Estudos Avançados* 21 (61): 139–57. https:// doi.org/10.1590/S0103–40142007000300010.

2011. "Crime Organizado e Crime Comum No Rio de Janeiro." *Revista de Sociologia e Política* 19 (40): 13.

Moncada, Eduardo. 2009. "Toward Democratic Policing in Colombia? Institutional Accountability through Lateral Reform." *Comparative Politics* 41 (4): 431–49. https://doi.org/10.5129/001041509X12911362972511.

2013. "The Politics of Urban Violence: Challenges for Development in the Global South." *Studies in Comparative International Development* 48 (3): 217–39.

2021. *Resisting Extortion: Victims, Criminals, and States in Latin America*. New York: Cambridge University Press.

Moore, Mark H., and Mark Kleiman. 1989. *The Police and Drugs*. United States Department of Justice, Office of Justice Programs, National Institute of Justice. www.ncjrs.gov/pdffiles1/nij/117447.pdf.

Moreira Franco, Wellington. 1991. *Em Defesa do Rio*. Rio de Janeiro: TopBooks.

Moskos, Peter. 2009. *Cop in the Hood*. Princeton, NJ: Princeton University Press.

Motta, Marly Silva da. 2000. "Mania de Estado: O Chaguismo e a Estadualização Da Guanabara." *História Oral* 3: 91–108.

Muggah, Robert, and Katherine Aguirre Tobón. 2018. *Citizen Security in Latin America: Facts and Figures*. Rio de Janeiro: Igarape Institute.

Neme, Cristina. 1999. "A Instituição Policial Na Ordem Democrática: O Caso Da Polícia Militar Do Estado de São Paulo." Universidade de São Paulo. www .nevusp.org/downloads/down147.pdf.

Nichter, Simeon. 2008. "Vote Buying or Turnout Buying? Machine Politics and the Secret Ballot." *American Political Science Review* 102 (01): 19–31. https://doi.org/10.1017/S0003055408080106.

O'Donnell, Guillermo. 1993. "On the State, Democratization and Some Conceptual Problems: A Latin American View with Glances at Some Postcommunist Countries." *World Development* 21 (8): 1355–69.

O'Donnell, María. 2005. *El Aparato: Los Intendentes Del Conurbano y Las Cajas Negras de La Política*. 1st edition. Crónica Argentina. Buenos Aires: Aguilar.

Ollier, María Matilde. 2010. *Atrapada Sin Salida: Buenos Aires En La Política Nacional, 1916–2007*. 1st edition. Ciencias Sociales. San Martín, Provincia de Buenos Aires: UNSAM EDITA.

Olson, Mancur. 1993. "Dictatorship, Democracy, and Development." *American Political Science Review* 87 (3): 567–76.

Ortega, Daniel. 2018. "The Challenge of Improving Police Behavior in Latin America." Washington, DC: Brookings Institution Press.

Osorio, Javier. 2013. "Hobbes on Drugs. Understanding Drug Violence in Mexico." Doctoral Dissertation in Political Science, University of Notre Dame.

2015. "The Contagion of Drug Violence: Spatiotemporal Dynamics of the Mexican War on Drugs." *Journal of Conflict Resolution* 59 (8): 1403–32. https://doi.org/10.1177/0022002715587048.

Palmieri, Gustavo, Josefina Martínez, Máximo Sozzo and Hernán Thomas. 2001. "Mecanismos de Control Interno e Iniciativas de Reforma En Las Instituciones Policiales Argentinas: Los Casos de La Policía Federal Argentina, La Policía de La Provincia de Santa Fe y La Policía de La Provincia de Buenos Aires." *Policía, Sociedad y Estado: Modernización y Reforma Policial En América Del Sur*, 177–220.

Pandolfo, Gabriel. 2010. *Ser o No Ser: Biografía Deportiva, Sentimental y Política de Carlos Reutemann.* Buenos Aires: Sudamericana.

Paoli, Letizia, ed. 2014. *The Oxford Handbook of Organized Crime. The Oxford Handbooks in Criminology and Criminal Justice.* Oxford: Oxford University Press.

Papachristos, Andrew V, David M Hureau and Anthony A Braga. 2013. "The Corner and the Crew: The Influence of Geography and Social Networks on Gang Violence." *American Sociological Review*. https://doi.org.10.1177/0003122413486800.

Penglase, Ben. 2014. *Living with Insecurity in a Brazilian Favela: Urban Violence and Daily Life.* New Brunswick, NJ: Rutgers University Press.

Pereira, Anthony, and Mark Ungar. 2004. "The Persistence of the 'Mano Dura': Authoritarian Legacies and Policing in Brazil and the Southern Cone." In *XXV International Congress of the Latin American Studies Association*, 6–8. http://lasa.international.pitt.edu/members/congress-papers/lasa2004/files/UngarMark_xCD.pdf.

Peres, Maria Fernanda Tourinho, Juliana Feliciano de Almeida, Diego Vicentin, Magdalena Cerda, Nancy Cardia and Sérgio Adorno. 2011. "Queda Dos Homicídios No Município de São Paulo: Uma Análise Exploratória de Possíveis Condicionantes." *Revista Brasileira de Epidemiologia* 14 (4): 709–21. https://doi.org/10.1590/S1415-790X2011000400017.

Pérez Correa, Catalina, Carlos Silva Forné and Ignácio Cano. 2020. "Monitor of the Use of Lethal Force in Latin America: A Comparative Study of Brazil, Colombia, El Salvador, Mexico and Venezuela (2019)." Región Centro and Aguascalientes, México: Centro de Investigación y Docencia Económicas.

Perlman, Janice E. 1979. *The Myth of Marginality: Urban Poverty and Politics in Rio de Janeiro.* Berkeley, CA: University of California Press.

Pierson, Paul. 2004. *Politics in Time: History, Institutions, and Social Analysis.* Princeton, NJ: Princeton University Press.

Pinheiro, Paulo Sérgio. 1997. "Violência, Crime e Sistemas Policiais Em Países de Novas Democracias." *Tempo Social, Revista de Sociologia Da USP* 9 (1): 43–52.

Pinheiro, Paulo Sérgio, Eduardo A. Izumino and Maria Cristina Jakimiak Fernandes. 1991. "Violência Fatal: Conflitos Policiais em São Paulo (81–89)." *Revista USP* 0 (9): 95. https://doi.org/10.11606/issn.2316-9036.v0i9p95–112.

Polga-Hecimovich, John, and Alejandro Trelles. 2016. "The Organizational Consequences of Politics: A Research Agenda for the Study of Bureaucratic Politics in Latin America." *Latin American Politics and Society* 58 (4): 56–79.

Post, Alison E. 2014. *Foreign and Domestic Investment in Argentina: The Politics of Privatized Infrastructure*. Cambridge: Cambridge University Press.

2018. "Cities and Politics in the Developing World." *Annual Review of Political Science* 21: 115–33.

Prado, Mariana Mota, Michael Trebilcock and Patrick Hartford. 2012. "Police Reform in Violent Democracies in Latin America." *Hague Journal on the Rule of Law* 4 (2): 252–85.

Punch, Maurice. 2009. *Police Corruption: Deviance, Accountability and Reform in Policing*. Cullompton, Devon: Willan Publishing.

Ragendorfer, Ricardo. 2002. *La Secta del Gatillo: Historia Sucia de la Policía Bonaerense*. Buenos Aires: Planeta.

Raghavan, R. K. 2002. "The India Police: Expectations of a Democratic Polity." In *Transforming India: Social and Political Dynamics of a Democracy*, 288–313. Delhi and Oxford: Oxford University Press.

Rauch, James E., and Peter B. Evans. 2000. "Bureaucratic Structure and Bureaucratic Performance in Less Developed Countries." *Journal of Public Economics* 75 (1): 49–71.

Reiner, Robert. 2010. *The Politics of the Police*. 4th edition. Oxford and New York: Oxford University Press.

Reiss, Albert J. 1992. "Police Organization in the Twentieth Century." *Crime and Justice*, 51–97.

Resende, Juliana. 1995. *Operação Rio*. 1st edition. História Imediata. São Paulo, Brazil: Scritta.

Reuter, Peter. 1982. *Licensing Criminals: Police and Informants*. Santa Monica, CA: Rand Corp.

2009. "Systemic Violence in Drug Markets." *Crime, Law and Social Change* 52 (3): 275–84. https://doi.org/10.1007/s10611-009-9197-x.

2014. "Drug Markets and Organized Crime." In *The Oxford Handbook of Organized Crime*, 359–80. Oxford: Oxford University Press.

Riccio, Vicente, Marco Aurélio Ruediger, Steven Dutt Ross and Wesley Skogan. 2013. "Community Policing in the Favelas of Rio de Janeiro." *Police Practice and Research* 14 (4): 308–18. https://doi.org/10.1080/15614263.2013.816494.

Rios, Viridiana. 2012. "How Government Structures Encourages Criminal Violence: The Causes of Mexico's Drug War." Doctoral Dissertation in Political Science, Harvard University.

2015. "How Government Coordination Controlled Organized Crime: The Case of Mexico's Cocaine Markets." *Journal of Conflict Resolution* 59 (8): 1433–54. https://doi.org/10.1177/0022002715587052.

Rodrigues, Rute I., and Patricia S. Rivero. 2012. "Áreas de Concentração Das Vítimas Da Violência No Município Do Rio de Janeiro (2002–2006)." Instituto de Pesquisa Econômica Aplicada, Document No. 1698.

Roebuck, Julian B., and Thomas Barker. 1974. "A Typology of Police Corruption." *Social Problems* 21 (3): 423–37.

Rose-Ackerman, Susan, and Bonnie J. Palifka. 2016. *Corruption and Government: Causes, Consequences, and Reform*. Cambridge and New York: Cambridge University Press.

Rosúa, Fernando. 1998. "La Reforma Policial En La Provincia de Santa Fe." Seminario: Las reformas policiales en Argentina. Centro de Estudios Legales y Sociales (CELS).

Sabet, Daniel M. 2012. *Police Reform in Mexico: Informal Politics and the Challenge of Institutional Change*. Standford, CA: Stanford Politics and Policy.

Sain, Marcelo F. 2004. *Política, Policía y Delito: La Red Bonaerense*. 1st edition. Claves Para Todos. Buenos Aires: Capital Intelectual.

———. 2008. *El Leviatán azul: policía y política en la Argentina*. Buenos Aires, Argentina: Siglo Veintiuno Editores Argentina.

———. 2019. *Por Qué Preferimos No Ver La Inseguridad (Aunque Digamos Lo Contrario)*. Buenos Aires: Siglo XXI Editores.

Santos, Germán de los, and Hernán Lascano. 2017. *Los Monos: Historia de La Familia Narco Que Transformó a Rosario En Un Infierno*. Buenos Aires: Sudamericana.

Sapori, Luiz Flávio. 2007. *Segurança Pública no Brasil: Desafios e Perspectivas*. Rio de Janeiro: FGV.

Saviano, Roberto. 2010. *Gomorra Viaggio Nell'Impero Eonomico e Nel Sogno di Dominio Della Camorra*. Milan: Edizioni Mondadori.

Schmidt, Walter, and Pablo Ibáñez. 2015. *Scioli Secreto: Cómo Hizo Para Sobrevivir a 20 Años de La Política Argentina*. Buenos Aires: Sudamericana.

Schneider, Ben Ross. 1992. *Politics within the State: Elite Bureaucrats and Industrial Policy in Authoritarian Brazil*. Pittsburgh, PA: University of Pittsburgh Press.

Seigel, Micol. 2018. *Violence Work: State Power and the Limits of Police*. Durham, NC: Duke University Press.

Sento-Sé, João Trajano. 1999. *Brizolismo: Estetização Da Política e Carisma*. Rio de Janeiro: Espaço e Tempo: Editora FGV.

Shelley, Louise. 2010. *Human Trafficking: A Global Perspective*. Cambridge and New York: Cambridge University Press.

Sherman, Lawrence W. 1978. *Scandal and Reform: Controlling Police Corruption*. Berkeley, CA: University of California Press.

Simon, Jonathan. 2007. *Governing through Crime: How the War on Crime Transformed American Democracy and Created a Culture of Fear*. Oxford and New York: Oxford University Press.

Sirimarco, Mariana. 2009. *De Civil a Policía: Una Etnografía del Proceso de Incorporación a La Institución Policial*. Buenos Aires: Teseo.

Skarbek, David. 2014. *The Social Order of the Underworld: How Prison Gangs Govern the American Penal System*. Oxford and New York: Oxford University Press.

Skolnick, Jerome H. 2011. *Justice without Trial: Law Enforcement in Democratic Society*. New Orleans, LA: Quid Pro Books.

Snyder, Richard. 2001. "Scaling Down: The Subnational Comparative Method." *Studies in Comparative International Development* 36 (1): 93–110. https://doi.org/10.1007/BF02687586.

Snyder, Richard, and Angélica Durán-Martínez. 2009. "Does Illegality Breed Violence? Drug Trafficking and State-Sponsored Protection Rackets." *Crime, Law and Social Change* 52 (3): 253–73.

Soares, Luiz Eduardo. 1996. "Violência e Política No Rio de Janeiro." In *Violência e Política No Rio de Janeiro*, 309–309. Rio de Janeiro: Relume Dumara.

    2000. *Meu Casaco de General: 500 Dias No Front da Segurança Pública do Rio de Janeiro*. São Paulo: Companhia das Letras.

Soares, Luiz Eduardo, André Batista and Rodrigo Pimentel. 2008. *Elite Squad*. New York: Weinstein Books.

Soares, Luiz Eduardo, and João Trajano Sento-Sé. 2000. "Estado e Segurança Pública no Rio de Janeiro: Dilemas de um Aprendizado Difícil." Rio de Janeiro: Federal University of Rio de Janeiro.

Souza, Fátima. 2007. *PCC: A Facção*. Rio de Janeiro: Record.

de Souza, Stefanie Israel. 2019a. "Pacification of Rio's Favelas and the "Pacification of the Pacification Police": The Role of Coordinating Brokerage in Police Reform." *Sociological Forum* 34 (2): 458–82.

    2019b. "Expiration Date: Mega-Events and Police Reform in Rio De Janeiro's Favelas." Doctoral Dissertation in Sociology, University of Notre Dame, IN.

Sozzo, Máximo. 2005. *Policía, Violencia, Democracia: Ensayos Sociológicos*. Ciencia y Técnica. Santa Fe, Argentina: Ediciones UNL, Secretaría de Extensión, Universidad Nacional del Litoral.

Spiller, Pablo, Ernesto Stein and Mariano Tommasi. 2007. "Political Institutions, Policymaking, and Policy: An Introduction." In *Policymaking in Latin America: How Politics Shapes Policies*, 1–28. Washington, DC: Inter-American Development Bank.

Staniland, Paul. 2012. "States, Insurgents, and Wartime Political Orders." *Perspectives on Politics* 10 (02): 243–64.

Stepan, Alfred C. 1988. *Rethinking Military Politics: Brazil and the Southern Cone*. Princeton, NJ: Princeton University Press.

Stevens, Elijah. 2017. "Narco-Planes Landing on Argentina's Rivers: Report." *InSight Crime* (blog). March 27, 2017. https://insightcrime.org/news/brief/narco-planes-landing-on-argentina-river/.

Stokes, Susan Carol. 2013. *Brokers, Voters, and Clientelism: The Puzzle of Distributive Politics. Cambridge Studies in Comparative Politics*. New York: Cambridge University Press.

Sweigart, Emilie. 2017. "Reducción de Homicidios: Lo Que Están Haciendo Los Presidentes." *Americas Quarterly* (blog). 2017. www.americasquarterly.org/fullwidthpage/reduccion-de-homicidios-lo-que-estan-haciendo-los-presidentes/.

Szwarcberg, Mariela Laura. 2015. *Mobilizing Poor Voters: Machine Politics, Clientelism, and Social Networks in Argentina*. Structural Analysis in the Social Sciences. New York: Cambridge University Press.

Taylor, Brian D. 2013. *State Building in Putin's Russia: Policing and Coercion after Communism*. New York: Cambridge University Press.

The Economist. 2013. "El Salvador's Gangs: The Year of Living Less Dangerously | The Economist." Accessed April 27, 2013. www.economist .com/news/americas/21573109-unusual-armistice-has-lasted-longer-many-predicted-year-living-less-dangerously.

Tilly, Charles. 1985. "War Making and State Making as Organized Crime." In *Bringing the State Back In*, edited by Peter B. Evans, Dietrich Rueschemeyer and Theda Skocpol, 169–91. Cambridge: Cambridge University Press. http://ebooks.cambridge.org/ref/id/CBO9780511628283A015.

2003. *The Politics of Collective Violence*. Cambridge: Cambridge University Press.

Tokatlian, Juan Gabriel. 2019. *Qué Hacer Con Las Drogas: Una Mirada Progresista Sobre Un Tema Habitualmente Abordado Desde El Oportunismo Político y Los Intereses Creados*. Buenos Aires: Siglo XXI Editores.

Trejo, Guillermo, and Sandra Ley. 2020. *Votes, Drugs, and Violence: The Political Logic of Criminal Wars in Mexico*. Cambridge and New York: Cambridge University Press.

Tsebelis, George. 2002. *Veto Players: How Political Institutions Work*. Princeton, NJ: Princeton University Press.

Tulchin, Joseph S., and Meg Ruthenburg, eds. 2006. *Toward a Society under Law: Citizens and Their Police in Latin America*. Washington, DC and Baltimore, MD: Woodrow Wilson Center Press and Johns Hopkins University Press.

Ungar, Mark. 2009. "La Mano Dura: Current Dilemmas in Latin American Police Reform." In *Criminality, Public Security, and the Challenge to Democracy in Latin America*, 93–118. Notre Dame, IN: University of Notre Dame Press.

2011. *Policing Democracy: Overcoming Obstacles to Citizen Security in Latin America*. Washington, DC and Baltimore: Woodrow Wilson Center Press and Johns Hopkins University Press.

UNODC. 2012. *World Drug Report 2012*. New York: United Nations.

Varese, Federico. 2013. *Mafias on the Move: How Organized Crime Conquers New Territories*. Princeton, NJ: Princeton University Press.

Vargas, Robert. 2016. *Wounded City: Violent Turf Wars in a Chicago Barrio*. New York: Oxford University Press.

Veloso, Fernando, and Sérgio Augusto Guimarães Ferreira, eds. 2008. *É Possível: Gestão Da Segurança Pública e Redução Da Violência*. Rio de Janeiro: Contra Capa: IEPE/CdG.

Volkov, Vadim. 2002. *Violent Entrepreneurs: The Use of Force in the Making of Russian Capitalism*. Ithaca, NY: Cornell University Press.

Wacquant, Loïc J. D. 2009. *Punishing the Poor: The Neoliberal Government of Social Insecurity. Politics, History, and Culture*. Durham, NC: Duke University Press.

Weitz-Shapiro, Rebecca. 2014. *Curbing Clientelism in Argentina: Politics, Poverty, and Social Policy*. Cambridge and New York: Cambridge University Press.

Wilkinson, Steven. 2006. *Votes and Violence: Electoral Competition and Ethnic Riots in India. Cambridge Studies in Comparative Politics*. Cambridge and New York: Cambridge University Press.

Wilson, James Q. 1968. *Varieties of Police Behavior: The Management of Law and Order in Eight Communities*. Cambridge, MA: Harvard University Press.

WOLA, Washington Office in Latin America. 2011. "Tackling Urban Violence in Latin America: Reversing Exclusion through Smart Policing and Social Investment." Washington, DC: Washington Office on Latin America.

Wolff, Michael Jerome. 2015. "Building Criminal Authority: A Comparative Analysis of Drug Gangs in Rio de Janeiro and Recife." *Latin American Politics and Society* 57 (2): 21–40. https://doi.org/10.1111/j.1548-2456.2015.00266.x.

Yashar, Deborah J. 2018. *Homicidal Ecologies: Illicit Economies and Complicit States in Latin America*. Cambridge and New York: Cambridge University Press.

Zaluar, Alba Maria, and Christovam Barcellos. 2013. "Mortes Prematuras e Conflito Armado Pelo Domínio Das Favelas No Rio de Janeiro." www.arca.fiocruz.br/handle/icict/9699.

Zarazaga, Rodrigo. 2014. "Brokers Beyond Clientelism: A New Perspective Through the Argentine Case." *Latin American Politics and Society* 56 (3): 23–45. https://doi.org/10.1111/j.1548-2456.2014.00238.x.

Index